PLEASE, GENERAL CUSTER, I DON'T WANT TO GO

PLEASE, GENERAL CUSTER, I DON'T WANT TO GO

True Tales of the Old West

RUSSELL W. ESTLACK

TWODOT®

GUILFORD, CONNECTICUT
HELENA, MONTANA

A · TWODOT® · BOOK

An imprint of The Rowman & Littlefield Publishing Group, Inc.
4501 Forbes Blvd., Ste. 200
Lanham, MD 20706
www.rowman.com
A registered trademark of The Rowman & Littlefield Publishing Group, Inc.

Distributed by NATIONAL BOOK NETWORK

British Library Cataloguing in Publication Information available

Library of Congress Control Number: 2019951364

ISBN 978-1-4930-4255-5 (paperback)
ISBN 978-1-4930-4256-2 (e-book)

♾™ The paper used in this publication meets the minimum requirements of American National Standard for Information Sciences—Permanence of Paper for Printed Library Materials, ANSI/ NISO Z39.48-1992.

This book is dedicated to the loving memory of my parents,
Elmer and Ethel Estlack, and to my siblings John, Warren, and Lois.
Though they are gone, they will never be forgotten.

CONTENTS

Acknowledgments

This book is the result of the collective efforts of a number of people who helped make it a reality. When writing about so many personalities and events of the Old West, it requires a smart and strong editor who knows what it takes to bring it all together. I was fortunate to have that person in Courtney Oppel at TwoDot. She is a pleasure to work with, and I hope I have an opportunity to work with her on future projects. I would like to thank the fine Western writers and historians who have done such a wonderful job preserving the traditions and history of the American West for future generations. A special debt of gratitude goes to the librarians and archivist who were kind enough to provide much of the research material for this book. My eternal thanks to my beautiful wife, Luisa, for believing in me and supporting me during the difficult times and the good times. Without her encouragement, this book would never have seen the light of day. I want to give a heartfelt thanks to my daughter Allison Estlack Peckumn who took time from her medical studies at Michigan State University to edit my work and correct my mistakes. Throughout the process of writing this book, she challenged me to organize my thoughts and clarify my writing into a more enjoyable format. Lastly, a special thank you to my sixth-grade teacher, Marie Chester of Wildwood, New Jersey. She taught me that the pen is indeed mightier than the sword.

The Comic Opera
Outlaw of California

ONE OF THE MOST FASCINATING CHARACTERS TO RIDE OUT OF THE pages of the Old West was a little-known outlaw named Dick Fellows. Not only was he a dismal failure as a bandit, but for some unknown reason, horses hated him. On more than one occasion it was a horse that led to his incarcerations at San Quentin.

Dick's career as a road agent began in 1869, when he attempted to rob the Soledad stage on the outskirts of Santa Barbara. He hid behind a large tree in a boggy area and waited for the stagecoach to come down the road. He then jumped out and shouted at the driver to stop. As soon as the stage came to a halt, a soldier opened the door, scampered out of the coach, and hid in the bushes. While Dick was occupied with the soldier, the driver took off with the stage. Dick missed getting the strong box, but he did collect three hundred dollars from the soldier.

Persistent in his efforts to earn a living as a highwayman, Dick decided to rob the stage that traveled down the Cahuenga Grade from Santa Barbara. He once again hid in a grove of oak trees, and waited for the coach to come down the hill. Waving his gun in the air, he jumped from his hiding place and shouted at the driver to stop. One of the passengers took a couple of shots at Dick, and the bandit dived for cover. The noise of the gunshots spooked the horses, and they tore down the road, precariously weaving from one side of the road to the other. Keeping the stage from turning over, the driver was able to bring it under control and continue on his way.

Dick mounted his horse and raced over a shortcut that brought him to a place the stagecoach had to pass. Jumping off of his horse, he hung his hat and coat on a stick and placed it on a hill overlooking the road. When the driver reached the spot where Fellows was waiting, he saw what looked like a man standing on the hill. Afraid of being shot, he threw down the strongbox and drove on. Dick waited until the stage was out of sight before he opened the box. He got 435 dollars for his trouble. Not bad for an hour's work.

All of this strenuous activity made Dick hungry. Later that night, on the way back to town, he stopped at a roadside cafe. Unfortunately for Dick, some of the local ranchers recognized him before he could sit down to eat. One of the men drew his pistol and ordered Dick to surrender. Dick grabbed the gun just as the man fired, and the bullet hit him in the foot. He blew out the lantern and dove through the window into the darkness. Later that night, he found a doctor to patch up his foot.

The next morning, a posse caught up with Dick; he was arrested on the spot. On January 31, 1870, he was sentenced to ten years in San Quentin for attempted murder and highway robbery. In prison, Dick took advantage of his job in the library to read and educate himself. He got religion and set up a Sunday Bible school for some of the inmates. He convinced the warden that he was a changed man and that he had seen the error of his ways. He had served only five years, when the State of California granted him a pardon.

Dick wandered around California for the next year. He managed to keep out of trouble, and in November 1875 he checked into a Bakersfield hotel under his real name, Richard Perkins. A month later, in a crowded train station in Caliente, California, the outlaw watched armed guards transfer 240,000 dollars in gold coins from a train to a waiting stage-coach. As soon as it was loaded, the stagecoach, four armed guards, and the gold coins headed out of town toward Los Angeles.

Dick realized the job would take at least two men, so he told a part-ner he had acquired somewhere along the way to ride on ahead and wait for him at a deserted spot in the road. Renting a gentle-spirited mare with kind eyes, the highwayman took off in hot pursuit. The horse didn't like him, and a mile and a half from town it bucked him off and returned to the stable. Dick flew through the air and landed in the middle of the road. After several minutes of sitting in the dust, he stood up, dusted himself off, and walked back to Caliente.

Dick Fellows held up stagecoaches like this. COURTESY SANTA BARBARA HISTORICAL MUSEUM

Before long, Dick came up with a new idea. He decided to rob the northbound stage from Los Angeles. Stealing a horse from the hitching post in front of a general store, he climbed into the saddle and rode out of town. Stopping the stage about a mile outside of town, Dick ordered the driver to throw down the strongbox. The driver complied, and when the box hit the ground, the stage continued on its way. Dick dismounted, dragged the box toward his horse, and tried to load it on the horse's back. The horse had no intention of carrying that heavy box. It bolted and took off for town, leaving the outlaw and the box in the middle of the road.

Night was fast approaching, and Dick knew he had to get away before a posse showed up. Dragging the box off the road into the brush and stumbling around in the dark, he missed his footing and fell fifteen feet into a ditch. The fall broke his left leg above the ankle, and the box tumbled into the ditch after him, landing with a thud on his left foot. Dick screamed as it crushed his instep. Despite the intense pain, he smashed the lock with the butt of his gun, lifted the lid, and removed eighteen hundred dollars. He then crafted crutches from an old tree branch, hobbled to a nearby farm, stole another horse, and headed into the valley flatlands.

The next morning, James Hume, one of Wells Fargo's best detectives, took off with a large posse and caught up with Dick. The horse had a mule shoe on one hoof, so it was easy to track. Dick was arrested without a fight and incarcerated in the Kern County jail to await trial.

Dick pleaded guilty to robbery and was sentenced to eight years in prison. The day before he was to be transferred to San Quentin, Dick used the new crutches the county provided him to make a hole in the floor of his cell. He tunneled his way under the jail and shuffled down the street.

The escapee hid in some trees on the banks of the Kern River for two days while posses scoured the countryside for him. Cold and hungry, he crawled into a farmer's corral to steal another horse. Dick found one he liked and tied it to a railing while he went into the barn to get a saddle. This horse didn't like Dick any better than the other horses had and wanted no part of him. Using its teeth, the horse managed to untie the rope from the rail and take off for town at a fast gallop. The outlaw stood in the corral and stared as the horse disappeared down the road. Dick was recaptured later that day and was held under guard until he could be transferred to San Quentin.

After five years of hard labor, Dick was released from prison. He tried to go straight, but honest employment didn't suit him. The lure of easy money was too tempting for him to ignore. After a few months of freedom, he returned to robbing stagecoaches. Dick knew that most of the lawmen and Wells Fargo detectives in the Bakersfield area would recognize him on sight, so he moved his operations to the area between San Jose and San Luis Obispo.

Dick pulled off several successful robberies, but it wasn't long before the law was on his trail. They found him hiding at a ranch in Santa Clara County and placed him under arrest. Even though he was under heavy guard, he somehow managed to escape. A posse recaptured him in the Santa Cruz Mountains and returned him to the county jail.

The trial was held in Santa Barbara, and he was sentenced to life in prison. Jail was the last place he wanted to be, and he had no intention of

Dick Fellows arrives at San Quentin to serve his third term. COURTESY SANTA BARBARA HISTORICAL MUSEUM

staying there. At the first opportunity, he broke out of jail and sprinted down the street. Spotting a horse tied to a stake in an empty field, he ran over to it. Pulling up the stake, Dick grabbed the rope and leaped on the horse's back.

Earlier that morning, the horse had ingested some locoweed and was suffering from its effects. As soon as Dick climbed on its back, the horse bucked and thrashed around in a narcotic-induced frenzy. Dick flew through the air and landed on his head. The animal raised such a ruckus that it attracted the attention of the sheriff and his deputies. They arrested the unconscious outlaw and took him back to jail. Safe from cantankerous horses at last, Dick spent the remainder of his life in prison.

Stagecoach Mary

Mention the Wild West and people picture pioneers crossing the plains, gunfighters, lawmen, blue-coated soldiers, and wild Indians. Most of these men were pretty tough customers, but there were also some pretty wild women who played a big part in the settling of the West. One of the roughest, toughest hellions to ride the western trails was a black female nicknamed "Stagecoach Mary," the second woman in history to drive a US mail coach.

In the entire West, Mary Fields had no equal. She was a six-foot, two hundred pound, cigar-smoking giant, and she packed a pair of six-shooters and a 10 gauge shotgun. Short-tempered, she settled her arguments with a fist or a gun. She could outshoot, outride, outcurse, and outdrink any man in the Montana Territory. Mary believed she was the equal of any man of any color, and she never stepped aside for anyone. The Great Falls *Examiner* reported that she broke more noses than any other person in central Montana.

Born in 1832, Mary started life as a slave but was freed at the end of the Civil War. Many ex-slaves chose to work for their former masters after the war, and Mary was no exception. Responsible for raising the five children of Judge Edmund Dunne on his plantation in Hickman County, Tennessee, Mary worked for the Dunnes until 1883, when Edmund's wife, Josephine, passed away. Stricken with grief and unable to care for his children, Edmund asked Mary to take the children to their aunt, Mother Mary Amadeus, the mother superior of an Ursuline convent in Toledo, Ohio. After delivering her charges to the nuns, her services were no longer required. Mary then took a job on a Mississippi riverboat, the *Robert E. Lee*, as a chambermaid, laundress, and servant to the families who sailed on the Mississippi River.

Mary was on board the steamboat in June 1870 when the *Robert E. Lee* and the *Natchez VI* raced up the Mississippi River from New Orleans to St. Louis. She loved to tell anyone who would listen how during the race, some crewmen tossed anything they could get their hands on, including barrels of resin, sides of ham, and bacon, into the boiler, while other crewmen closed the relief valves to build up the steam pressure. In a 1914 interview she told a reporter for a local newspaper in Cascade, Montana: "It was so hot in the cabins that passengers were forced to stay out on deck. It was expected that the boilers would burst, but they didn't. The *Robert E. Lee* won the race by several hours."

Mary worked on the riverboats for many years and became tired of her life on the river. Missing one of Dunne's daughters, whom she had raised into adulthood, she decided to search for her. Boarding a northbound steamboat, Mary traveled up the Mississippi. Reaching Toledo, Ohio, she found her former charge, who had since become Mother Annunciation at the Ursuline convent.

Mother Mary Amadeus was no longer at the convent. She had been transferred to a convent in Helena, Montana. Mother Amadeus Dunne, a cousin of Annunciation, was now in charge of the convent. She took Mary in, provided her with room and board, and paid her to guard the convent garden and cloister courtyard. She saw to it that Mary was always attired in a black dress, cape, and black cap, and gave her a special place for her prayers in the convent chapel. She overlooked Mary's insistence on carrying a .38 Smith & Wesson under her apron, her attachment to a pet dog, and her custom of smoking big black cigars, drinking from a whiskey jug, and driving a hack around town at breakneck speed. According to the convent archives, Mary was musically inclined, and the nuns taught her to read music and sign her name. Convent records also show that on many occasions the sisters lent her money and she always repaid them.

Mother Amadeus finished her term as mother superior and in 1884 was selected to lead six nuns to Miles City, Montana, to establish schools for the children of settlers and Indians in the area. The work was hard, and Mother Amadeus took sick with pneumonia. She wrote to the nuns in Ohio to send Mary to help her. Mary had become much more cantankerous toward the public since Mother Amadeus left Ohio, so the nuns were happy to send her out west. Mary was happy to go.

St. Peter's Mission and Indian School was a simple frontier facility. Most of the buildings were in dire need of repair, and Mary was hired to chop wood, perform stone work and rough carpentry, dig ditches, wash clothes and sacristy linens, care for more than four hundred chickens, and tend a large vegetable garden for the sisters. When the mission reserves ran low, she made her customary supply runs to the train station. On occasion she hauled freight to the mission from Great Falls to Helena, Montana.

One cold winter night, Mary was returning to the convent with a wagonload of supplies. Surrounded by a pack of wolves, the terrified horses bolted. The wagon hit a large boulder and overturned, dumping Mary and the supplies onto the prairie. Throughout the long, dark night, she held the wolves at bay. The next morning, the nuns found her sitting on the overturned wagon with a rifle across her knees, guarding her team and the supplies.

The citizens of Helena didn't know what to make of this black hellion in their midst. The Native Americans called her "White Crow" because she acted like a white woman but had black skin. A schoolgirl wrote an essay about Mary saying she drank whiskey and swore, and that being a Republican made her a low, foul creature in the public's eye.

In the extreme cold of the Montana winters, Mary dressed like a man. An unforgettable sight in her wool cap, boots, a long dress, and a pair of men's pants—a .38 Smith & Wesson strapped under her apron and carrying her shotgun—Mary was ready for anything.

On more than one occasion, Mary engaged in open warfare with some of the men in the area, and she always came out on top. She had a standing bet that she could knock out any man with one punch, but she never found anyone foolish enough to take her up on it. When a local drunk made the mistake of making faces and insulting her, she picked up a rock and adorned his face. The last time anyone saw him, he was running for the Canadian border. In a shootout with a cowboy, her bullet came a little too close for his comfort. The cowboy took the hint and got out of town.

In spite of her rough edges and wild behavior, the sisters loved Mary and appointed her foreman over the workers at the school. In return for their love and trust, Mary declared herself the protector of the Ursuline nuns at St. Peter's Catholic Mission, safeguarding them from drunken cowboys, Indians, and four-legged predators.

Always ready for trouble, Mary was quick to settle it. A disgruntled Chinese hired hand confronted her and wanted to know why she earned two dollars a month more than he did. "You're nothing but an uppity colored woman. What makes you think you're worth nine dollars a month anyway?" he yelled.

Mary ignored him until she heard him repeat his complaint once too often at a local saloon, where she happened to be a regular customer. She chased the hired man behind the nunnery, where he had been digging a latrine. Grabbing her gun and firing a shot at him, she missed; he fired back. Bullets flew in every direction, and the nuns dove for cover. Mary escaped unscathed, but one of her bullets ricocheted off a stone wall and hit her enemy in the left buttock, ruining his new $1.85 trousers.

Some of Mary's bullets passed through the bishop's laundry that was hanging on a clothesline. The underwear and two white shirts he had had shipped from Boston the week before were riddled with bullet holes. The bishop was not amused. He fired Mary and gave her opponent a raise. Mary traveled to Helena to plead her case, but the bishop told her that nothing she could say or do would change his mind.

Mother Amadeus couldn't bear to let Mary leave the convent under such circumstances, but she had to follow the bishop's orders. She gave Mary the money to open a restaurant in Cascade twice, but both times the business went belly-up. Mary had a big heart and fed anyone who was hungry, whether they could pay for it or not. Since Mary wasn't a very good cook, the food wasn't very good anyway, so she attracted few paying customers.

Now that Mary was sixty years old and unemployed, Mother Amadeus refused to abandon her friend. In 1895 she bought Mary a wagon and a team of horses and helped her secure a government position as a mail coach driver. Mary soon developed a reputation for delivering letters and parcels in any kind of weather over any terrain. She became

Mary Fields was the first African-American woman to be employed as a mail carrier in the United States (1895). COURTESY OF THE URSULINE CONVENT ARCHIVES, TOLEDO, OHIO

famous throughout the Montana Territory for carrying the mail to lonely mountain cabins and remote outposts through blinding snowstorms and blistering heat. She cut quite a figure as she drove through town perched atop the mail coach, smoking a big black homemade cigar.

The job was fraught with hardships and danger. Thieves and wolves roamed the countryside, but they never messed with Mary. When heavy snows blocked the trails, Mary was forced to leave her horses on the side of the road and walk through the snowdrifts to deliver the mail. She earned the nickname "Stagecoach Mary" for her unfailing reliability and dedication to her job.

As she approached her seventieth birthday, Mary decided it was time to give up her mail route and find a less strenuous way to earn a living. In 1903 Mother Amadeus was sent to Alaska to establish another mission and was no longer available to provide sustenance to Mary. The sisters at St. Peter's Mission took up a collection and helped Mary open a laundry in her home. Mary didn't wash many clothes. She preferred smoking her foul cigars and drinking whiskey with her friends. It didn't matter that it was against the law for women to drink in saloons with men; the mayor gave her special permission to drink in any bar in town. The owner of the Cascade Hotel gave strict orders to his staff that Mary was to be given free meals and drinks in his establishment for the rest of her life.

The years hadn't mellowed Mary. She could still outcuss, outfight, outshoot, and outdrink any man in three counties. Once while having a few drinks at a local saloon, she spotted a man who owed her two dollars for his laundry. Following him into the street, she grabbed him by his shirt collar and flattened him with one punch. As she later told her drinking companions, the satisfaction she got from laying him out was worth more than the money he owed her. As far as she was concerned, his laundry bill was paid. Over the years, Mary did much for the people of Cascade. She gave a helping hand to anyone who asked her, sharing her time and money with those in need.

Mary babysat for most of the children in the area, and then spent her own money buying gifts and candy for them. An avid baseball fan, she adopted the local baseball team as her own. For each game, she prepared a bouquet of flowers from her garden for every player, with larger bouquets reserved for the home-run hitters. She attended every game, and any man who made disparaging remarks about her team could expect a fistful of knuckles in the face.

Mary couldn't remember her exact birthday, but she celebrated twice a year, giving the townspeople plenty of notice. When the day arrived for the celebration, the town fathers declared a holiday and closed the school in her honor. When fire destroyed Mary's home in 1912, the entire town turned out to rebuild it at their expense.

Two years later, in failing health and sensing the end was near, Mary wrapped herself in blankets and lay down to die in the tall weeds near her small, two-room house. She was found by three brothers playing nearby and taken to Columbus Hospital in Great Falls, Montana. She died of liver failure at eighty-two years of age.

Without exception, everyone in Cascade turned out to honor her. The only building in town large enough to hold the crowds was the newly constructed Pastime Theater. Every seat in the auditorium was filled, and people waited in long lines for hours to pay their last respects. So many flowers surrounded Mary's casket that it was hidden from view.

Mary was laid to rest in Hillside Cemetery at the foot of the mountain trail that led to St. Peter's Mission. The single white cross that marked her grave has since been replaced by a large rock. Perhaps like the rock that guards her final resting place, her fighting spirit still protects the town.

The Outlaw Priest

PRIEST, OUTLAW, GUNFIGHTER, AND LAWMAN, CLEOPHAS J. DOWD WAS one of the most enigmatic characters to ride the outlaw trail. Even though most Western writers have ignored him, and few people today have ever heard of him, he is considered by some historians to be one of the fastest gunfighters of his era.

In 1845 blight struck the Irish countryside like a plague of locusts. The Irish Potato Famine lasted for five long years; took the lives of more than a million men, women, and children; drained the people's spirits; and drove them across the sea to America. Like so many of their countrymen, Michael O'Dowd and Bridget Matilda Foley fled from County Cork and boarded a ship for Boston. After a long sea voyage and a shipboard romance, they moved into the dilapidated tenements in the city's Irish section with Michael's brother, Patrick. Michael and Bridget were married in 1855.

The dream of most Irishmen was to own their own land, and cheap land was available in California to anyone who wanted it. Patrick made up his mind to leave the overcrowded tenements and mean streets of Boston. Booking passage on a ship bound for California, he tried to convince the newlyweds to join him.

Bridget had suffered from long bouts of seasickness on the voyage across the Atlantic and had no desire to endure the hardships of another long voyage. So in the early spring of 1856, Michael loaded his pregnant wife and their meager belongings into a wagon he had purchased with their savings and joined a wagon train heading west.

An arduous journey brought them to the outskirts of San Francisco. Bridget went into labor, and Michael went in search of a doctor. Most of the doctors were out in the hills prospecting for gold, and those who did practice medicine charged exorbitant fees. They refused to help anyone who couldn't pay, so Michael was forced to look elsewhere for help.

At the Old Dolores Mission, an Irish priest gave them shelter, and on July 26, 1856, with the assistance of the nuns, Bridget gave birth to a healthy baby boy. They christened him Cleophas J. Dowd, for one of the men who walked with Jesus on the road to Emmaus. Irish tradition dictated that the first-born son would be consecrated to the priesthood. Cleophas was left in the care of the nuns at the old Spanish mission until he was old enough to attend school and receive religious instruction. At age five he entered into a routine he hated. Rising from his bed before sunrise, he attended catechism classes and an hour of prayer before he was allowed to eat breakfast. A long day of rigorous study was followed by afternoon and evening chores, a sparse evening meal, and an early bedtime. Depending on the situation, for any infraction of the rules or perceived disobedience, the priests and nuns meted out equal measures of punishment or penance. Of all of the indignities he was forced to endure, the thing he detested the most was kneeling before the priest and kissing his ring.

Unburdened with the care of a baby, Michael, Bridget, and Patrick moved on to Marin County, across the bay from San Francisco. Over the next few years, they acquired a large parcel of land in the surrounding hills and began raising and racing Thoroughbred horses. An inveterate gambler, Patrick lost a bet on a horse race, thereby losing a large section of his ranch to Senator Leland Stanford, founder of Stanford University.

On special occasions Cleophas was permitted to visit his parents at the ranch. It was an exciting place for a young boy whose world consisted of adobe walls, cell-like rooms, and the harsh regimen imposed upon him by the priests and nuns. He felt alive as he rode with his father's vaqueros, wild and free over the open spaces of Marin County. The ranch hands taught him Spanish and how to use a lariat and a gun, and he reveled in the knowledge. Michael considered it unseemly for a future priest to engage in such mundane activities, so he forbade Cleophas to ever leave the mission and visit the ranch again.

Cleophas had no intention of following his father's orders. Having experienced the freedom of the outside world, he had no desire to remain in the purgatory of the mission. At age thirteen he climbed over a wall and ran away to the Barbary Coast, a notorious area of San Francisco defined by saloons, gambling parlors, whorehouses, and the dregs of California's criminal society. Life was cheap on the Coast. Murder, robbery, and kidnapping were the order of the day. Cleophas joined a gang of young thieves, pickpockets, cutpurses, and delinquents, and by the time he was fifteen years old, he was their undisputed leader.

Michael was ready to disown him until Jim Murray, an old sailor from a whaling ship out of Nantucket, Massachusetts, took an interest in the boy. Through his patience and guidance, Murray convinced Cleophas to quit the gang and straighten out his life. With Michael's consent, Jim became Cleophas's guardian. He purchased a dairy on Strawberry Point and gave Cleophas a job delivering milk and butter by rowboat to customers across the bay in San Francisco.

Under the terms of the guardianship agreement, Cleophas was required to complete his schooling and become a priest. Returning to the life he detested, he resumed his studies. When he was old enough, he attended classes at the University of San Francisco and completed his training for the priesthood. By the time he graduated, he was a voracious reader, spoke seven languages, and became an expert in the art of calligraphy. Since war with Mexico was looming on the horizon, he excelled in the study of weapons and ballistics.

On his twenty-first birthday, Cleophas took his final vows. Dressed in his long black robes, he strapped two pistols to his waist and headed for the nearest bar in Sausalito. Celebrating his newfound freedom, he had a little too much to drink. After shooting up the town and killing a cowboy in a saloon brawl, he hurriedly hoofed it out of town to escape retribution from the law and fled to his father's ranch.

Arriving at the ranch, the fugitive created such a clamor that he rousted his father out of a sound sleep. Michael stuck his head out of a second-story bedroom window to see what all the noise was about. Cleophas yelled at his father and blamed him for his wasted life in pursuit of the priesthood. In a fit of anger, he fired a shot at Michael, then ran to the corral and mounted his father's prize Thoroughbred stallion. Without ever looking back, he rode east.

Cleophas was certain the law was after him. In the mountains he shared a camp with a group of surveyors. Informing his newfound friends that he was on the run and needed a place to hide, he was told about an outlaw stronghold called Brown's Hole located somewhere near Vernal, Utah. A lot of men on the run hid out there, and any lawman crazy enough to come after them would never leave the stronghold alive.

Cleophas rode hard until he reached Brown's Hole, where the rustlers, gunfighters, and other outlaws welcomed him with open arms. He felt safe there and could always get a hot meal at one of the ranches that dotted the area. Residents never asked questions. Shallow, unmarked graves were scattered over the landscape, and a few makeshift headstones marked the final resting places of those who were just a little too curious.

Many of the ranchers in Brown's Hole were otherwise law-abiding citizens who saw nothing wrong with rustling a few steers from the large cattle companies and providing money, food, shelter, and horses to men on the dodge. In return for the favors, the outlaws helped out with round-ups and other chores. Butch Cassidy and the Wild Bunch often "laid over" after a robbery, and it was not unusual to see them riding fence or changing brands on stolen cattle.

James Warren's ranch on Diamond Mountain was home to many notorious outlaws, rustlers, and horse thieves. Warren, a huge man and former priest, was worse than any of the outlaws who took shelter there. Cleophas took refuge at the ranch, and before long he had his first violent confrontation with the Herrera Gang, one of the most vicious gangs in the Hole. "Mexican Joe" Herrera, his brother Pablo, and more than a dozen Mexican banditos ruled the Hole through intimidation and murder. Those who disagreed with Mexican Joe met their end on the blade of his knife, their bodies tossed into the Green River.

Joe met his end when he was caught cheating in a game of stud poker. Following an extreme run of bad luck, he began dealing from the bottom of the deck. The hombres he was playing with didn't cotton to his manipulation of the cards. An argument ensued, someone pulled a knife, and Joe died at the table. Dragging his body outside, they buried him in a shallow unmarked grave near the south wall of the cabin. In a hurry to get back to their cards and whiskey, they went back inside and resumed playing as soon as they planted him.

Horse racing was a favorite pastime for the residents of Brown's Hole, and large sums of money were bet on the outcome of each race. The race between the Thoroughbred stallion Cleophas had stolen from his father and Charley Crouse's undefeated bay mare precipitated the trouble between Cleophas and the Herrera Gang. The Herreras bet on Charley's horse to win, but when the stallion beat the bay, Pablo became furious. Unaware that Cleophas understood the language, Pablo began to curse him in Spanish. Cleophas replied to his tirade in Spanish, and Pablo kicked the stallion in the flanks. The horse bucked and bolted, throwing Cleophas to the ground.

Pablo assumed Cleophas was unarmed. Screaming in Spanish and pulling a knife from a sheath concealed behind his neck, he leaped through the air toward the fallen man. With lightning speed, Cleophas pulled a hidden pistol from his pocket and fired, the bullet hitting Pablo between the eyes, blowing out the back of his head.

With blood still oozing from the wound in his head, his hands folded and tied across his chest, Pablo was laid out on a canvas tarpaulin in an open grave. In his official capacity as a priest, with his black robes blowing in the wind, a Bible in his hand, and a Colt .44 strapped to his waist, Cleophas administered the last rites. Bending down and scooping up a handful of sand, he let it trickle through his fingers onto the dead man's face while mumbling aloud, "Rest in peace, you Mexican son of a bitch!"

During the summer months, the Mormon bishop of Vernal drove his cattle into Brown's Hole. In 1883 his teenage daughter, Ella Rophena, accompanied him, and since women were in short supply, she attracted the attention of every bachelor for miles around. The bishop knew how cowboys behaved around a pretty girl and was taking no chances. He kept a close watch on her whenever possible.

While the bishop guarded Ella's virtue, the cowboys had other ideas. Splitting into two groups, they hid in a stand of cedars, waiting for Ella to pass by on her morning ride. As she approached the trees, the first group of cowboys rode out into the open, firing their guns in the air. The sound of gunfire spooked her horse and it raced down the trail as if its tail were on fire. The terrified girl held on and somehow managed to keep her seat while the second group rode hard to the rescue.

Cleophas was riding nearby when he heard the shots. Digging his spurs into his horse's flank, he raced to the scene of the action in time to see Ella's horse step into a prairie dog hole and throw her to the ground. The pursuing cowboys saw Cleophas ride up with a gun in his hand and scurried for cover. Ella was thrown clear, but she hit the ground hard and broke her hip. He scooped her up in his arms and took her to the Bassett ranch where, under the tender care of Elizabeth Bassett, her injuries mended.

Cleophas was her hero, and Ella fell in love with him. But the bishop felt that Cleophas would not be a fit husband for his daughter. He had a bad reputation as a gunfighter, he was too old for her, and, worse yet, he wasn't a Mormon. Forbidding his daughter to ever see Cleophas again, the bishop took her back to Vernal.

Cleophas never let anyone stand in the way of his happiness. Crashing Ella's eighteenth birthday party, he kidnapped her and rode to a cabin in Crouse Canyon with a posse in hot pursuit. Charley Crouse and some of the outlaws from Brown's Hole held off the posse long enough for a justice of the peace to perform the wedding ceremony.

A few weeks before Cleophas got married, he took a job as a government hunter. Along with other hunters, he set up his camp at an army encampment in the Uinta Mountains. Early one morning, they were approached by George "Sol" Solomon, owner of a large spread in Connor Basin a few miles north of the camp. The Al Connor Gang had taken over and moved into the ranch house. Sol offered to give each man a part of his land that consisted of three valleys if they would help him drive the gang out of the basin.

Sol and the hunters checked their guns, mounted their horses, and galloped at a fast pace to the ranch. Cleophas and his friends remained in the background with their hands on their guns while Sol cantered up to the house and called Connor out. Someone in the house opened fire and Sol dived for cover. The bullets flew in both directions, and when the smoke cleared, Connor and four of his associates lay dead. Two of the gang members had been lounging near the corrals when the shooting started. They scurried to safety up a narrow canyon while Sol and his friends walked away from the fight without a scratch.

Once the bodies had been dragged away and buried, each man selected the piece of land he wanted. Cleophas chose an isolated section of land on Sheep Creek Canyon. He built a dugout in the side of a hill, and after the wedding, Cleophas and Ella spent their honeymoon there. A few weeks later, with the help of his friend and mentor, Jim Murray, they constructed a frame-and-log cabin.

In an effort to make life a little easier for the newlyweds, Ella's uncle appointed Cleophas deputy sheriff of Uintah County, Utah, and the adjoining county of Sweetwater, Wyoming. Cleophas upheld the law when it suited him, and his position provided a perfect cover for his outlaw enterprises. Raising and selling horses to the McCarty Gang, he robbed a few banks and held up a few trains along the way. He also dug a tunnel through the hill between the dugout and the corral, where he kept horses saddled and ready for a fast getaway. After he moved into the house, he used the dugout to hide men on the dodge.

His salary as a deputy sheriff and the money from his criminal activities were not enough to support his growing family. In 1888 Cleophas took a job as a detective for the Union Pacific Railroad. He rode the rails between Ogden, Utah, and Cheyenne, Wyoming, and it isn't known if he prevented any of his outlaw friends from holding up the trains.

Cleophas was away from home for long periods of time, and that suited his family fine. He was abusive to them, and they lived in fear of his ire. Over the years Ella gave birth to six children, but only four lived to maturity. One of Ella's pregnancies was terminated when a cow she was milking kicked her in the stomach, causing a miscarriage. Another child died in infancy as a result of Cleophas's violent temper. When Ella beat him in a game of checkers, he became so angry that he picked up the checkerboard and threw it across the room. The corner of the board struck the baby in the temple as it slept in its cradle, killing it instantly. Both babies were buried on a little knoll overlooking Canyon Ranch.

Cleophas still had family in California, and in 1897 his brother George came to Canyon Ranch for a visit. Cleophas sent his oldest son, also George, to Fort Bridger to pick up a package of fireworks for the upcoming Fourth of July celebration. On the return trip home, the harness broke and the team of horses pulling the wagon got away from young George. When Cleophas saw the broken harness, he pulled his son from the wagon and threatened to beat him. When brother George stepped between father and son and refused to allow it, Cleophas picked up a large stone and threw it at his brother, hitting him in the shoulder. Brother George drew his pistol and shot Cleophas in the groin.

The winter of 1897–98 was a difficult time for the Dowd family. Snowbound in their cabin, Cleophas made life unbearable. As soon as the spring thaw came, Ella gathered up the younger children and took a train to California. Cleophas became irate when he discovered they were gone. Even though his wound hadn't healed, he mounted his horse and went in search of his family. Unable to find any trace of them, he went on a three-week drinking binge.

Returning to the ranch, Cleophas was surprised to find that his two oldest sons, fourteen-year-old George and ten-year-old Charles, had remained behind to take care of the place. Cleophas had a suspicious nature and didn't trust his sons. When asked why they hadn't gone with their mother, they replied that they had been in the mountains rounding up livestock when the rest of the family left.

On the pretense of rounding up strays, Cleophas took his sons into the canyons near the Green River. George waited until their father rode on ahead and then, pulling Charley aside, said, "Papa brought us here to kill us. Now, whatever I say to him, you agree with me, you hear?" Charley looked down at the ground and nodded.

They sat around the campfire that night, and Cleophas asked once again why they hadn't gone with their mother. George thought about it for a moment before he spoke. Knowing it wouldn't take much to set his father off, he phrased his words carefully. "Because we love you, Papa," George lied. "Mama abandoned us too. We want to stay with you." Cleophas asked Charley the same question, and Charley gave him the same reply. Their answers seemed to satisfy him.

Cleophas's wound was so painful that he was unable to work around the ranch. George and Charley did the best they could, but the chores were too much for them. On a clear spring day, a man named Charles

Reaser arrived at the ranch looking for work. He was a rat-faced man who chewed tobacco and spit after every few words. His nose and chin were so close together, they nearly touched when he talked. Desperate, Cleophas hired him on the spot.

George and Reaser spent many long hours together, and it wasn't long before George told him how abusive Cleophas was. Reaser offered to help him put an end to it. On the morning of April 11, 1898, they put their plan into action. They knew that due to a hunting accident, Cleophas had stopped carrying a gun and was therefore unarmed an easy target.

Cleophas went into the barn to repair a broken harness, and Charley went across the creek to drive the milk cows home. George walked over to his brother and told him not to go back to the house because something was about to happen. Charley hid in some bushes near the barn and waited. George went into the house and emerged a few minutes later with his father's gun. Reaser took the gun and walked to the barn. As Charley watched, two shots rang out. Reaser ran to the corral, mounted his horse, and rode away from the ranch.

An inquest was held at the Dowd Ranch, and Charles Reaser pleaded self-defense. He claimed that when he went into the barn, Cleophas drew a gun and fired at him. The bullet missed and lodged in the doorjamb. Reaser stated that he returned fire, one bullet hitting Cleophas in the head and the other bullet hitting the wall. The justice of the peace accepted the plea of self-defense, and he and Reaser went out and got drunk.

Brown's Hole hasn't changed much in the last 150 years. It is still a wild, rugged land. On a small knoll overlooking the old ranch that Cleophas called home, the outlaw priest and two of his children rest in eternal sleep.

The Great Train Robbery of 1895

Near the small desert town of Wilcox, Arizona, a valuable treasure of Mexican silver pesos lies scattered in the sand, the result of one of the zaniest train robberies in the history of Arizona.

Times were tough in the Arizona Territory in 1895, and jobs and money were hard to come by. Most of the cowhands were broke or unemployed, and Grant Wheeler and Joe George were no exception. Leaning against the hitching rail in front of a saloon, they decided to do something to change their situation. Since the Southern Pacific Railroad had plenty of money, they would rob the westbound train.

Grant and Joe had never robbed a train before. How difficult could it be to stop a slow-moving train, break into the express car, and make off with the contents of the safe? If all those other guys could get away with it, why couldn't they?

Posing as prospectors, the two men purchased a large supply of blasting caps and a case of dynamite. They stashed the explosives a few miles west of town, tied their horses to a nearby tree, and walked two miles along the track until they came to a steep grade. As the train approached, it slowed down long enough for Grant and Joe to jump aboard.

Grant held the engineer and fireman at gunpoint and ordered the engineer to stop the train while Joe jumped down from the cab and uncoupled the passenger cars. On a signal from the outlaws, the engineer moved the engine and express and baggage cars forward to the spot where the dynamite was hidden. The outlaws broke into the express car expecting to find the guard waiting for them with a loaded shotgun. To their surprise, the car was empty. The guard had jumped out the door and disappeared down the tracks.

In the center of the car, the bandits found a large Wells Fargo safe and dozens of sacks of "dobe dollars" (silver pesos) piled against a wall. Believing that a few well-placed sticks of dynamite would do the job, they lit the fuses and ducked for cover. The blast made a lot of noise, but the safe remained intact.

Undaunted by their failure to open the safe, they packed dynamite against the safe's door and added a few extra sticks just to be sure. The resulting explosion blew out the doors and windows of the express car, but only scratched the paint on the safe and scattered a few silver pesos across the car's interior.

The frustrated desperados weren't quite ready to give up yet. They packed their remaining explosives against the safe, covered them with eight large sacks of "dobe dollars" to hold the dynamite in place, lit the fuse, and ran for cover. The blast shook the ground like a California earthquake and turned the express car into kindling. Large pieces of wood flew through the air in every direction, followed by thousands of silver pesos.

Perhaps it was just dumb luck that Grant and Joe weren't hurt or killed by the flying silver. The airborne coins filled the air like shrapnel from an artillery barrage, sowing the desert with bent and twisted pesos. They embedded themselves in everything they hit, including the telegraph poles and cacti along the tracks.

Once the smoke cleared, the robbers returned to the remains of the express car. The explosion had torn the door of the safe off its hinges and blown it several feet away. Except for a few American dollars, the safe was empty. The only things on the train worth taking were the silver pesos, and they were scattered all over the landscape.

Disappointed with their take, the outlaws picked up a few coins and rode off into the desert. When news of the fiasco reached Wilcox, the good citizens of the town grabbed their rakes and rushed to the crime scene. The silver-laden telegraph poles and the bent and twisted coins became valuable souvenirs. Many years after the robbery, people were still uncovering silver coins.

Grant and Joe must have believed the old adage "If at first you don't succeed, try, try again." On February 26 they stopped another Southern Pacific train near Stein's Pass in southwestern New Mexico. As luck would have it, the engineer and fireman were the same ones they'd held up in their previous robbery.

Grant kept them covered while Joe uncoupled the cars. They ordered the engineer to move the train two miles up the track to the place where they had stashed the dynamite. With the trainmen in front of them, they walked back to the express car. To their dismay, it wasn't there. Joe had uncoupled the wrong car. The express car was two miles down the track, still coupled to the passenger cars. The robbers released their captives; when the train was out of sight, they lit the fuse on the unused dynamite. Without looking back, they rode away.

Wells Fargo and the Southern Pacific didn't take too kindly to having their property treated in such a cavalier manner. W. M. Breakenridge, the agent in charge of the Southern Pacific in southern Arizona, was directed to organize a posse and capture the outlaws. He caught up with Grant near Mancos, Colorado, on April 25. Rather than allowing himself to be taken alive, Grant committed suicide.

As for Joe, it isn't certain what became of him. According to the official Arizona State Historian Marshall Trimble, he was eventually tracked down and killed. Fred Moore, who settled in southern Arizona in 1875, told a different story. As a young man, he had befriended the outlaws and knew them quite well. In an interview with Helen Smith of Cochise County, Fred stated, "Joe was tracked down, arrested, and sent to the territorial prison in Yuma. I ran into him in a restaurant in Cochise many years later. He was dressed in fine clothes, a diamond stickpin in his cravat and a large ring on his finger. He looked like a highly successful gambler.

"He started a conversation with me," Fred continued, "and he seemed vaguely familiar. I tumbled to his identity when I noticed that his trigger finger was missing. Joe's trigger finger had been shot away. As to what became of him, I have no idea, nor have I heard more about him. An instinctive distrust made me hurry to the caboose and keep out of sight until I knew he was not aboard the train."

But for the lure of easy money, we might never have heard of Grant Wheeler and Joe George. Unlike the James brothers, who made a serious living robbing trains, the antics of Grant and Joe gave everyone a good laugh. They weren't the most successful train robbers in the history of Arizona, but they may have been the funniest.

Vigilante Justice

FEW CHARACTERS IN THE OLD WEST HAVE FIRED OUR IMAGINATIONS like the gunfighters who rode the Western trails. Their legends have been told and retold for generations, and people never seem to tire of them. Movies, television, and popular fiction have presented these men as romantic heroes, but in reality many of them were vicious killers. One such hombre was a hard-living gunslinger named Joseph A. "Jack" Slade. Slade's story is a tale of mayhem and murder on the high plains of Colorado.

Jack Slade was born to wealth and influence in Carlyle, Illinois, in 1829. As a young boy he had an uncontrollable temper, and he displayed murderous tendencies at an early age. By the time he reached the tender age of thirteen, he had killed his first man. The man was annoying Jack and his school friends, and he felt justified in killing him. Picking up a rock, he threw it at the man and hit him in the head. To avoid prosecution, his parents hustled him off to Texas.

In 1847 Jack enlisted in the army and went off to fight the Mexicans. When the war ended, he took a job driving freight wagons over the Oregon Trail and later hired on as a stagecoach guard. Once, while riding shotgun over a particularly dangerous stretch of road, his coach was attacked by four mounted Indians. Jack killed three of them and took the fourth one prisoner. He sliced off the ears of the dead men and gave them to the surviving Indian along with a warning to his chief not to attack any more stagecoaches. As Jack's prowess with a gun grew, the demand for his services increased.

In the late 1850s the settlement of Julesburg in northeastern Colorado was home to a way station for the Overland Stage Company and a trading post that had been established a decade earlier by a French trader named Jules Beni, the reputed leader of a band of cutthroats. The company had hired Jules to serve as superintendent of the Overland Sweetwater Division, but they soon realized their mistake. The Sweetwater Division stretched for two hundred miles over some of the most dangerous territory in the West, and the stations along the line of travel were prime targets for the gangs of outlaws who infested the territory.

Jules was a vile character with a reputation to match. The horses he swapped to travelers crossing the plains somehow found their way back to his corrals. The supplies he sold were robbed from the buyers and returned to the trading post to be sold again. Haystacks meant to provide feed for the teams of horses that pulled the stagecoaches mysteriously caught fire on a regular basis. Jules bought replacement hay at exorbitant prices and split the profits with his friends. Over time, reports of Jules's nefarious activities filtered back to the company offices. Ben Ficklin, general superintendent for the Overland, made a surprise visit to the station to verify the reports. Discovering they were true, he fired Jules on the spot and hired Slade to replace him.

Being fired didn't set too well with Jules. Angry with his treatment at the hands of the superintendent, he threatened to get even. Each time Jack attempted to upgrade the stage stations under his control, Jules interfered. On one occasion, Jack went to Jules's ranch to recover some horses that belonged to the stage company. As Jack led the horses out of the corral, Jules swore vengeance against him. Over the next few months, Jules continued to create problems for the new superintendent.

On a quiet spring morning in 1859, Jack rode onto the grounds of the Julesburg station. Unarmed and not expecting trouble, Jules and a few hired hands were engaged in conversation near the corral. When Jules saw his nemesis heading for the bunkhouse, he pulled out a pistol and pumped six slugs into Jack's body. Jack staggered around the corner of the ranch house. Seeing that Jack was still alive, Jules grabbed a loaded double-barreled shotgun and took off after him. He caught up with his quarry and emptied both barrels into him at point-blank range.

Jules stood over the bleeding body of his enemy and examined his handiwork. "There's an empty dry-goods crate in the barn," he said. "When he's dead, you can put him in it and bury him." Jules turned and walked away.

Legend has it, and witnesses swear it's true, the wounded man pushed himself to his feet and confronted Jules. "You needn't trouble yourself about my burial. I don't intend to die. I'll live long enough to wear one of your ears on my watch-guard."

One of the ranch hands lifted Jack onto his horse, tied him to the saddle, and took him back to Julesburg. The doctor worked on his shattered body for hours removing bullets and buckshot, and Jack refused to die. As soon as he was strong enough to travel, he took a stagecoach back to the family home in Illinois to complete his recovery.

While Jack was being doctored, the hired hands decided to invite Jules to a necktie party. They tossed a rope over a large beam between two freight wagons, dropped a noose around his neck, and strung him up. Someone must have been watching over Jules. At that exact moment, Ben Ficklin rode into the station and cut him down. Upon hearing the details of the shooting, Ficklin ordered Jules to clear out of the territory forever or face vigilante justice. Realizing that if he stayed he'd end his days swinging at the end of a rope, Jules climbed on his horse and disappeared.

Jules moved his operations west to the Rocky Ridge Division near the Wyoming border where his outlaw gang was creating the same kind of trouble they had inflicted on the Sweetwater Division. The Overland Stage Company needed their most feared enforcer, and Jack was not about to pass up his chance to exact revenge.

Jack returned to Colorado and took over as superintendent of the Rocky Ridge Division. The records aren't clear, but somewhere along the way he married an alleged prostitute named Virginia Dale. Weighing in at 160 pounds, she was described as tall and voluptuous; in reality she was a rather nasty character, forever interfering in her husband's business. There is no doubt in anyone's mind that she was the cause of most of their problems.

Virginia was an expert horsewoman and almost as good with a gun as her husband. When a gang of outlaws captured her husband, he asked to be allowed to say goodbye to his wife before they killed him. The outlaws brought Virginia to the cabin where they were holding her husband. She had several pistols hidden under her skirt and started firing as soon as she walked through the door. Jack grabbed one of the guns and joined the fray. After the smoke cleared, the gun-toting young couple walked out unhurt, leaving the dead outlaws in their wake.

Jules and his band of cutthroats continued to terrorize the countryside, and Jack was determined to put a stop to his activities once and for all. He recruited a posse and caught up with Jules driving a herd of stolen horses toward Julesburg. When the posse opened fire on the rustlers, Jules was wounded. Jack ordered him tied to a post at the Virginia Dale stage stop, a station he had built and named for his wife.

Jules had plenty of time to reflect on his fate. Throughout the night, he remained tied to the post. In the morning Jack emerged from the bunkhouse and walked over to his captive. He raised his pistol, took careful aim, and fired. The bullet struck Jules in the arm. Leaving the wounded man hanging from the post, Jack turned and walked back into the station to eat his breakfast. When he finished his meal, he walked outside and shot Jules again. Perhaps it was Jack's need for vengeance or the whiskey he had consumed that caused him to continue using his enemy for target practice. Late in the afternoon, he put an end to it with a fatal shot to Jules's head. He pulled his knife and carved off Jules's ears as souvenirs. He attached them to his watch chain and carried them for the rest of his life.

Through he was exonerated, Jack was becoming a major problem for the Overland Stage Company. He was blamed for hangings, shootings, beatings, and assaults. In a drunken rage, he smashed up the settlers' store at Fort Halleck, shooting canned goods off the grocery shelves. Now that the lawless element that had preyed on the stagecoaches was gone, Jack's services were no longer needed. The Overland Stage Company terminated his employment.

With his job gone, Jack and Virginia pulled up stakes and moved on to Virginia City in the Montana Territory. He bought a small ranch a few miles outside of town and was hired as a supervisor of a toll road. He was responsible for collecting tolls, maintaining the road, and keeping travelers safe from outlaws.

As was to be expected, Jack spent his time drinking, gambling, fighting, and carousing while Virginia did most of the work around their home. Whenever he went on a bender, Jack and his friends galloped their horses up and down the streets. Yelling like wild Indians, they shot out windows and streetlamps and rode their horses into stores and saloons, destroying them from within. It wasn't long before Jack wore out his welcome.

Virginia City was a wild place, but Jack's shenanigans were too much for the townspeople to stomach. Convening an emergency session of the Vigilance Committee, they issued a warrant for Jack's arrest on charges of disturbing the peace. Jack tore the writ into little pieces, grabbed his gun, and went in search of the judge who had issued it and the deputy who had served it.

At the same instant Jack spotted the judge, the vigilantes spotted Jack. They took him into custody and read the charges against him. They informed him that he had one hour to live, so if he had any business to attend to, he'd better do it straightaway.

Some of Jack's friends among the vigilantes tried to intervene on his behalf, but to no avail. Someone tossed a rope over the crosspiece of a corral gate. Standing on some boxes with a rope around his neck, he pleaded for his life. When Jack's hour had passed, the crowd shouted, "Times up!"

When the leader of the vigilantes learned that Virginia was on her way, he kicked the boxes out from under the condemned man, sending him to his death. Perhaps he had heard how Jack and Virginia wiped out a gang of outlaws in Colorado and didn't want to give her the opportunity to rescue her husband again.

Virginia arrived in town too late to save her husband. Seeing him swinging at the end of a rope, she cursed the men who killed him and the crowd for allowing it to happen. She swore that Jack would never be buried in "this damned territory." The mob was in no mood to put up with her tirade. They told Virginia to take her husband's body and get out of town. If she ever came back, they'd string her up too.

The bereaved widow had the undertaker place the body in a zinc-lined casket. She filled it with whiskey to preserve Jack's corpse and kept it under her bed to wait for the end of winter. As soon as the snow in the mountain passes melted, she hired a wagon and shipped his remains to Salt Lake City, to be transferred to an eastbound stage to his family's home in Illinois.

By the time the wagon reached Utah, it was mid-July, and summer is not a good time to haul a body almost two thousand miles. Jack's coffin was buried in the "Stranger's Lot" in the Salt Lake City Cemetery with instructions "to be removed to Illinois in the fall." No one ever came to claim Jack's body. To this day he waits in his whiskey-filled coffin for the eastbound stage to Illinois.

The Gentleman Bandit

IMAGINE A WESTERN OUTLAW WHO WALKS EVERYWHERE BECAUSE HE'S afraid of horses, doesn't carry a loaded gun because he doesn't want to shoot anyone, and doesn't belong to a gang, and you have a picture of one of the most unusual highwaymen in the history of the West. From 1875 to 1883, this elusive bandit robbed twenty-nine stagecoaches; and escaped twenty-nine times.

Charles Bolton, alias "Black Bart," was a mild-mannered, middle-aged gentleman whose targets were the Wells Fargo stagecoaches that traveled from the foothills of the Sierras to the Sonoma coast of California. His weapon of choice was an empty double-barreled 12 gauge shotgun, and he often left verses of poetry behind to amuse his victims and taunt his pursuers. He eschewed profanity and was polite to the ladies. He took only what was in the strong boxes, and he never robbed the passengers.

One of seven children born to John and Maria Boles, Charles first saw the light of day in Norfolk County, England, in 1829. When Charles was two years old, the family migrated to Jefferson County in upstate New York and settled in Alexandria Township. John earned his living from farming a one-hundred-acre homestead; over the next few years, two more children were born.

Charles had no desire to be a farmer; he craved adventure. Life on the farm was too tame for him, and he planned to leave at the first opportunity. When gold was discovered in California in 1849, Charles and his cousin David set out for the gold fields. They spent the winter months in St. Joseph, Missouri, and reached California in 1850. The cousins panned for gold on the North Fork of the American River, but since pickings were slim, they moved on to other gold strikes in Butte, El Dorado, and

Tuolumne Counties. They did manage to find small quantities of gold along the rivers in Shasta and Trinity Counties. With a few dollars in their pockets, Charles and David headed home to New York.

Life on the farm was pretty dull compared to the excitement of the mining camps. Charles returned to California, but after two unsuccessful years of panning for gold, he called it quits. On his way home to New York, he stopped in Decatur, Illinois, long enough to marry Mary Elizabeth Johnson. By the time the Civil War erupted in 1861, she had given birth to two daughters.

Charles didn't care much for the humdrum existence of married life. He was restless and looking for any opportunity to escape. The excitement of war was what he needed, and he enlisted in the 116th Regiment of the Illinois Infantry. Life in the military agreed with Charles, and he enjoyed marching more than twenty miles every day and sleeping on the hard ground. Fighting in most of the major battles of General Grant's Central Mississippi Campaign, he was promoted to first sergeant of Company B during the siege of Vicksburg. Wounded in battle, he recovered in time to join General Sherman's march from Atlanta to the sea and his Campaign of the Carolinas. Mustering out of the army at the end of the war, Charles moved his family to a small farm near New Oregon, Iowa.

The peace and quiet of civilian life was alien and suffocating to someone who missed the excitement of battle. Charles knew he'd never find adventure and excitement if he stayed on the farm, so he said goodbye to his wife and family and went on his way to the silver mines of Idaho and Montana. In 1871 Charles wrote to his wife from Silver Bow, Montana, that dishonest Wells Fargo agents had cheated him and he was going to head to California to take back what was his. That was the last letter his wife ever received from him, so she eventually assumed he was dead.

The legend of Black Bart began on a lonely mountain pass near Copperopolis, California, on July 26, 1875. A solitary figure stood in the middle of the road with a double-barreled shotgun draped over his arm. John Stine, the driver of the coach, was startled to see a strange apparition in a long white linen duster, a flour sack with two holes cut out for eyes, a derby hat perched on top of his head, and his boots wrapped in flour sacks. Stine wasn't about to argue with a double-barreled shotgun.

Bringing his team up short, he stopped the stage a few feet from where the outlaw waited.

In a deep resonant voice that brooked no disobedience, the bandit uttered the words that became his trademark: "Throw down the box." To ensure that Stine complied with his command, the bandit shouted another order, "If he dares shoot, give him a solid volley, boys!" Stine looked up and saw six rifles pointing at him from behind the boulders that lined the sides of the road. Reaching under the seat, the driver grabbed the strongbox and tossed it to the ground. He warned his charges not to do anything stupid.

A woman passenger panicked and threw out her purse. Bart picked it up, bowed to the lady, and returned it to her. "Madam, I do not wish your money," he said. "In that respect I honor only the good office of Wells Fargo." In a quiet voice, he suggested that Stine drive on.

Stine drove down the road for a short distance and stopped. When he was certain that the bandits had left the area, he walked back to look for the strongbox. He was surprised to see the rifles still protruding from the boulders. He stood rock still until he realized the outlaws weren't moving. Afraid of being shot, he cautiously approached the boulders, only to find that what he thought were rifles were nothing more than sticks pointing at the trail.

Wearing his linen duster, his flower sacks, and his derby hat, on December 2, 1875, Charles robbed the stage from North San Juan to Marysville in Yuba County. Six months later he held up the stage from Roseburg to Yreka in Siskiyou County. The Wells Fargo detectives thought the outlaw must be an amateur because he always went after the smaller stagecoaches and left the big ones alone.

In the early 1870s, "dime novel" adventure stories that appeared in the local newspapers were all the rage. The *Sacramento Union* ran a serial called *The Case of Summerfield*. The villain was a black-bearded character named Bartholomew Graham. Dressed in black from head to toe and riding a black stallion, he called himself "Black Bart." Wanted by the law for crimes against humanity and Wells Fargo & Co., Charles decided to expand the legend and build his reputation on this fictional character's exploits. Before long, he was also known as "Black Bart."

On August 3, 1877, Charles stopped the stage from Point Arena to Duncan's Mill in Sonoma County and escaped with three hundred dollars in coins and a check for $305.52. The posse returned to the scene and found a rather whimsical poem penned on the back of a waybill placed under a stone on top of a tree stump. Each sentence was written in a slightly different manner to confound the handwriting experts.

> I've labored long and hard for bread—
> For honor and for riches
> But on my corns too long you've tred,
> You fine-haired sons of bitches.
> Black Bart
> The PO 8

Bart's antics and his pretensions toward poetry were the talk of California. The board of directors for Wells Fargo was not amused and placed their offices up and down the California coast on high alert. Company detectives and lawmen were as mystified by the letters and number at the bottom of the poem as they were about the name Black Bart. The posse scouring the countryside for the elusive bandit found no trace of him, leading a few superstitious souls to spread the rumor that a ghost had robbed the stagecoaches.

Bart lay low for almost a year, until he held up the Wells Fargo stage traveling between Quincy and Oroville, California. Ordering the driver to "Throw down the box," he got away with $379. When the posse arrived, they found an empty strongbox and another poem.

> Here I lay me down to sleep
> To wait the coming morrow,
> Perhaps success, perhaps defeat
> And everlasting sorrow
> Yet come what will, I'll try it once,
> My conditions can't be worse,
> And if there's money in that box,
> 'Tis money in my purse.

Wells Fargo Building, Virginia City, 1866. COURTESY OF THE LIBRARY OF CONGRESS

With each holdup, Bart's legend grew. The governor of California posted a three hundred-dollar reward for Bart's capture and conviction. The US Post Office contributed an additional two hundred dollars, and Wells Fargo added three hundred. A Wells Fargo flyer described him as follows: "He is polite to all passengers, and especially to the ladies. He comes and goes from the scene of the robbery on foot; seems to be a thorough mountaineer and a good walker." The eight hundred dollars was never collected.

Bart became more elusive than ever. All of his crimes were committed far away from civilization, and he never left any clues behind. His usual routine was to leave his home in San Francisco and board the evening boat for Stockton, arriving there the next morning. Since he was afraid of horses, he walked forty miles into the mountains and camped out under the stars to wait for the stage. Upon completion of his nefarious deed, he removed any traces that he had ever been there and walked out of the mountains to his next destination.

Bart disliked Wells Fargo, but he wasn't vindictive. He might stop three or four stages in a row and then disappear for six months. He was considered a gentleman by most of the drivers because he was always polite and never shot anybody. When ordered to "Throw down the box," the drivers generally complied.

One cantankerous hard case named George Hackett refused to accede to his demands. Hackett was driving the stage along a mountain road near Strawberry, California, when Bart jumped out from behind a boulder and stopped the coach. In a quiet voice, Bart requested, "Please throw down your strongbox," but Hackett refused. Instead he grabbed a rifle from under his seat and fired a shot at the bandit. The bullet grazed the top right side of Bart's forehead, leaving a permanent scar. Not waiting for a second shot, Bart dashed into the woods and vanished.

Wells Fargo had become the laughingstock of the country and the butt of many jokes. James Hume, chief investigator for Wells Fargo, was determined to end the highwayman's career. His first big break came when he found some people who claimed they'd seen him, or dined with a man who might be Black Bart, or encountered him walking cross-country in the areas where many of the robberies occurred. One man reported that the stranger had graying hair with patches of baldness at the temples, two missing front teeth, a mustache, and slender hands that showed no evidence of hard work. All the witnesses spoke of his gentle manner and wondered if such a well-mannered man could be the notorious bandit Hume was looking for.

Hume's second break, which became Bart's undoing, came with the robbery of the Sonora–Milton stage. Just as he always did, Bart planned this holdup with meticulous care. Over a few drinks, the miners he befriended at the Patterson Mine told him that the Sonora stage would be carrying a significant amount of gold dust and amalgam, the date of the shipment, and what route the stage would take. With this information, Bart put his plan into action.

Bart spent the night in Reynolds Ferry at an inn operated by Madame Rolleri and her nineteen-year-old son, Jimmy. Early the next morning, the stage rolled to a stop in front of the inn. The driver climbed down from his perch and went inside for breakfast. Jimmy wanted to do some small-game hunting along the stagecoach road and asked if he could hitch a ride. As the stage started up the steep grade of Funk Mountain, Jimmy grabbed his rifle and jumped off. He headed into the brush to see if he could flush some game for dinner. McConnell, the driver, continued up the slope; when the stage reached the top, Bart jumped from his hiding place behind a boulder.

"Where's your passenger?" asked Bart. He had watched the stage approach and knew there had been two men on board.

"It wasn't no passenger," McConnell replied. "It was just young Jimmy Rolleri, who hoped to get a shot at a deer or a fox with his new rifle."

Bart told the driver to unhook the team and take it down the road. The driver chocked one of the wheels on the rig so it wouldn't roll down the hill and led the horses away. When he had gone about forty yards, Bart motioned for him to stop, climbed into the coach, and smashed the box with an ax.

McConnell spotted Jimmy coming around the hill and motioned him over to the horses. Together, they made their way back up the hill. They took cover and watched as Bart backed out of the coach with his loot. McConnell grabbed Jimmy's rifle, took two shots at Bart, and missed. Jimmy took the rifle, fired once, and scored a hit. Clutching his loot, Bart rabbited into the brush and skedaddled down the hill, losing his derby in the process. He dropped a blood-splattered bundle of mail in his haste to escape, but by the time the posse arrived, he had vanished.

Wells Fargo detectives descended on Funk Mountain in the hope of corralling Bart and retrieving the stolen money. They searched the area and discovered two bags of crackers and a tin of sugar, a pair of field glasses, a couple of flour sacks, three dirty linen cuffs, a razor, and a bloodstained handkerchief bearing a laundry mark in one corner reading "F.X.0.7." Sometime later, they located a woman who had sold the provisions to Bart and two men who'd seen a stranger who matched a physical description of the bandit.

The detectives were convinced the mark in the corner of the hand-kerchief belonged to one of San Francisco's numerous laundries, and that it would lead to Bart's arrest. Wells Fargo detective Henry Morse spent an entire week checking out more than a hundred San Francisco laundries, and his determination paid off. The owner of Ware's Bush Street Tobacco Shop & California Laundry identified the laundry mark as belonging to Charles E. Bolton, a retired mining engineer who lived down the street at the Webb House.

While Morse was questioning Ware, Charles walked through the door to pick up his laundry. Morse engaged him in conversation by stating he understood Charles was interested in mines. Morse told him that if Charles would give his expert opinion on a piece of property Morse owned, Morse would be happy to show him some of the ore samples from the mine. Morse sounded sincere, and Charles fell for his story. He accompanied the detective to his office, and when he entered and took in his surroundings, Charles knew without a doubt he had been caught. He threw up his hands and exclaimed, "Gentlemen, I pass." Morse later told reporters his first impressions of Charles were that of a man elegantly attired and carrying a little cane. He wore a natty little derby hat, a diamond stickpin, a large diamond ring on his little finger, and a heavy gold pocket watch and chain. "One would have taken him for a gentleman who made a fortune and was enjoying it," said Morse.

The police thought Black Bart would be much younger than the man they held in their jail. They were amazed to learn that a fifty-year-old man could rob so many stagecoaches and elude the law for so long. The police report stated, "He exhibited genuine wit under most trying circumstances. He is extremely proper and polite in behavior, eschews profanity, and he is a person of great endurance." The report went on to describe Charles as being five feet, eight inches tall, 160 pounds, with an arrow-straight posture, deep-set blue eyes, a light complexion, a broad white mustache, and a pointed beard.

In his hotel room, investigators found a Bible that had been given to him by his wife in 1865. It bore the name of Charles E. Boles. They also discovered a linen duster, flour sacks, a shotgun, and clothes inscribed

Charles Bowles, aka "Black Bart," American stagecoach robber.
COURTESY OF THE LIBRARY OF CONGRESS

with the same laundry mark as the handkerchief. There was no doubt in anyone's mind that Charles Bolton and Black Bart were the same person.

When Charles was booked, he gave his name as T. Z. Spalding, the proud owner of a gold mine on the California–Nevada border. He denied his name was Charles Bolton or that he had ever robbed a stagecoach. It wasn't until he was identified by the people he encountered during the planning stages of his last robbery that he confessed to robbing the Sonora–Milton stage. Charles surmised that if he confessed to this one holdup, the statute of limitations on the robberies he had committed prior to 1879 would protect him from prosecution, and the judge agreed with him.

The judge could have sentenced Charles to life in prison for his crimes but instead gave him a sentence of six years in San Quentin. After serving four years and two months, Charles walked out of prison a free man. He disappeared and was never heard from again. For a while it was thought that he had returned to his bandit ways when a Wells Fargo stage was robbed. The bandit left a note that read:

> So here I've stood while wind and rain
> Have set the trees a'sobbin'
> And risked my life for that damned stage
> That wasn't worth the robbin'.

Chief of Detectives James Hume examined the note and compared it to Bart's poetry. He declared the note a hoax and stated that, in his opinion, Black Bart had permanently retired. Hume's statement gave credence to the rumor that Wells Fargo was paying Bart a large lifetime annuity if he would stop robbing their stagecoaches.

No one is certain what became of Charles Bolton. Reporters and writers had the outlaw living in luxury in New Orleans, St. Louis, Mexico City, or a hundred other places. Although his death was never confirmed, several New York newspapers printed an obituary claiming that Charles died in 1917.

The wit who said crime doesn't pay never met Charles Bolton. As Black Bart, Charles robbed twenty-nine stagecoaches and got away with an estimated forty thousand dollars. It goes without saying that for Charles E. Bolton, crime did pay.

Whatever Lola Wants, Lola Gets

In 1849 the Forty Niners came seeking gold and the land was changed forever. In 1853 Lola Montez came to San Francisco, and California was never the same. When the sailing ship *Northerner* tied up to the pier, the waiting crowd pushed and shoved toward the gangplank, hoping to catch a glimpse of this legendary femme fatale who deigned to honor their city with her royal presence. As she strolled down the gangway, someone yelled, "Lola has come!" and the crowd went wild. It was a phrase that would be repeated many times throughout the California gold camps.

Lola's parentage and place of birth were so obfuscated that for many years no one was certain who her parents were or where she was born. At times she claimed to be the illegitimate daughter of the poet Lord Byron or the offspring of a famous matador. To hear her tell it, she was born in such romantic cities as Madrid, Lucerne, Calcutta, or Constantinople. The public image she created for herself was far removed from the truth.

The daughter of a British Army officer, Lieutenant Edward Gilbert, and a Spanish danseuse from Madrid, Lola was born Eliza Rosanna Gilbert in County Sligo, Ireland, on February 17, 1821. Before she was a year old, her father was ordered to India, and it wasn't long after the family arrived in Calcutta that he died of cholera.

Eliza's mother didn't stay a widow for very long. She remarried and Eliza was sent to Scotland to live with her stepfather's parents. This wild and beautiful young girl jolted their strict Presbyterian sensibilities by running naked through the streets of town. Without waiting to hear from her mother, they shipped her off to a private boarding school in Paris. In addition to learning foreign languages and other things every young girl needed to know to find her place in society, she also honed her fiery temper to perfection.

When Eliza turned eighteen, her mother arranged for her to marry Sir Abraham Lumley, an eighty-year-old judge of the Supreme Court of England. Lola disobeyed her mother's wishes and eloped with Lieutenant Thomas James, a young officer her mother had sent to plead the judge's case. Eliza and her new husband moved to India, but before long another woman caught the lieutenant's fancy; he eloped with the wife of his regiment's adjutant.

Eliza's mother and stepfather weren't too happy with this scandalous situation. To protect their good name, they gave her a check for one thousand pounds and sent her back to England. Arriving in London, she became the mistress of the aide de camp to the military governor of India. A few months later, her wandering husband caught up with her and publicly accused her of misconduct. After dragging her through the courts, he was granted a legal separation, but not a divorce. Eliza's mother was so ashamed of her daughter that she went into mourning as if Lola were dead.

Now that Eliza's mother wanted nothing more to do with her, Eliza had to find a way to earn a living. She wanted to be an actress, but since she didn't have the talent for it, she decided to become a professional dancer. Knowing that no one would pay to see Eliza Gilbert dance across the London stage, she changed her name to Lola Montez.

Lola's first performance was a disaster. She couldn't dance any better than she could act. The audience became angry when they discovered that the Spanish dancer they had come to see was none other than the notorious Mrs. James. They booed her off the stage with their hisses and catcalls and threw a few rotten vegetables at her for good measure. It didn't matter to Lola that these oafs couldn't recognize talent when they saw it. As far as she was concerned, a star had been born.

Lola left England for a short time and studied Spanish dances in Madrid. She toured the capitals of Europe and accepted dancing engagements whenever she could get them. In St. Petersburg, Russia, Lola was granted a private audience with the czar. He rewarded her with one thousand rubles for services rendered.

In Warsaw, Lola enraged her audiences by pouting and flinging her garters at them. On one occasion, she performed an impromptu striptease, removing her skirt and most of her undergarments. The manager fired her on the spot and banned her from ever dancing in the theater again.

The viceroy of Poland was so enraptured with Lola's beauty that he fell hopelessly in love with her. He offered to give her the finest estates in Poland and drape her body in diamonds if she would become his mistress. Lola found this sixty-year-old reprobate so repulsive that she refused his advances. Insulted by her refusal, he tried to get her fired from the theater. At her next performance, she told her audience what was going on. Much to the chagrin of the viceroy, the audience rioted and almost destroyed the theater.

In Dresden, Lola was introduced to famed composer Franz Liszt. They carried on a fiery romance until she became jealous of all the attention her paramour was receiving from his adoring fans. After a particularly heated argument, Lola became so angry with her lover that she crashed a banquet he was hosting. Leaping up on a table, she started to dance among the dishes, spilling hot soup on some of the guests.

Liszt had a reputation as the greatest lover in Europe, but after a few months with Lola, he was exhausted. One night while she was asleep, he slipped out of their hotel room, locking the door behind him. As he climbed into his waiting coach, he told the coachman, "It is true that I understand women. I have already paid for the furniture she will break when she discovers my absence."

Lola tried dancing in Paris, but the French treated her worse than the English. She did, however, create a sensation with her famous temper. She always carried a whip, and any man who annoyed her was a target. When one of her lovers disappointed her, she chased him down the street, firing her pistol at him. With his pants down around his knees, he dodged her bullets and quickly hobbled away. On one occasion, she horsewhipped a bodyguard for the king of Prussia.

An English writer who followed her antics with great interest wrote, "There is nothing wonderful about her except her beauty and her impudence. She has no talent or any of the graces which make women attractive; yet many men of talent rave about her."

Before she left Paris, she had a brief affair with Alexander Dumas, Sr. Within a week of being introduced to Charles Dujarier, a distinguished French journalist, she became his mistress. As if he had a premonition, Dumas warned his friend, "She has an evil eye and is sure to bring bad luck to anyone who closely links his destiny with hers."

Failing to heed his friend's warning, a short time later the journalist was killed in a duel with one of his readers over an unpublished manuscript. In his will he left Lola twenty thousand francs, some stock, and a letter that read:

My ever dearest ever Lola: I want to explain why it was I slept by myself and did not come to you this morning. It is because I have to fight a duel. All my calmness is required, and seeing you would have upset me. By two o'clock this afternoon everything will be over. A thousand fond farewells to the dear little girl I love so much, and the thought of whom will be with me forever.

During Lola's lifetime, Dujarier may have been her only true love. Upon learning that the man she loved was mortally wounded, she rushed to his bedside and flung herself on his dying body. Crying in despair, she covered his face with kisses. Even though she wasn't involved in the argument between Dujarier and his opponent, Lola was blamed for his death.

In 1846 Lola accepted an engagement to dance at the theater in Munich, and there are many stories of how she became the consort of King Ludwig of Bavaria. According to one story, the theater manager was appalled with Lola's dancing. He claimed it was so bad that no one would ever pay to see her prance around the stage and said she was the worst dancer he had ever had the misfortune to witness. He fired her on the spot.

Infuriated, Lola went to the palace to present her case directly to the king. Still in costume, she stormed past the startled palace guards into Ludwig's private study. In an angry voice, she demanded that the king fire the manager and reinstate her in the theater. Surprised by this unexpected interruption to the affairs of state and not knowing what to say, he inquired if her lovely figure was a work of nature or a work of art.

Lola Montez (1861 or earlier). COURTESY OF THE LIBRARY OF CONGRESS

Lola knew how to use her charms to make men do what she wanted. Picking up a pair of scissors from his desk, she slit her dress open to the waist. To Ludwig's astonishment, she thrust her breasts into his face. The king fired the manager and gave Lola a long-term engagement at the Munich Theater.

In another version of this story, Ludwig attended Lola's opening night performance and, smitten with her beauty, summoned her to the palace. Other writers insisted that Lola sought and was granted an interview with the king. While they may not agree on how Lola and Ludwig met, they do agree that in a very short time, she became his mistress.

Ludwig was as eccentric as Lola was beautiful. He never rode in his royal coach, not even to occasions of state. Night and day he prowled the streets of the city, knocking the hats off the heads of anyone unlucky enough to cross his path. Dressing like an English gentleman on a fox hunt, he wore an outlandish hat with a long plume. When the mood struck him, he wrote poetry, and he kept a portrait gallery of all the beautiful women he met.

The king was now desperately in love with Lola. Within a few weeks, he conferred on her the title of Countess of Landsfeld and gave her a generous allowance from the public treasury. Granting her a pension of twenty thousand florins, he built a lavish palace for her. For the courtyard of her new home, Ludwig even designed a magnificent marble fountain that sprayed an arc of perfumed water into the air. This aging lothario was so mesmerized by Lola's beauty that he allowed her to rule his kingdom.

Lola took control of king and country, and in a very short time alienated the royal court and the king's subjects. She was rude to the queen and meddled in the politics of the kingdom. Angry with Lola for instituting democratic reforms in the government, the Jesuits conspired to eliminate her. The king's advisors tried to warn him that unless he got rid of this scheming female who now ruled in his name, he might lose his throne. He became angry, refused to listen, and ordered them out of his chambers.

While the citizens of Bavaria may have been amused with Ludwig's harmless eccentricities, they were angry with Lola's hateful behavior. She swore in public and buggy-whipped anyone she disliked. Feeling threatened by the huge bulldog that accompanied her everywhere, they plotted against her.

The final showdown between the countess and the people of Bavaria came when Lola tried to change the policies and traditions of the University of Munich. When the students rioted, Lola convinced the king to close the university. Joined by the merchants who stood to lose the students' business, the students rioted again. Mob rule became the order of the day, and revolution was imminent unless Lola left the country.

The princes of the realm held an emergency meeting and presented the demands of the people to the king. "I will never abandon Lola," the king said. "I would rather lose my crown." Ludwig was forced to abdicate in favor of his son. Lola's Bavarian citizenship was revoked, and she was banished from the kingdom.

Lola returned to England where, even though she was legally married to Thomas James, she wed a young army officer. To avoid arrest on a charge of bigamy, the couple fled to Spain. According to some reports, her husband drowned and she had to leave Spain in a hurry.

Lola arrived in America in 1851 and, even though she couldn't dance, played to packed houses for more than a year in New York. One theater manager described her dancing as "unusually modest and inoffensive, even though her behavior often shocked the audience." He later stated, "She danced through a certain routine of steps without regard to time, music, or anything else."

Moving on to New Orleans, Lola crossed the Isthmus of Panama and booked passage on the *Northerner* bound for California. While on board ship, she met Patrick Purdy Hull, a man who bore an uncanny resemblance to her former lover Charles Dujarier. Like Dujarier, he too was a journalist and part owner of a newspaper. During the long voyage he fell in love with her and wanted to marry her, but she wasn't sure she needed another husband just yet. Hull's partner was waiting for them at the dock, and the two men, one on each side, escorted Lola through the mob to the seclusion of a hotel.

Just as the San Franciscans rushed to the waterfront to welcome the countess to their city, the newspapers waxed wild over her visit. The *San Francisco Examiner* wrote, "This distinguished wonder, this world-bewildering puzzle, the Countess of Landsfeld, has come to San Francisco and her coming has acted like the application of fire to combustible matter. She sways hearts and potentates, editors and public opinion."

Lola agreed to appear on stage as Lady Teazle in *The School for Scandal.*

The May 23, 1853, issue of the *Daily Alta California* reported:

The public of San Francisco will have an opportunity to gratify its long awakened curiosity, on Thursday night next, by visiting the American Theatre, where and when Lola Montez will make her debut before a California audience. An engagement has been made with her by Mr. Baker, and she will appear on that night. We can say nothing of her theatrical ability, never having seen her upon the stage. But who has not heard of her and her gallant spirit, her independent Republican nature? Who has not heard how the sins of the aristocracy were heaped upon her because she possessed the royal favor, and how her troublesome Democracy was got rid of by the usual tyranny of despotism exile? Are not these things written in the books of history of Bavaria?

The demand for tickets was so great, they were auctioned off to the highest bidders. The crowd hadn't come to see Lola act, they wanted to see her famous Spider Dance. In describing this dance that Lola had invented, one reporter wrote:

Lola looked her loveliest as she pirouetted into view, her long slender legs in flesh-colored tights, for she no longer danced without the requisite maillot. Her glossy hair, wreathed in flowers, fell to her shoulders. Her skirt consisted of tiers of tinted chiffons, creating the illusion of a spider's web, entrapping her as she spun around, constricting her step. With the music slowing down she struggled to free herself and shake off the spiders lurking in her chiffons. As the dance grew more frantic she shed the spiders and stamped them underfoot. When the music changed to a jig, Lola spread out her hands and feet like a spider and leaped from one side of the stage to the other. The effect was as grotesque as it was riveting. It all ended with fire and abandon as she stomped on the last of the fallen spiders.

Lola played to packed houses in an autobiographical epic titled *Lola Montez in Bavaria*. Despite the fact that the prompter was kept busy correcting her mistakes, the play ran for a whole week, a record for San Francisco theaters.

William and Caroline Chapman, a well-known brother-and-sister act, wrote and starred in *Who's Got the Countess*, a satirical burlesque of Lola Montez. During intermission, William put on a frilly dress and performed his own version of the Spider Dance, which he called "The Spy-Dear Dance." The audience had a good laugh at Lola's expense.

When it came to her reputation, Lola had no sense of humor. She became angry with the Chapmans, the newspapers, and San Franciscans in general. Perhaps it was their cruel laughter and harsh ridicule that prompted her to do the unexpected. In July 1851, Lola and Hull were married at Mission Dolores in San Francisco.

After a contentious honeymoon in Monterey, California, the couple settled in Sacramento. They spent their time arguing, horseback riding, and hunting in the hills near their home, and soon Lola became bored with the solitude of country living and a husband she disliked. Her decision to return to the stage was just one more disaster in a long line of disasters.

The moment Lola began to dance, she realized she'd made a mistake. The crude, woman-starved miners of Sacramento made fun of her and laughed as she pranced across the stage. With tears streaming down her cheeks, she ordered the orchestra to stop playing. In an angry voice that carried to all corners of the theater, she challenged her audience to a duel. "Apes, give me your pants and take my petticoats. You're not fit to be called men. Lola Montez is proud to be what she is. But you, who have not the courage to fight with her—yes, this woman, who has no fear of you all despises you."

The miners were so outraged by her outburst that they showered her with the fruits and vegetables they had brought to the theater just for this purpose. With drawn pistols, a small cordon of Lola's loyal admirers gathered around her and escorted her back to her hotel.

Later that night, a mob of angry miners gathered beneath her window to voice their displeasure with her. In epithets too vulgar to print, they screamed out her name and banged pots and pans together to attract her attention. Holding up a lamp so the miners could see her,

Lola stepped out on her balcony and fearlessly repeated her speech for their benefit. This was the kind of courage the miners understood and appreciated, and they gave her a rousing cheer.

Lola forgave the miners for their rude behavior, and a few nights later she returned to the theater. Each time she appeared on stage, she never knew what to expect from her audiences. One night they might cheer her; the next night they might hiss and boo her off the stage. The editor of Sacramento's leading newspaper, the *Daily Californian*, ran an editorial accusing Lola of hiring some of her friends to sit in the audience and lead the applause. In a letter to the editor, she wrote:

> *After such a gross insult you must don petticoats. I have brought some with me for the occasion. I leave the choice of weapons with you for I am very magnanimous. You may choose between my dueling pistols or take your choice of a pill out of a pillbox. One shall be poison and the other not and the chances are even.*

The editor refused her challenge.

Lola's marriage was less than picture perfect. She and her husband fought constantly, and she would have left him if she hadn't discovered that he suffered from an advanced case of tuberculosis. Stung by harsh criticism in the press and convinced that she could nurse her quarrelsome mate back to health, she decided to move to Grass Valley.

After much cajoling and nagging, Lola persuaded the reluctant Hull to build her a two-story, ivy-covered house. She furnished it with Louis XVI cabinets, ormolu mirrors, a swan bed, a large red-topped billiard table with dragons carved on its legs, and gold leaf everywhere. In her wine cellar, she kept the finest wines, imported from all over the world.

Lola developed such a strong love for her new home that she had no intention of ever leaving it. When Hull demanded that she come to her senses and return to Sacramento with him, she refused. He took to hard liquor to soothe his bruised ego, and his nightly bouts with the bottle became legendary. He died a few months later, and Lola was left to her own devices. However, Lola's grief was short-lived. Each week she danced for the miners in the nearby mining camps, and the price of admission was extremely high. They were hungry for any kind of diversion from their dreary lives in the mines and had little else to spend their money on except whiskey and women, so they gladly shelled out the price Lola demanded. As a result, her performances were always sold out.

Lola's home became the cultural center of Grass Valley. European royalty, senators, military officers, writers, actors, the famous, and the infamous attended her weekly soirees; no women were allowed. Along with champagne, cake, and fruit, she served up stories of her past and samples of her dancing. Her guests looked forward to the next party, and they all came back for more.

On the surface, it appeared that Lola wanted to surround herself with the most influential men of her day, but in reality she had an ulterior motive. In letters discovered after her death, she outlined her plan to gain influence and assistance to capture California from the United States. Once the state declared its independence, it would be renamed "Lolaland" and she would be its queen.

Lola enjoyed the company of her illustrious guests, but she also had an affinity for animals. She acquired a pet grizzly cub and proceeded to tame it. Believing she had succeeded in domesticating the bear, she tried to pet it; it bit her hand. The miners couldn't let the bear get away with this vicious attack on the "Lovely Lola." They got together and held a kangaroo court on the animal. In the case of the *State v. Bruin*, the bear was acquitted of the charge of attempted murder. The jury claimed that the bear had ample provocation. Hanging around Lola all the time, it couldn't resist the temptation to hug her.

During her quiet period in the valley, Lola loved to play with the neighborhood children. Of all the children who spent time with her, it was a seven-year-old wisp of a girl named Lotta Crabtree who won her heart. Lola taught her to sing and dance, and it wasn't long before the student surpassed the teacher. Though Lola would never admit it, Lotta possessed a natural talent and sense of rhythm that Lola never had. Perhaps because of Lola's teaching, or maybe in spite of it, Lotta Crabtree was destined to become one of the greatest musical stars of her era.

Lola missed the excitement of the theater and decided it was time to return to the stage. In 1855 she left California for the theaters of

Australia. Like all her previous performances, she was cheered or hissed depending on the audience. In one of his books, historian Michael Cannon wrote, "In September 1855 she performed her erotic Spider Dance at the Theatre Royal in Melbourne, raising her skirts so high that the audience could see she wore no underclothing at all." The local newspapers called her performance "utterly subversive to all ideas of public morality." An editorial that ran in the *Sydney Morning Herald* described her dance as "the most libertinish and indelicate performance that could be given on a public stage."

Lola found her most loyal following at the Victoria Theatre in Ballarat, which was in the midst of its own gold rush. She was so popular that after almost every performance, the miners showered her with gold nuggets and other tokens of their affection. On those rare occasions when someone heckled her, she would lose her temper and hurl insults at the audience in turn.

Lola was almost as famous for her temper as she was for her romantic affairs. On one occasion she got into a hair-pulling, nail-scratching catfight with the theater manager's wife over some disparaging remarks about Lola's character and her lack of talent. She also took a whip to the editor of the *Ballarat Times* because she didn't like one of his editorials.

Four years in Australia was enough for Lola. She wanted to return to Grass Valley, but on the long voyage home, she became involved in the mysterious disappearance of one of her lovers. While the ship was anchored in the harbor near the South Pacific island of Fiji, the natives reported that a man had been tossed overboard from one of the first-class cabins. Since most of the passengers had been driven off the ship by the wild music emanating from Lola's stateroom, it was impossible to find reliable witnesses. The authorities wanted to charge her with ritual murder in conjunction with a Black Mass in the jungle of a nearby island, but when nothing could be proven, they let her go.

Lola returned to California a changed woman. She still welcomed her friends with her usual hospitality, but now her soirees evolved into séances, and she became obsessed with mysticism and astrology. She wrote a book of her innermost beauty secrets and went on the lecture circuit. In her last public appearance she said, "I am content to leave the history of my heart and moral life without comment to defend itself by contrast with that of the other sex."

The former countess spent the last two years of her life wandering the streets of New York. Broke and in poor health, at forty-three years of age, she died of a paralyzing stroke on January 17, 1861. Alone and almost forgotten, she was buried in Greenwood Cemetery in Brooklyn, New York. A simple tablet marks her final resting place with the inscription "MRS. ELIZA GILBERT, BORN 1818, DIED 1861."

Diamonds in the Dust

IN MAY 1871 TWO DISHEVELED PROSPECTORS, PHILIP ARNOLD AND John Slack, wandered out of the Sierra Nevada and through the doors of the Bank of California. They carried bags of what they claimed were rough diamonds. "We found them on a deserted mountain section of the west," they said. With the receipt in their hands, they tramped out of the bank and headed for a hotel.

Word of the diamonds spread, and before long, William C. Ralston, the president of the bank, heard about them. The idea of owning a diamond mine intrigued him. He had done great things for San Francisco with the wealth he had accumulated from the Comstock. What might he accomplish for his beloved city with a diamond mine? Discoveries of gold, silver, and other minerals were being made every day, and diamond fields had opened in South Africa just a few years before. If there were diamond mines in other countries, could there not be diamond mines in North America?

Determined to gain control of this new discovery, Ralston sent for the miners; in a very short time, the two rough-clad prospectors showed up at his office. They appeared to be shy, bewildered, and uncomfortable amid the opulence of these unfamiliar surroundings, and at first they were reluctant to speak.

Ralston's gregarious manner soon put them at ease. He asked them where they found the diamonds, but they were evasive in their answers. Perhaps it was Arizona, Colorado, or Wyoming, but they weren't sure. They were looking for gold when they found the gems. "Would you be interested in selling?" Ralston asked. No, they didn't want to sell their rights to the mine. It was true they didn't have the resources to secure title to the land or to develop their discovery, but they might just sell a small interest in the mine if the price was right. They might be persuaded to take in a third party, but they didn't want an outsider.

Returning to Ralston's office for further negotiations later that week, the prospectors had thought things over, and Yes, they would part with a half interest in their diamond field, but only to men they trusted. Ralston pointed out that negotiations could not continue unless they disclosed the location of the mine and his engineers could inspect the sight. The miners proposed that they accompany two men selected by Ralston to conduct an on-site inspection, but the men would have to be blindfolded before they could enter or leave the area of the mine.

Ralston selected General David C. Colton of the Southern Pacific Railroad to conduct the investigation. Colton departed for the diamond fields and, on his return to San Francisco, reported that he had unearthed more diamonds than he ever knew existed—acres of diamonds, rubies, sapphires, and emeralds. To say that Ralston went wild would be an understatement. This was the place for Ralston and his friends to invest their millions. There would be no limit to what he could accomplish for San Francisco, not to mention how much he could increase his own wealth.

Ralston sent a cable to Asbury Harpending, an old friend, in London, asking him to drop everything, take the next ship to America, and help him develop the mine. Diamonds in North America? Impossible! Had Ralston taken leave of his senses? Ralston continued to bombard his friend with lengthy telegrams until Harpending relented. Giving up several lucrative London deals, he sailed for America.

After numerous delays and thousands of dollars the bank president had given to the two men, Arnold and Slack sensed that Ralston's enthusiasm for the project had begun to wane. As a sign of good faith, they offered to go back to the mine and collect a couple of million dollars' worth of diamonds, bring them back to San Francisco, and turn them over to Ralston. The offer was too good to pass up, and since it wouldn't cost him anything, Ralston accepted.

The days passed, and soon Ralston received a telegram informing him that Arnold and Slack were in Reno. They requested that he have a reliable person of good character meet them to share the responsibility of transporting the diamonds. The next morning, Harpending, who had just arrived from London, met the prospectors and accompanied them back to San Francisco.

A large group of potential investors waited for Harpending in the billiard room of his mansion. The excitement mounted to a fever pitch when he entered the room and walked to a table. Cutting the rawhide bindings from the buckskin bundle, he opened the bag and turned it upside down. A fiery shower of diamonds, rubies, emeralds, amethyst, garnets, and spinels of assorted sizes gushed forth and covered the sheet that had been placed on the table. The gems sparkled like a million stars in the candlelit room. Harpending returned the stones to the buckskin bag, retied it, and placed it in his vault for safekeeping.

Ralston, Harpending, and a small group of friends and associates formed a syndicate they called the San Francisco and New York Mining and Commercial Company. The company was responsible for exploiting the diamond fields and selling stock to finance the cost of operations. They sent Harpending to Tiffany & Company in New York with a small sample of gems for appraisal. If the value of the stones met or surpassed the expectations of the investors, a mining engineer would be selected to conduct a complete survey of the diamond field.

Tiffany stated that the gems were genuine, and valued them at 150,000 dollars. The sample they sent to Tiffany was only one-tenth of the stones in Harpending's vault, so the remaining stones must be worth 1,500,000 dollars.

The syndicate secured the services of Henry Janin, one of the best-known mining engineers in America. He had inspected more than six hundred mines across the West, and he never made a mistake. He was paid 2,500 dollars, and in a few days he arrived at the mine site. His report stated that gems were so plentiful that twenty miners could wash out a million dollars in uncut stones every month. His report confirmed everything Arnold and Slack had claimed, and it reinforced the report David Colton had made weeks earlier. Ralston and Harpending agreed that the mine was more than they expected. The prospectors received 660,000 dollars for their rights to the find—and immediately disappeared.

The syndicate was ready to commence operations. With 1,500,000 dollars in gems in Harpending's vault, it was easy to attract investors, and only men of national reputation and impeccable character were permitted to subscribe to the initial stock offering. Twenty-five captains of industry, including General George B. McClellan, Horace Greely, and Charles Tiffany, each invested eighty thousand dollars in the venture. The two million dollars raised from the sale of stock was deposited in Ralston's bank.

Arnold and Slack's scheme began to fall apart when renowned geologist and explorer Clarence King arrived on the scene. Determining that the field was located in the northern foothills of the Uinta Mountains, a remote area where Utah, Colorado, and Wyoming meet, he visited the site to ascertain the national significance of the discovery.

Diamonds, rubies, sapphires, and emeralds were scattered over a wide terrain. The anthills were powdered with diamond and ruby dust, while others were sprinkled with pulverized sapphire and emerald particles. In the heart of every anthill, he found a gem corresponding in color to the dust sprinkled over its surface. Nothing was found in the underlying bedrock, where nature would have placed them. An elderly mule skinner confirmed the miraculous nature of the discovery when he held up a faceted diamond he had unearthed in an anthill. "Look, Mr. King!" he exclaimed. "This is the bulliest diamond mine there ever was. It not only produces diamonds, it cuts them." In one day, they uncovered more than five hundred gems.

King's telegram arrived in San Francisco like a bolt of lightning. "The alleged diamond fields are fraudulent. Plainly they are salted. The discovery is a giant fraud. The company has been pitifully duped." Calling a meeting of the company, Ralston showed them the telegram. The investors examined Tiffany's appraisal and the reports from Janin and King in minute detail, acknowledging that they had been duped. Ralston accepted his loss and restored, dollar for dollar, the entire two million dollars to the investors. The 660,000 dollars paid to Arnold and Slack plus other out-of-pocket expenses depleted most of Ralston's fortune. When he had acquired all the receipts, he framed them and hung them on his office wall as a reminder of the faith and duplicity of man. It was the beginning of the end for Ralston. He lost most of his friends, and his reputation was ruined.

Ralston's bank failed, and the directors ordered him to relinquish control. Ralston was a broken man. With great sadness he walked out of the bank. Just as he had done every morning, he swam from North Beach Bluff in the general direction of Alcatraz Island. Bystanders on the shore watched as he thrashed around in the cold water of the Golden Gate, but they did nothing to save him. His body was later recovered, and there was talk of suicide. At the coroner's inquest, the doctors testified that, during the autopsy, they found evidence of an apoplectic stroke.

Harpending was denounced as the mastermind of the swindle, even though he continued to profess his innocence. Arson was suspected in the fire that destroyed some of his real estate holdings. After liquidating all his valuable assets, he departed for his home in Kentucky. Arnold was traced to Kentucky, where on threat of a lawsuit, he surrendered 150,000 dollars. He died of pneumonia a few years later. Slack disappeared and was never heard from again. It is believed he ended his days as a coffin maker somewhere in New Mexico.

The trustees of the company conducted an inquiry to determine how the fraud had been perpetrated and who was responsible. In the course of their investigation, they learned that Arnold had purchased thirty-seven thousand dollars worth of diamonds from different jewelers in London and large quantities of assorted gems and industrial diamonds in St. Louis and Arizona. The trustees never determined who the brain behind the swindle was, but the evidence pointed to Harpending. A grand jury was convened, and warrants were issued for the arrest of Arnold and Slack, but since they had disappeared, the warrants were never enforced.

In a strange twist of fate, gem-quality diamonds have been discovered just a few hundred miles from the location where Arnold and Slack said they made their discovery. Twenty-five miles south of Laramie, just over the Wyoming-Colorado border, the Kelsey Lake Mine has been producing gem-quality diamonds since 1996. This small but lucrative mine has yielded tens of thousands of diamonds, including a 17-carat giant that recently sold at auction for more than three hundred thousand dollars and 5.4-carat stone that sold for ninety thousand dollars.

The Man Who Almost
Stole Arizona

Land grabs have been a part of the Old West since the first mountain men crossed the continent. But all other such instances pale in comparison to the swindle perpetrated by James Reavis, the self-proclaimed Baron of Arizona. In the largest land fraud in US history, he created a fictitious Spanish land grant that encompassed almost twelve million acres of southern Arizona and western New Mexico and raked in millions of dollars from his unsuspecting victims.

James Addison Reavis was born to Fenton Reavis and his half-Spanish wife, Maria, in southern Missouri in 1843. Fenton worked at a succession of short-lived, menial low-wage jobs, and the family moved from town to town. James formed a strong attachment to his mother, a disappointed, defeated woman who in her mind lived in Spain's glorious past. She told him that he was descended from a long line of Spanish nobility, and it was his duty to reclaim his aristocratic birthright through heroic deeds.

With the onset of the Civil War, the Missourians, uncertain if theirs was a free state or a slave state, were forced to take sides. Maria convinced James that the Southern cause was a just cause, that Southerners were noble and chivalrous, that he was destined to perform great deeds and cover himself with glory. Donning the gray of the Confederate Army, he marched off to war.

The realities of army life in Vicksburg, Mississippi, didn't match his expectations of the noble life, and the incessant drills and long hours of guard duty dispelled his notions of romance and glory. The only vacation from the monotony of his daily regimen came from an occasional leave, but these furloughs were too infrequent to suit him. Whenever he wanted a few days away from the tedium of playing soldier, he would reproduce exact replicas of handwritten leave forms signed by his commanding officer. The guards never questioned the validity of these papers and passed him through the gates without challenging him. This was a golden opportunity for Reavis to make money with his newfound talent forging passes for anyone who met his price. He also created "official" orders for government supplies, which he then resold to local merchants.

Times were hard in the South in the spring of 1863, and the future looked bleak. Reavis decided it might be a good time to get while the getting was good. The Confederates had fought hard, but it was a losing battle. Vicksburg surrendered, and Reavis deserted before he could be taken prisoner. Crossing enemy lines, he joined the Union Army and resumed his forgery business. When his commanding officer discovered what he was doing and threatened to arrest him, Reavis deserted again.

James Reavis, Baron of Arizona

Reavis wandered from place to place for the next few years. He surfaced in St. Louis and took employment as a streetcar conductor, saving the money he earned and stole from his job to open a real estate agency. Business was good, but earning money by honest means was too slow for him. To remedy this problem, he forged documents and deeds on faded paper and used them to close lucrative deals.

A meeting took place in 1871 that changed the direction of his life and affected the fortunes of thousands of unsuspecting citizens of the American Southwest. Dr. George Willing, a well-respected eccentric on the Arizona frontier, entered Reavis's office and for the next two hours related a fantastic tale of Spanish land grants and destitute nobles.

Seven years earlier, Willing had been traveling along the Agua Fria River south of Prescott, Arizona, when he met an old Mexican. The Mexican claimed to be Don Miguel Peralta, the owner of a Spanish land grant that gave him ownership of more than two thousand square miles of land in Arizona Territory. Willing gave Peralta gold, mules, and supplies worth a few thousand dollars for a pack of old deeds. He informed Reavis that under the Treaty of Hidalgo, the US government had agreed to recognize Spanish deeds to territorial lands that had been created before the United States annexed California and the Southwest. Marital strife, a shortage of funds, and rampaging Apaches had made it impossible for Willing to register his grant, and he needed an accomplice.

Reavis was suspicious of Willing's story. He had seen documents like these before, and he had forged quite a few in his time. The tale just didn't ring true, but they spent the next two years searching for a way to make the deeds pay off. In 1873 the real estate market in the West crashed and Reavis was wiped out. The two men met for one last time, and Reavis agreed to travel to California to find financial backers for the project while Willing returned to Arizona. Once Reavis fleeced the suckers in California, they would meet in Prescott and split the profits.

Reavis arrived in San Francisco after a lengthy voyage around Cape Horn. He was dismayed to learn that his partner had died a few weeks earlier without leaving a will or any mention of the Peralta grant. The doctor's death was a shock to Reavis, but it was no reason for him to change his plans. He would search for financial backers and continue as if nothing had happened.

Reavis found a position as a reporter for a California newspaper. In the course of his employment, he met two of the robber barons who ran the Southern Pacific Railroad. With unbounded enthusiasm, he related the story of the Peralta grant and informed them that he was in the process of researching it. If the deeds proved to be authentic and the US government recognized his claim, he was prepared to grant right-of-way privileges to the railroad for their proposed line through Arizona for the paltry sum of fifty thousand dollars. They agreed to pay him an advance of two thousand dollars plus two thousand a month in royalties.

Reavis went to Phoenix to study Spanish land grants and how the territorial courts processed them. He believed he could prove the legality of his claim with the proper documents. He duped Willing's heirs out of the mound of tattered parchments the doctor left behind and proceeded to examine them. The faded words on the scrap of wrapping paper that Peralta had signed in 1864 were almost illegible. To ensure the legality of the agreement, Willing had bribed two drunks with the promise of a bottle of whiskey to act as witnesses.

Convinced that the Peralta land grant was a fraud, Reavis decided it would have been difficult, if not impossible, for Peralta to conclude an agreement with Willing in 1864. According to the locals, no one had seen the good doctor in the territory before 1867. If his backers in California were willing to pay him thousands of dollars, sight unseen, for a claim based on a story, then Reavis should be able to convince the courts to award him ownership of the Arizona Territory.

Reavis returned to San Francisco, told his story, and collected vast sums of money from California's wealthiest citizens. They were willing to fund his attempts to prosecute his claims in return for railroad interests and mineral rights. To bolster his claim, Reavis spent the next six weeks in the musty rooms of the state archives in Mexico City and Guadalajara, studying Spanish land grants, royal decrees, deeds, and maps. When the clerks weren't looking, he pocketed dozens of old documents to use as templates for the next phase of his scam.

For the next few weeks, Reavis buried himself in his hotel room, copying the stolen papers until his looked like the genuine article. He created a fictitious lineage for the Peralta family that he believed would fool the experts, elevating Don Miguel to the rank of baron. The counterfeit documents also showed that King Charles III had officially recognized the title and ownership of the land, and the Spanish High Court had confirmed them.

These spurious records included three generations of Peraltas starting with Don Miguel, who lived to age of 116, and ending with his great-grandson, who became destitute and was forced to sell his birthright. The documents also mentioned a large boulder inscribed with the Peralta coat of arms to mark the southwest boundary of the claim, and a small garrison fort situated near the Indian ruins at Casa Grande.

The grant that specified two thousand square miles was expanded to more than eighteen thousand square miles. Reavis filed his claim at the Tucson Land Office in 1882 and demanded that the surveyor general of the United States pass judgment on it. While waiting for his answer, Reavis hired gangs of thugs to harass the legal owners of the land to pay up or get off his claim. US President Grover Cleveland made it clear that he wanted Reavis gone, and that same year the surveyor general pronounced the deeds a fake.

Reavis fled to California with mobs of angry Arizonians close on his heels. He continued to refine his scheme, and over the next two years he put together another cartel of rich and powerful backers. He married a gullible fifteen-year-old servant girl and convinced her that she was the great-granddaughter of Don Miguel. After changing her name to Dona Carmelita de Peralta, he packed her off to a convent to learn reading, writing, and the social graces her position as the wife of a Spanish noble required. She later gave birth to twin boys.

Carmelita was kept busy with her studies while Reavis performed a series of actions he believed would lend credence to his scheme. Borrowing the birth register from a young priest at the San Salvador Catholic church in San Bernardino, he erased two entries for the year 1862 and inserted the names of Carmelita's mother and her uncle in their place.

He was unaware that the church kept a second set of birth records; they would come back to haunt him.

Later that year, Reavis made a trip to Phoenix for the express purpose of locating a large rock with a wide face. He found a boulder that met his needs, and on its smooth surface he carved the Peralta coat of arms. With all the elements of his scheme now in place, he resubmitted his claim.

Reavis lived a lavish lifestyle, and money was no object. The Southern Pacific and the mining companies were still making payments to him. Joining with a California banker, they formed the Arizona Development Corporation and sold millions of shares of worthless stock to unsuspecting investors. The baron and his entourage then moved on to New York City. Meeting with some of the most powerful men in America, Reavis used his powers of persuasion and his wife's charms to separate them from some of their money. He promised them influence and wealth through his vast land holdings in return for their financial help.

To gain credibility for his claim, the Reavis family boarded a ship and landed in Spain. The Royal Court welcomed them with open arms, and they were the darlings of Madrid's social set. The Reavis children played with the royal children in the palace nursery while their parents hobnobbed with high society. Queen Maria Cristiana granted them an audience, but Reavis was more interested in planting fake documents. He worked till late at night forging documents, and in the morning he placed them in the National Arcives.

Tiring of life at court, and unable to interest any of the nobility into financing his plans, Reavis moved his family across the channel to England. The baron and baroness reached London just in time to celebrate Queen Victoria's Golden Jubilee year of 1887. They were wined and dined and accepted as equals by British nobility.

The good life might have continued for years, but trouble was brewing back home. The Reavis family sailed for America, and upon their arrival in Tucson, they were greeted with the news that, once again, the surveyor general had declared the deeds to be fraudulent.

Reavis considered the government's decree to be a minor setback. He filed a new claim in Santa Fe, New Mexico, and almost immediately his scheme started to unravel. Don Pedro de Peralta had founded Santa Fe in the sixteenth century, and many of his descendants still lived there. They believed the grant belonged to them and wanted their share. The Feds were also hot on the baron's trail, and when the surveyor general declared these deeds also to be fraudulent, Reavis sued the US government for eleven million dollars.

The court convened in Santa Fe on June 3, 1895, and the attorneys for the United States presented their case. Federal agents had followed the baron's trail across America to Europe, and back to America. They had assembled a mountain of evidence and collected witnesses who would prove their case. Reavis was nowhere to be seen for the first three days of the trial, but on June 6 he made his initial appearance.

Reavis had been involved in some minor lawsuits prior to the trial and had made some bad financial decisions that rendered him unable to afford a lawyer, so he acted as his own attorney. Knowing it would be difficult to prove his case with all the evidence the government presented against him, he asked the judge to dismiss the lawsuit; his request was denied. Carmelita was called as a witness, but under heavy questioning by government lawyers, she broke down and cried. She told the court that the only crime she was guilty of was believing everything her husband told her.

In the case of *Reavis v. The United States of America*, the court ruled that the Peralta grant was fraudulent, that Miguel Peralta never existed, and that the documents were clever forgeries. Reavis walked out of the courtroom into the waiting arms of a US marshal. Arrested and charged with attempted fraud, he wasn't able to make his ten-thousand-dollar bail. He spent the next year in the city jail. At his trial, Reavis was found guilty, sentenced to six years at hard labor, and fined five thousand dollars.

Reavis was released after serving two years. He emerged from prison sick and dejected, his fabulous wealth and glamorous lifestyle gone forever. Carmelita filed for divorce, took the twins, and moved to Denver. Spending his days in the Phoenix Public Library reading about his exploits in faded newspapers, Reavis spent his nights wandering the streets, a lonely and broken man. He moved to Downy, California, and took up residence at the county poor farm, where his only income was what he earned from doing odd jobs and selling vegetables he grew on a small patch of county land.

The citizens of Downy thought he was a crazy old coot and did their best to avoid him. He ranted and raved about his estates in Arizona, and schoolchildren mocked him and called him "The Crazy Baron." No one knows when Reavis left Downy, but on November 20, 1914, at the age of sixty-one, the self-proclaimed Baron of Arizona died in poverty and obscurity in a dusty village somewhere in Mexico.

The Lieutenant Was a Lady

In 1876 a mysterious young woman known as Madame Loreta Janeta Velázquez created a sensation with the publication of her controversial Civil War memoir, *The Woman in Battle: A Narrative of the Exploits, Adventures, and Travels of Madame Loreta Janeta Valázquez, Otherwise Known as Lieutenant Harry T. Buford, Confederate States Army*. This tale of a beautiful woman who posed as a man to fight for the South is no ordinary war story.

The sixth child of an important Spanish government official and a French mother, Loreta was born on June 26, 1842, in Havana, Cuba. During her early years, the family employed an English governess to oversee Loreta's education, teaching her English, reading, writing, and the social skills every young girl needed. Opportunities for women in Cuba were limited, so when Loreta was eight years old her mother shipped her off to New Orleans to live with a maiden aunt.

The aunt was strict but kind with her young charge. After two years of living under her aunt's roof, Loreta was sent to a private academy run by the Sisters of Charity. She remained with the sisters until a chance meeting with a stranger and a clandestine marriage changed the direction of her life forever.

In Spain and its colonies in the 1800s, parents decided whom their children would marry. Following this ancient tradition, Loreta's parents betrothed her to Raphael, a young Spanish dandy from a good family. Although she didn't feel any affection for him, she bowed to their wishes and accepted Raphael as her future husband.

An arranged marriage was the last thing in the world this romantic twelve-year-old wanted. Loreta had no intention of becoming the wife of some useless Spanish fop. Her classmates told her that one of the chief blessings of living in the United States was that she was free to marry the man of her choice, and it was against the law for anyone to force her to marry a man she didn't love.

Loreta decided it was time to dump Raphael in favor of Bill, a handsome young army officer she met at a dance. To help her implement her plan, even though he knew she was betrothed, Bill asked for and received permission to call on Loreta at her aunt's home. Raphael objected strenuously to this arrangement, so the couple was forced to meet in secret. Bill wrote to Loreta's father asking for his blessing to marry his daughter. A harsh reprimand was not long in coming. How dare this brash American ask for his daughter's hand in marriage when he knew she was promised to another?

Fearing discovery, the two lovers carried on with their clandestine relationship. When Bill received orders to report for duty at one of the western frontier posts, he made plans to take this beautiful Southern belle with him. In a secret ceremony, Loreta and Bill exchanged wedding vows. At the tender age of fourteen, she was an army bride.

Her father's bitter hatred for the Americans overcame his love for his daughter. He informed Loreta that since she chose to ignore his wishes, she was no longer a member of the family and was removed from his will. Loreta's estrangement from her family devastated her, and Bill did his best to console her. "In time," he said, "your family will forgive you and accept you as their daughter again."

While Bill was off chasing Indians, Loreta spent her time studying military tactics. Like her childhood heroine Joan of Arc at the siege of Orleans, she dreamed of wearing a uniform and leading great armies into battle. How wonderful it would be if someone started a war and she could be there with her man to minister to his needs if he was wounded on the battlefield.

In 1857 Bill mounted his horse and, waving goodbye, rode off to fight the Mormons in Utah. Loreta wanted to go with him, but motherhood interfered with her plans. Reluctantly, she agreed with Bill that crossing the plains with an infant in her arms would not be good for her or the baby. Bill headed west and she headed east to St. Louis. With the birth of her first child, she reconciled with her parents.

At the successful conclusion of the Mormon expedition, Bill reunited with Loreta and the baby. For the next two years, the family lived in the desolation of Fort Leavenworth, Kansas. In *The Woman in Battle*, Loreta described her life at this remote Army post:

> *The living conditions at this place were miserable, and the cooking especially, was atrociously bad. I bore every discomfort however, without a murmur, out of deference to my husband's feelings, and in every way endeavored to make myself as little a burden to him as possible. In course of time I became a good American in thought and manner, and despite the inconveniences of life at a frontier post, was as happy as I could wish to be.*

Sometime during her stay in Kansas, Loreta gave birth to a second baby.

In the spring of 1860, Bill was transferred to Fort Arbuckle, somewhere in Indian territory, and Loreta returned to St. Louis. With two small children to care for and a third one on the way, life was hard for this nineteen-year-old Southern belle. During her separation from her husband, Loreta's third child died in childbirth and the two older children died of fever. Bill's letters gave her the strength she needed to endure her grief.

The country was being torn apart by political differences, and war was on the horizon. Perhaps it was Loreta's grief that revived her desire to win fame and glory on the battlefield. As a little girl, Loreta had dreamed of being a man. When war came, she wanted to be part of it. Knowing that women weren't allowed to join the army, she decided it was time to put her plan into action.

When Texas seceded from the Union, Loreta saw her chance. Using every female trick at her command, she persuaded Bill to resign from the US Army and accept a commission in the newly formed Army of the Confederacy. It grieved him to give up his union-blue uniform and the stars and stripes of the American flag for Confederate gray and the bars and stars of the secessionist South. Despite believing that secession was a big mistake, he yielded to his wife's wishes.

Day and night for six weeks, Loreta schemed and plotted. She tried everything to gain Bill's consent to go to war with him, but he refused to listen. Arguing with her was useless; no matter what he said, he couldn't shake her resolve. "I won't permit my wife to become a camp follower," he said. "These are rough, coarse, untrained troops. An army camp is no place for a delicately refined woman."

Realizing that his words failed to dampen her ardor for war, Bill thought he might cure Loreta of her irrational fantasies if he exposed her to the least pleasing aspects of male behavior. The night before his departure to report for duty with the Confederate Army in Richmond, he told her, "Since you insist on acting like a man, I'll take you to the bar rooms and other places of male resort. I'll show you what you'll be compelled to go through if you persist in unsexing yourself."

Braiding her long tresses, Loreta dressed in one of Bill's old uniforms, tucked the pantaloons into her boots, put on a man's wig and pasted a false mustache on her face. Though the uniform was too big for her, she did her best to look like a soldier. Before embarking on her great adventure, Bill instructed her in the finer points of being a man and told her to drink nothing stronger than cider lest she become drunk and give herself away.

Bill took Loreta on a tour of Memphis at night. They visited the principal gambling parlors and saloons, places where women were forbidden to enter. She was fascinated by the scene that greeted her in each of these establishments. The smoke-filled rooms were crowded with hard-drinking patrons, many of them in uniform. In language so vulgar and blasphemous it would do justice to a drunken sailor on leave, the men did some tall talking on a variety of subjects. They talked about the war and how they'd wipe out any damned Yankee that dared to set foot in their beloved South.

Before the night was over, the couple encountered two old friends from Bill's regiment. Loreta was afraid they might see through her disguise when Bill introduced her as a young fellow on leave in Memphis to see the sights and gather war news. To Loreta's delight, they failed to recognize her. If she could fool her friends into believing she was a man, then she could fool anybody.

Bidding Bill's friends goodnight, Bill and Loreta returned to their hotel room. Bill hoped she would be so shocked by the vulgarity and profanity she saw and heard that she would give up her insane plan to dress like a man and fight beside him. Loreta was more determined than ever.

"Well, don't you feel pretty much disgusted?" Bill asked.

Knowing what he wanted to hear, Loreta replied, "Yes, but then I can stand anything to be with you, and serve the sunny South."

"Now, Loreta," Bill said in a condescending voice, "I have done this tonight for the purpose of showing you how men behave when they're out of sight and hearing of decent women whom they are forced to respect. What you have seen and heard, however, is nothing compared to what you will be compelled to see and hear in camp, where men are entirely deprived of female society and are under the most demoralizing influences. It is out of all reason that you should even think of associating in the manner you propose with soldiers engaged in warfare."

Loreta knew Bill would never give his consent. She pretended to accept his arguments, but her resolve only grew stronger. Bill should have known better than to think that Loreta would allow a few words to stand in her way. As soon as he left for Richmond, she went to work.

To be convincing in her role as an officer and a gentleman, Loreta needed uniforms that would hide her female attributes, but she wasn't certain how to obtain them. Then she remembered seeing a tailor shop hidden away on a small tree-lined street near her hotel.

She took scissors to her long brown hair and cut away until her beautiful locks lay at her feet. Hiding her female figure in wire body shields and loose undergarments, she dressed in one of Bill's old uniforms and went to visit the tailor. Purchasing the desired uniforms, Loreta returned to her room with her forbidden treasures.

Loreta decided that the only way Bill would permit her to fight at his side was to raise and equip a battalion of soldiers at her own expense and present them to her husband as a gift. She could imagine the look on Bill's face when he recognized his wife as the officer in charge of men who had joined up to fight for the Southern cause. If her husband still withheld his consent after she turned turned over command of the troops, she would play her part in the war without his permission.

With a definite purpose in mind, Loreta was eager to start her recruiting drive. Donning her disguise, she changed her name to Lieutenant Harry T. Buford, CSA, and boarded a train for New Orleans. Confiding in a fellow passenger, Loreta explained that she was on a recruiting mission. She asked him if he knew where she could find the men she needed. The gentleman suggested that a lot of strong young fellows ready to take on the Yankees were living at Hurlburt Station in Arkansas.

The little hamlet in the Arkansas hills exceeded her wildest expectations. In four days she enrolled 236 recruits. Using her inheritance,

Cover drawing by John Rea Neal for *The Woman in Battle* by Loreta Janeta Velázquez. DUSTIN, GILLMAN, AND COMPANY, VIRGINIA AND CONNECTICUT, 1876. REPRINTED BY THE UNIVERSITY OF WISCONSIN PRESS, MADISON, WISCONSIN, 2003.

she equipped them with tents, blankets, weapons, and ammunition, and marched them to Pensacola, where Bill was encamped, to organize a fighting force. Bill didn't recognize the young officer leading his men into camp. Imagine his shock when Loreta took him aside and revealed her true identity. Even though she had brought more than two hundred men with her, he wasn't too happy to see her. Taking command of the company, he commenced to train them, ordering Loreta back to New Orleans to purchase supplies and equipment.

Arriving at her destination, Loreta received a telegram announcing Bill's death and a request that she return to Pensacola immediately. Distraught over the loss of her husband, she did as ordered, only to learn that Bill had been drilling the men in the proper use of firearms when the carbine he was demonstrating to one of his sergeants exploded in his hands, killing him instantly. The young widow was more determined than ever to become a soldier. After turning command of the battalion over to one of Bill's friends, she headed north to Virginia to find her own destiny on the battlefield.

Dressed in her counterfeit uniform, Loreta reported to the headquarters of the Confederate Army of the Potomac. She had heard that a battle was shaping up at Manassas Junction, and she hadn't come all this way to sit on the sidelines. She tried to buy a regular commission for five hundred dollars from an officer she knew, but he refused to sell. Introducing herself to Brigadier General Bonham, commanding officer of the troops holding Mitchell's Ford on the road to Richmond, she saluted her superior officer. "General Bonham, sir, I am Lieutenant Harry T. Buford reporting for duty."

"What company do you belong to?" asked the General.

To this she replied, "I am an independent, paying my own expenses. The only thing I want is to take a hand in the coming fight. I belong where there is work to do."

"Well," said Bonham, "you are the right sort to have around when a when a fight is going on. If you stay here a little while, I reckon you'll be able to find plenty of work."

On July 18, Union troops advanced in force and attacked Longstreet's brigade at Blackburn's Ford. In a series of skirmishes that lasted for almost an hour, Longstreet's infantry halted the enemy's advance. With Longstreet reinforced by Jubal Early's brigade, the Federals broke and ran. Chasing the enemy across the battlefield, Loreta picked up a dead soldier's musket and fired at the retreating bluecoats.

According to information from their spies, the Confederates knew the Federals planned to attack on July 21. Loreta was placed in temporary command of a company that had lost its senior officer. Along with reinforcements from Alabama and Georgia, she marched to the front to face the enemy. In the early morning hours, the Union troops charged the rebel lines. Loreta's company was in the center of the line and bore the brunt of the attack. Her childhood dreams were about to be realized.

The battle raged throughout the day, with neither side giving ground. On each side, as men fell dead or wounded, others moved forward to take their place. Braving cannon shot and musket fire, Loreta spurred her horse onward, leading her comrades forward to drive the enemy from the field.

The Union lines broke under the weight of the unstoppable onslaught, and their retreat became a mindless rout. Northern troops rushed headlong back to Washington, DC, discarding most of their equipment along the way. The first battle of the Civil War was a decisive victory for the South, but sheer exhaustion prevented them from pursuing the fleeing enemy and capitalizing on their triumph.

The Confederates were elated with their victory, and many of them thought the war was over. Scores of soldiers went home to their families, lounged around camp, or went to Richmond to have a good time. Brothels, gambling halls, and saloons reaped a rich harvest from young men who'd never been away from home before, and army discipline fell apart. Disgruntled and disgusted with her comrades, Loreta refused to join in their debauchery.

After their hard-won battle, Loreta thought the army would use the victory to their advantage, but the generals seemed content to take a wait-and-see attitude. She was too restless and impulsive to endure this prolonged inaction for very long. Camp life was too confining, the city's amusements too demoralizing, and the slow progress of the military annoyed her. For this young firebrand, the time had come to take action.

Loreta tried to get herself attached to a regular command, but since she was an independent, the generals ignored her. She knew the difficulty the generals were experiencing in obtaining reliable information concerning the enemy's movements, and she wanted to do something about it. To solve their problem and help the cause, Loreta decided to go to Washington and spy on the enemy.

Loreta exchanged her uniform for a borrowed dress and made her way past the federal troops guarding the approaches to the city. Renting a room at Brown's Hotel, she contacted one of Bill's old friends, a high-ranking Union officer. He was happy to see her and unwittingly provided her with sensitive information that was useful to the Confederacy. Unaware that she was a spy, her companion showed her different points of interest, including the Patent Office, the Treasury Department, the War Office, and the White House. To her delight, the officer even went so far as to introduce her to the secretary of war and President Lincoln.

Loreta returned to Memphis and once again put on her uniform. Traveling to Columbus, Kentucky, she reported to the commander of the military district. For her courageous act of spying on the North and returning with important information, he assigned her to the detective corps.

Loreta was overjoyed with her new assignment, until she discovered that she would be a military conductor for the railroad. Examining travel documents, passes, and leave orders, spying on her passengers, and arresting anyone who didn't have the right papers was distasteful to her. She made up her mind to try her luck in some other line of duty.

In the West, the war was heating up. On the Cumberland River in western Tennessee, Union forces prepared to lay siege to Fort Donelson. The Confederates expected the fighting to be fierce, and Loreta wanted to be in the middle of it. Arriving at the fort in time to participate in its defense and subsequent surrender, she narrowly escaped capture by hiding for hours in the tall grass that grew along the river. Waiting until nightfall, she slipped through the Yankee patrols and returned to the safety of her own lines.

In a skirmish with Union troops at Balls Bluff, Loreta received a minor wound in the foot. Afraid that the surgeon who examined her would discover she was a woman, she lit out for New Orleans, and it wasn't long before she was arrested on a charge of spying for the North. After questioning her at length, the provost marshal decided there was no justification to hold her. Arrested again the next day on suspicion of being a woman in disguise, she was fined ten dollars and sentenced to ten days in jail.

Once Loreta was released, she hurried to a recruiting office and enlisted in the 21st Louisiana Regiment. Having no desire to be a common soldier, she presented her commission to her commanding officer with a request to be transferred to the army in eastern Tennessee. Her request granted, she rejoined the army at Corinth, Mississippi.

The battle of Shiloh was Loreta's last battle. On the first day of battle, the rebels swept the Yankees from the field in a surprise attack. During the fighting, Loreta was reunited with the battalion she had recruited in Arkansas. When the commanding officer was killed, she took command and under intense fire led her troops to engage the enemy. The Federals brought up reinforcements and forced the Confederates to retreat back to Corinth.

Loreta joined a cavalry unit and returned to the battlefield. The Yankees were still lobbing artillery shells at the retreating army when a random shell exploded nearby, sending shrapnel into the air. Wounded in the arm and shoulder and thrown from her mount, Loreta was shaken from the fall and in great pain. Climbing back on her horse, she rode back to camp and sent for a surgeon.

The doctor examined her and began to suspect that something wasn't right. Deciding further concealment was useless, Loreta told him the truth. He was astonished that a woman would engage in such a wild adventure. Dressing her wounds, he put her arm in a sling and placed her on a train taking the wounded south.

Loreta returned to New Orleans to recover from her wounds, but with the arrival of Union gunboats and Federal troops, she gave up her male disguise. In her memoir she wrote:

I felt that the time was now come for me to make a display of my talents in another character than that of a warrior, and with the arrival of the fleet in front of the city found me in the anxious and angry

crowd on the levee, not inelegantly attired in the appropriate gar-
ments of my sex—garments that I had not worn for so long that they
felt strangely unfamiliar, although I was not altogether displeased at
having a fair opportunity to figure once more as a woman, if only for
variety sake.

For the next two years, Loreta served in the Confederate secret service as a spy and courier. She used a number of aliases and posed as a
man or woman as circumstances dictated. She ran the Federal blockade
to Cuba, crossed into Canada to support the Copperheads (Northerners
who supported the Southern cause), and organized a failed rebellion of
rebel prisoners of war in Indiana and Ohio.

Loreta participated in draft-dodging swindles in New York City
and smuggled Confederate money out of occupied New Orleans in a
currency-changing enterprise. She also smuggled badly needed medicines
through Union lines, reaping a handsome profit for herself. Her activities
created so many problems for the North that the Federal secret service
hired her to find this female Confederate spy.

As a double agent, Loreta was assigned to distribute counterfeit
Confederate money in the South in an attempt to destroy its economy.
She continued to actively support the Southern cause while causing
problems for the North until the final days of this bloody war.

After the war, Loreta tried her hand at a number of different ventures, including acting as an agent for Confederate officers who wanted
to immigrate to Venezuela. Traveling extensively throughout the West,
this former Confederate officer speculated in gold mining, and while
in Salt Lake City, she gave birth to a son. Married and widowed two
more times, she settled somewhere in Texas. After the publication of her
memoirs in 1876, this mysterious woman who fought so fervently for the
Southern cause vanished from the pages of history.

The Legend of Oofty Goofty

IN THE LATE 1800s, SAN FRANCISCO WAS A WILD AND DANGEROUS place, a mecca that lured immigrants from every corner of the globe to its golden shores. The city by the bay that started as a collection of mud huts, a military fort, and a few Spanish missions had become a bustling metropolis. Shops of every type, bars, brothels, and dance halls lined its crowded streets. Every few years, firestorms swept the city clean; each time, the inhabitants built it bigger and better.

Since its humble beginnings, California has attracted some of the strangest characters in the history of the United States. One such individual was a man known only as Oofty Goofty, a name he acquired during his first public appearance as a wild man in a freak show on Market Street.

This strange looking man wandered aimlessly through the muddy streets of San Francisco in search of his destiny. No one knew whence he came or where he was going, and no one cared. Like most of the inhabitants of Kearny Street, this nocturnal nomad joined the nightly parade of humanity. He loved the night, and he reveled in the glare of the bright lamps that shone from Pacific to Market Street. Dressed in an ill-fitting black suit, an oversized top hat, and boots that were too small for his feet, this scarecrow of a man stood out among his peers.

One night, Oofty strayed up Market Street into the heart of the Barbary Coast, the most depraved section of the city. Never in his life had he seen such wonderful sights. He was fascinated by the loud music emanating from the saloons and dance halls, and the painted ladies who offered their services to any gentleman who could afford them. He was drawn to the vicious street fights and offers of lewd entertainment that permeated the entire district. After the serenity of his life on Market Street, the excitement of the Barbary Coast was just what he needed.

Each night, Oofty walked the streets in search of employment. He needed money and was willing to do almost anything short of murder or robbery to get it. While Oofty was walking past a dark alley one night, a short, rotund con man in a red-and-white-checkered suit and black derby ran out and grabbed him. The large "diamond" stick pin in his lapel and numerous jeweled rings on his fingers were as phony as he was. The fast-talking scalawag had little trouble convincing the gullible young man that he would be a roaring success and become rich beyond his greatest expectations as the one and only, the original "Wild Man of Borneo."

Oofty believed everything his new friend told him. He followed the man to a small room in the back of a rundown saloon, where two large, gorilla-like toughs in turbans and robes ambled over to Oofty, undressed him, and pushed him down into a hard wooden chair. With great dexterity and a pair of shears, the pseudo-Turks removed the luxuriant curly locks from his head. From the top of his head to the soles of his feet, they coated his naked body with hot tar and covered it with a layer of black horsehair. Painting his face with black dye, they gave him such a savage and ferocious appearance that it would frighten his own mother and give his audiences nightmares.

Once the transformation was complete, Oofty was installed in a large iron cage. He was an immediate success, and people came from all over the territory to see the recently captured wild man from the jungles of Borneo. While curious onlookers gathered around the cage, the Turks told them how they had captured this primitive savage and that they had spared no expense to bring him to San Francisco. In a loud voice that could be heard over the roar of the crowed, one of the Turks warned them to step back and be ready to run for the exits if the beast broke free of his prison.

The Turk beat the cage with a club to rile up the wild man and threw enormous chunks of meat at him through the bars. As part of the act, the wild man tore the meat apart with his bare hands and gobbled it down. Red dye that resembled blood ran down his chin and dripped onto the floor of the cage. Gripping the bars with both hands, he shook them violently to terrorize his audience while jumping up and down in frenzy. In a high-pitched voice that frightened his audience, he yelped out those fearsome words, "Oofty Goofty! Oofty Goofty!"

The wild man's antics delighted the crowd. Each time he shook the bars and screamed at them, they moved closer to the exits. They didn't know if he could get loose, but they weren't taking any chances. Since the wild man didn't have a name, someone in the audience christened him Oofty Goofty, a name he carried for the rest of his life.

For more than a week, Oofty was the biggest draw on the Pacific coast. It was standing room only. The patrons felt it was worth every penny of their hard-earned money to see the legendary "Wild Man of Borneo." Oofty was enjoying his newfound fame and fortune when he suddenly became ill, he couldn't perspire through the thick covering of tar and horsehair. When he passed out, the Turks rushed him to the Receiving Hospital of San Francisco.

For several days, the physicians tried in vain to remove Oofty' costume without also removing his skin. They soaked him in every solvent they could find, but nothing seemed to work. They found a tar solvent at a local hardware store, placed him in a tub, and doused his body with the solvent. For three days he lay on the roof of the hospital in the hot sun until the tar melted.

After his disastrous stint as the Wild Man of Borneo, Oofty refused to accept any more outlandish character roles. Instead, he decided to try his luck as a singer and dancer. The manager of Bottle Koenigs, a Barbary Coast beer hall that catered to the dregs of society, hired him. He was uncoordinated and fell off the stage, to the great amusement of his audience. His voice was so bad that as soon as he started to sing, the audience threw rotten tomatoes at him and told him to shut up. It was a good thing their aim was bad. Most of the missiles soared past him and splattered against the backdrop, but a few hit him dead center. In a voice that sounded like a cross between a sawmill and a jackhammer, he belted out a romantic Irish ballad.

The audience was in no mood to be trifled with. After working in the mines day and night, the miners demanded better entertainment. Ignoring their taunts and tomatoes, Oofty continued to sing until the

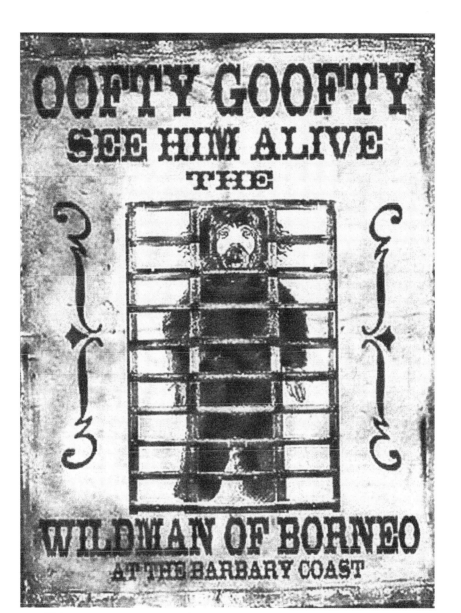

This poster was hung around town to draw attention to Oofty Goofty's act.

crowd became so violent that they rushed the stage. Four drunken miners grabbed the would-be singer and kicked and punched him. Lifting him off his feet, the miners tossed him like a sack of flour to the waiting crowd. Oofty fought them every step of the way, but they were too strong for him. They carried him to the batwing doors at the front of the bar and tossed him onto the sidewalk. A few seconds later, his top hat flew through the air and landed near his supine body.

Oofty picked himself up, placed his hat on his head, and walked away from his latest debacle. He was amazed to discover that he was unhurt and felt no pain. He had been kicked and pummeled by dozens of angry drunks and had landed with great force on a stone sidewalk, yet he had no broken bones, sprains, or any other injuries. Perhaps, he thought, the treatment to remove his wild man costume had made him insensitive to pain.

Oofty was always looking for ways to earn a living. He soon realized that the violent incident in the saloon was in reality a fortunate event. He decided that since he was immune to pain, he would capitalize on his great gift or, as Oofty called it, his "work." For the next fifteen years, he eked out a precarious existence by allowing himself to be kicked and punched for a price. Advertising himself as a human plank, he boasted, "For a price, one can kick or hammer my carcass at will, but the glamour of gladness will hang round me still."

Oofty traveled from town to town and played his unusual talent for all it was worth. In each town, he stationed himself in front of a saloon looking for customers. Once he found a willing participant, Oofty invited him to kick him or whack him with a cane or the baseball bat he always carried. For ten cents, a man might kick Oofty as hard as he pleased, for a quarter, he could hit him with a walking stick, and for fifty cents, he would become the willing recipient of a blow from the baseball bat.

Oofty's peculiar vocation carried him through the towns and many painless whacks until the day he met the first heavyweight boxing champion of the world, the mighty John L. Sullivan. Hearing that the great pugilist was in town, Oofty went looking for him. He found the fighter in front of a local sporting house amusing himself with a bottle of whiskey and a few of the town's soiled doves.

Oofty Goofty Meets World Champion Boxer John L. Sullivan. COVER ILLUSTRATION FOR
THE LEGEND OF OOFTY GOOFTY BY RUSSELL ESTLACK, ILLUSTRATED BY RICK ESTRADA, 2006.

In a manner befitting his presumed status as a major attraction, Oofty explained his bizarre service to the boxer. Sullivan was always looking for diversions, and with unbounded enthusiasm he accepted Oofty's offer. The crowd smelled blood, and bets were placed on the outcome.

Sullivan paid his fee, took off his coat, and rolled up his sleeves. He grasped a pool cue in his oversized hands and waited until Oofty's back was turned. Like Babe Ruth hitting a four-bagger in the World Series, the pool cue connected with its target. Sullivan dealt Oofty the whack of his life. Oofty flew through the air and landed in a prone position. He lay on the sidewalk moaning in agony as intense pain coursed through his tortured body. With his mighty bat, John L. Sullivan had accomplished what no one else could—shatter two of Oofty's vertebrae.

Oofty's career had come to a painful end. He never recovered from his encounter with Sullivan, he walked with a limp,and he whimpered at the slightest touch. To earn a living, he was forced to swamp out saloons and clean out stables. With his claim to fame gone, people soon forgot him. He died a pauper and was buried in an unmarked grave.

Norton I, First Emperor
of the United States

ON JULY 4, 1776, REPRESENTATIVES FROM THIRTEEN COLONIES MET IN Philadelphia to declare their independence from the yoke of tyranny. Since that historic day, forty-five men have held the title of President of the United States. But in 1859, America had another head of state: a self-proclaimed emperor, who ruled by proclamation.

Unlike the presidents, Joshua Abraham Norton was not a natural born citizen of the United States. The second of nine children, Joshua was born to John and Sarah Norton on February 14, 1819, at Shropshire, England. In response to a call for immigrants to populate the new settlements in South Africa, the Norton family took advantage of free land in a new country. Along with other Jewish families, they settled on Algoa Bay near the Cape of Good Hope.

The cape was a major port of call for ships of many nations, and John became wealthy by providing them with provisions and needed services. As a young man, Joshua worked in his father's chandlery, but the job didn't last long. In 1848 John, Sarah, and two of their sons became ill and died. Joshua inherited the bulk of his father's estate, which amounted to about forty thousand dollars.

Joshua was thirty years old, wealthy, and restless. When news of a major gold strike in California reached South Africa, Joshua saw an opportunity to increase his fortune. Booking passage on the Dutch schooner *Franzika*, he landed in San Francisco in 1849.

Joshua was different from the majority of forty-niners. While most of them headed for the gold fields of the Sierra Nevada to search for gold, he set himself up in the import brokerage business. Renting a small adobe cottage, he hung a large sign over the door advertising his business, Joshua Norton & Company, General Merchants. To store his merchandise, he purchased one of the hundreds of derelict ships that littered the harbor, abandoned when their crews jumped ship and joined the rush to the gold fields.

Selling supplies to miners and prospectors was much more profitable than searching for gold. Joshua's customers were more than willing to pay the exorbitant prices he charged, and he was more than willing to take their money. In 1851 his shop burned to the ground and Joshua moved his operations into a granite building in a fashionable section of the city. With so much money coming into the company coffers, he decided to diversify and expand his empire.

The San Francisco real estate market was booming, and land was scarce. Only the wealthy could afford to buy it. Through shrewd business dealings, Joshua acquired three parcels of land on a busy street. He opened a cigar factory, a small wooden office building, and a rice mill. The lots he purchased along the bay increased in value when the Pacific Mail Steamship Company built a passenger terminal and warehouse nearby. He also acquired several lots in North Beach, an undeveloped section of the city.

Joshua's wealth continued to grow, and by 1853 his assets were estimated at 250,000 dollars. Considered one of the most respected and successful businessmen in San Francisco, and always on the lookout for new opportunities, he attempted to corner the rice market.

The Chinese were the largest ethnic group in the city, and the main ingredient in their diet was rice. Most of the rice came by ship from China, but a disastrous famine in the Orient had cut off their supplies. With rice in short supply, the price rose from four cents a pound to thirty-six cents a pound.

A banker at the Merchant's Exchange showed Joshua a handful of rice from Peru and told him there were two hundred thousand pounds in the holds of the *Glyde*, a ship anchored in the harbor. Joshua could buy it for twelve cents a pound or twenty-five thousand dollars for the entire cargo, resell it at thirty-six cents a pound, and make a handsome profit.

Joshua put two thousand dollars down and agreed to pay the balance in thirty days. Before he could take advantage of the inflated prices, however, a ship loaded to the gunwales with Peruvian rice sailed into the harbor. When other rice-laden ships followed, the price dropped to three cents a pound. Joshua tried to nullify the contract on the grounds that he had been misled and argued vigorously that the rice on the *Glyde* was inferior to the sample the banker had shown him. When Joshua refused to pay, the owner of the *Glyde* sued.

Over the next three years, Joshua's life was a nightmare. One of his clients accused him of embezzlement, and the Lucas Turner and Company Bank foreclosed on his North Beach properties. His holdings became worthless, and he filed for bankruptcy. On August 25, 1856, a brief notice appeared in the newspapers: "Joshua Norton filed a petition for the benefit of the Insolvency Law. Liabilities $55,811; assets stated at $15,000, uncertain value." During the years of litigation that followed, Joshua lost it all.

With his life in ruins, Joshua disappeared. When he emerged from his self-imposed exile, it was apparent to everyone that in addition to losing his fortune, he had also lost his sanity. On a warm September morning this down-on-his-luck businessman donned an admiral's uniform complete with gold braid, gilt epaulets, and shiny brass buttons, climbed up a flight of stairs, strode into the office of the editor of the *San Francisco Bulletin*, and placed an official-looking proclamation on his desk. The editor had a rich sense of humor and decided to publish the proclamation on the front page of the morning edition. The headline read: "Have We An Emperor Among Us?" The proclamation read as follows:

At the pre-emptory request of a large majority of the citizens of these United States, I Joshua Norton, formerly of Algoa Bay, Cape of Good Hope, and now for the last nine years and ten months past of San Francisco, California, declare and proclaim myself the Emperor of These United States, and in virtue of the authority thereby in me vested do hereby order and direct the representatives of the different States of the Union to assemble in Musical Hall of this city, on the first day of February next, then and there to make such alterations in the existing laws of the Union as may ameliorate the evils under which the country is laboring, and thereby cause confidence to exist, both at home and abroad, in our stability and integrity."

Norton I
Emperor of the United States
September 17th 1859

The citizenry had a good laugh and decided it was a great idea. By unanimous acclamation, they accepted Norton as their emperor. Humoring his delusions, they were proud that Norton had chosen their city as his empire's capital. As he strolled along the streets as though he did rule the city, the people gave him a wave or a bow as they passed him and addressed him as "Your Majesty."

Norton played his role to the hilt and looked and acted like an emperor, even if his royal uniform was ill fitting and a little worse for wear. With a ceremonial sword at his side and an umbrella as his scepter, he topped off his attire with a beaver hat decorated with colored peacock feathers. Norton was short and stocky, but the hat added inches to his stature, making him seem taller than he really was.

Few monarchs in history ever had Norton's common touch. He related to the people, and they loved him. During his daily patrols, the emperor made certain the sidewalks were unobstructed and the police were on duty. Checking on the progress of street repairs, His Imperial Majesty inspected buildings that were under construction and called on City Hall to enforce all the city's ordinances. Whenever Norton felt that taxes were too high, he ordered the city to lower them; if public facilities were inadequate, he ordered them fixed.

When Norton noticed someone performing an act of kindness, he made them part of his royal entourage. He would place a hand on their shoulder and ennoble them with the title of "king or queen for a day." To be a duke, lord, or earl in Norton's court was high praise indeed. Gangs of children followed him everywhere he went. They picked up litter and helped old ladies across the street in hopes of being named a "prince of the realm."

His Imperial Majesty, Emperor Norton I, aka Joshua A. Norton.

The citizens of San Francisco were proud to adopt this eccentric ex-merchant as their own, and they afforded him the royal treatment he commanded. He enjoyed free meals in the city's finest restaurants as the guest of the owners, and the proprietors vied for his royal patronage, placing brass plaques in their entrances that declared, "By Appointment to his Imperial Majesty, Emperor Norton I of the United States."

Associating the emperor with a restaurant, clothing store, or saloon generated free publicity for the merchants and guaranteed a substantial increase in their profits. Business owners soon learned that any time Norton was involved, the newspapers were happy to give them free publicity. One business advertised, "Gentlemen's Outfitters to his Imperial Majesty." A popular tavern posted a sign in its window that read, "Fine wines and spirituous liquors by Appointments to his Majesty, Norton I." Occasionally he would become angry with merchants who used his name without his permission. He threatened to take action, but never did.

When the troops of Napoleon III invaded Mexico in 1862, Norton added a new title, "Protector of Mexico." "Mexico," he said, "beseeched him to expel the foreign invaders and rule over them." He soon dropped the title, explaining that it was "impossible to protect such an unsettled nation."

Norton printed his own money. Since US currency was considered unreliable, his dollars were accepted almost anywhere without question. If he owed debts or was in a financial bind, he paid with his imperial "legal tender" in denominations ranging from fifty cents to ten dollars. His picture and the denomination were imprinted on the front of each bill, with a promise to pay to the holder hereof with interest at 7 percent per annum from date; the principal and interest to be convertible, at the option of the holder, at maturity, into twenty years at 7 percent. Bonds were payable in gold coin.

One day Norton walked into the lobby of the First National Bank of San Francisco. He attempted to cash one hundred dollars of imperial currency, but the bank refused to honor his request. He then issued a proclamation that foreclosed on the bank.

Norton also levied taxes on his subjects. He would often walk into an office building and announce an imperial assessment of ten million dollars. The owner would satisfy him with a cigar, which he smoked as he walked out of the building.

The emperor rode for free on all of the city's ferries and streetcars. Leland Stanford, the president of the Central Pacific Railroad, gave Norton a free lifetime pass that he used to attend sessions of the state legislature and review military troops around the Bay Area. The city gave him a bicycle for his royal transport and thirty dollars a year to pay for his uniforms. The local Masonic lodge took care of his rent.

Norton never traveled alone when he made his daily rounds. He was accompanied by Bummer and Lazarus, two stray dogs with an uncanny ability to keep the city's rat population in check. The dogs had been together ever since Bummer saved Lazarus from being killed by a larger dog. They were often seen at the free lunch counters in the city's saloons, waiting for Norton or other patrons to toss them a few choice morsels. No play or musical performance would dare open its doors to the public without reserving seats for Norton and his two companions.

Bummer and Lazarus were as popular as the emperor. Newspapers competed with one another to report their escapades. One day a new dogcatcher mistakenly took Lazarus into custody. An angry mob surrounded City Hall and demanded that Lazarus be turned loose. The city council met in an emergency session and announced that both dogs were to have free run of the city.

When Lazarus was run over by a San Francisco fire truck, the city entered into a period of mourning. Thousands of tearful citizens turned out for his funeral, and Norton received hundreds of condolence letters. The *Daily Evening Bulletin* ran a lengthy obituary, "Lament for Lazarus." Two years later, Bummer died a painful and lingering death. He was kicked by a drunk when he entered his favorite saloon for a free lunch. Mark Twain, a well-known reporter for the *Virginia City Territorial Enterprise*, wrote Bummer's obituary: "Bummer died full of years, and honor, and disease, and fleas." The *Bulletin* described Lazarus and Bummer as "Two dogs with but a single bark, two tails that wagged as one."

Any politician who failed to show proper respect for the emperor had to face the wrath of his constituents. In 1867 Constable Armand Barbier arrested His Imperial Majesty on a charge of vagrancy. His fellow officers pointed out that since the emperor had $4.75 in his pocket and lived in a lodging house, he wasn't a vagrant. Barbier declared that Norton was of unsound mind and a danger to himself and others. He wanted to commit him to a psychiatric hospital. Norton was placed in a cell to await a mental examination by the commissioner of lunacy "for involuntary treatment of a mental disorder."

The public was outraged. Every newspaper in the city printed scathing editorials denouncing the police department. Fearing a riot, Police Chief Patrick Crowley opened the door to Norton's cell and ordered his release. He issued a formal apology to His Majesty on behalf of the police force. Norton accepted the apology with magnanimity and pardoned Officer Barbier for his act of treason. From that day forth, every member of Norton's "Imperial Constabulary" saluted him each time he passed them on the street. A special chair was reserved for the emperor at each precinct. Norton also marched at the head of the annual police parade and reviewed the cadets at the University of California.

Norton may have been a madman, but he refused to accept racial intolerance. A number of anti-Chinese demonstrations had broken out against the residents of some of the poorer sections of the city, and many of them died in the riots that followed. One night, a gang of vigilantes marched into San Francisco's Chinatown. The only thing that blocked them from reaching their intended target was the solitary figure of Emperor Norton standing in the middle of the street.

Norton could have reasoned with them or could have ordered them to cease and desist in the name of his imperial authority, but he knew they wouldn't listen. This situation called for stronger measures, and Norton was up to the task. Removing his hat, he bowed his head and repeated the Lord's Prayer several times. Within a few minutes, the agitators retreated in shame.

Norton ruled his kingdom by proclamation, and he enjoyed the powers and privileges befitting an emperor. He spent most of his time inspecting his domain, but he never neglected his paperwork. During his reign, he drafted a wide variety of royal edicts and proclamations. As loyal subjects, the newspaper editors followed his commands and printed them.

Norton believed that the United States was now a monarchy and there was no longer a need for a federal legislative body. On October 12, 1859, he issued a decree that dissolved the US Congress and ordered "all interested parties" to gather at Platt's Music Hall in San Francisco.

On the date of the scheduled meeting, the *Bulletin* urged folks to get there early for a good seat. When the emperor arrived at the hall, the doors were locked and not a soul had shown up. Since Congress had failed to comply, he ordered the commander of the army, General Winfield Scott, to assemble his forces, march on Washington, and "clear the halls." General Scott didn't comply either.

Each week, Norton issued a new decree. He abolished the California Supreme Court and fired Governor Henry A. Wise of Virginia for hanging abolitionist John Brown, replacing him with Governor John C. Breckenridge of Kentucky. In 1869 he abolished both the Republican and Democratic Parties, and in 1872 he issued the following edict:

> *Whoever after due and proper warning, shall be heard to utter the abominable word "Frisco" which has no linguistic or other warrant, shall be deemed guilty of a High Misdemeanor, and shall pay into the Imperial Treasury as penalty the sum of twenty-five dollars.*

Bay Area newspapers competed for the honor of publishing his proclamations and on more than one occasion, published fake decrees to generate sales. Some of the local citizens submitted their own bogus proclamations to the newspapers when they wanted to express a political view or make fun of the emperor. Anything that made a good story sold papers, and Norton was grist for the tabloids.

There was genius in Norton's madness, and he may have been a man before his time. He ordered a suspension bridge to be built from Oakland to Goat Island to Telegraph Hill, provided it could be built without injury to the navigable waters of San Francisco Bay. He further ordered that the Central Pacific Railroad Company be granted franchises to lay down tracks and run cars from Telegraph Hill along the city front to Mission Bay. The idea of building a bridge across the bay may have been a ridiculous idea in 1872, but sixty-four years later, it became a reality.

Norton was convinced that travel by air would one day be a common mode of transportation. Commissioning panels of researchers and designers to create plans for airships, he commanded his loyal subjects to provide the financial means to guarantee the success of the venture.

His Imperial Majesty proposed a worldwide League of Nations that would meet on a regular basis to resolve international problems through diplomacy. He wrote to many of the heads of state around the world, including Abraham Lincoln, King Kamehameha of Hawaii, and Queen Victoria of England. They all replied to his letters. King Kamehameha was so impressed with Norton that he refused to recognize the US State Department, saying he would deal only with representatives of the empire.

In the 1870s San Francisco had become a major tourist destination, and Norton was one of the main attractions. Visitors to the city had read about the emperor in travel books and newspapers, and they wanted to meet him. Golden Gate Park and the botanical gardens, the zoo, the seals, and the sea lions were okay, but they wanted to see His Imperial Majesty. Almost every store, hotel, and saloon displayed a sign that read "By Appointment to Norton I." The most popular items were picture postcards of the emperor, Emperor Norton dolls dressed in a military uniform and a plumed hat, Emperor Norton Cigars with his portrait on the label, and colored lithographs that were suitable for framing.

The glorious reign of Norton I came to an abrupt end on a cold and rainy evening. On January 8, 1880, he was walking along the street toward Nob Hill to attend the monthly debate of the Hastings Society at the Academy of Natural Science. As he passed Old St. Mary's Church, he had an attack of apoplexy and collapsed. A passerby saw him fall and raised the alarm. According to one newspaper, "The police officer on the beat hastened for a carriage to convey him to the City Receiving Hospital, but the Emperor passed away before the carriage arrived. As a large crowd gathered in front of the church, the police lifted Norton's body into the carriage and took it to the city morgue."

In the pockets of the emperor's uniform they found several telegrams, a gold piece worth $2.50, three dollars in silver, a French franc dated 1828, and a bundle of fifty-cent Imperial Treasury notes. A horde of reporters invaded his tiny apartment in search of a final story. They discovered that all he had left behind were his collection of walking sticks, his tasseled saber, numerous news clippings, his correspondence with Queen Victoria and President Lincoln, and 1,098,235 shares of stock in a worthless gold mine.

The next day, the *San Francisco Chronicle* published his obituary under the headline "Le Roi est Mort": "On the reeking pavement, in the darkness of a moonless night under the dripping rain . . . , Norton I, by the grace of God, Emperor of the United States and Protector of Mexico, departed this life." The entire city mourned the loss of their beloved emperor. One newspaper announced, "San Francisco without Emperor Norton will be like a throne without a king." Out of respect for their friend, flags flew at half-staff and businesses closed their doors.

Despite the rumors that Norton had amassed a fortune during his twenty-year reign, it soon became quite evident that he had died in poverty. The initial funeral plans called for him to be buried in a pauper's coffin of simple redwood, but to the members of The Pacific Club, a San Francisco businessmen's association, these arrangements were unacceptable. They raised enough money to purchase a handsome rosewood casket and pay for a funeral fit for an emperor at the Masonic Cemetery.

Ten thousand people came to the morgue to see their emperor lying in state. The *San Francisco Chronicle* reported, "The visitors included all classes from the capitalist to the pauper, the clergyman and the pickpocket, the well-dressed ladies, those bowed with age, and the prattling child."

The funeral procession that followed the coffin from the morgue to the cemetery was more than two miles long and was headed by the city's top officials. At 2:39 p.m. on January 10, 1880, as the coffin was lowered into the grave, San Francisco experienced a total eclipse. The mourners took it as a sign of Norton's passing into the afterlife.

In 1934 the city of San Francisco closed its cemeteries to make way for office space and new housing. Norton's remains were moved to Woodlawn Cemetery in Colma, California. Flags were once again lowered to half-staff, and businesses closed their doors in his honor. Sixty thousand people looked on as he was reinterred with full military honors.

The 3rd Battalion of the 159th Infantry Division fired three volleys into the air in salute while a lone bugler played taps. Carved into the new granite tombstone that covered his final resting place are the words: "Norton I, Emperor of the United States, Protector of Mexico, Joshua A. Norton, 1819–1890."

She Was a Hell of
a Good Woman

SARAH BOWMAN WAS A MOUNTAIN OF A WOMAN. SHE STOOD SIX FEET two inches and had a reputation as the roughest, toughest fighter on the Rio Grande. Because she was intrepid and reckless while at the same time possessing all the finer qualities of her sex, and alluding to her great size, she was nicknamed "the Great Western," for the largest steamship afloat.

Sarah didn't fit the stereotype of the frontier woman. Weighing two hundred pounds, she was described as having dark eyes, enormous breasts, an hourglass figure, and long black, red, or blonde hair. She packed two pistols, and she knew how to use them. People said she was so tall you had to hug her in installments.

Sarah was born in 1812 in Clay County, Missouri, and not much is known of her early years. She married young, and along about 1845 her husband joined the army to fight the Seminoles. Not wanting to be deprived of his company, she signed on as a cook and laundress and followed him to Florida. When her husband took sick, she left him behind and moved on with General Zachary Taylor's army to Fort Texas (later called Fort Brown) near the site of present-day Browns-ville, Texas.

Tensions ran high on both sides of the border in 1846. In early May, Taylor received word that thousands of Mexican troops were crossing the Rio Grande. Unless the general acted at once, the Mexicans would cut off his supply lines to Fort Texas and endanger the supply depot at Port Isabel on the Gulf of Mexico.

Determined to save the army's crucial supplies, Taylor marshaled most of his forces and marched them toward the coast. Hoping they could withstand an attack from the Mexican Army stationed across the river in Matamoros, the general left five hundred soldiers, one hundred women, and a dozen artillery pieces behind to defend the fort.

This was what the Mexicans had been waiting for. With most of Taylor's army gone, they laid siege to the fort. Once the cannonballs started to fly, the women were ordered to the dugouts for safety. Sarah refused to go. Exhibiting great courage under fire, Sarah began to care for the wounded and dying, and she brought food to the women in the dugouts and tended to their needs. At one point, the fighting was so fierce that a piece of shrapnel tore through her sunbonnet and a stray bullet knocked a bread tray out of her hands.

The siege lasted for seven days before the Mexicans were driven off. For her bravery, the soldiers called her "The Heroine of Fort Brown." Her legend grew when she offered to join a charge against a band of Mexican cavalry on the opposite bank of Arroyo Colorado Lagoon. In a loud voice she said, "I'll wade the river and whip the enemy single-handed if only someone will loan me a stout pair of tongs." A few minutes later, she saved numerous soldiers from drowning when their flatboat sank.

President Polk used the siege of Fort Brown as an excuse to invade Mexico. Under direct orders from the US government, Taylor's troops crossed the Rio Grande and marched into Northern Mexico. As a cook and laundress for the army, Sarah went with them. In the town of Saltillo, near the city of Monterrey, she opened the American House, an establishment providing weary soldiers with food, drink, and women.

Surrounded by thousands of soldiers, Sarah had plenty of male companionship. Not knowing or even caring if the husband she left in Florida was alive or dead, she married for a second time. Her second husband was a member of the 5th Infantry, and his name has been listed as Bourjette, Bourget, or Bourdette. No other record about him exists. He may have been killed in the attack on Monterrey; then again, maybe he wasn't.

At the Battle of Buena Vista, a few miles south of Saltillo, Sarah was once again in the thick of the fighting. With grapeshot and mus-

Sarah Bowman (center) as innkeeper/saloon owner during the Mexican/ American War

ket balls flying in every direction, she moved along the front lines giving aid and comfort to the troops. She provided hot meals for them, nursed the wounded where they fell, and picked them up and carried them to safety.

Sarah could whip almost any man in a rough-and-tumble fight, but she also had a gentle side. During the hardest fighting, she learned that her good friend Captain George Lincoln had been killed. It grieved her to think that he might lie undiscovered and not receive a proper funeral. She walked the bloody battlefield until she found him. Wrapping him in a blanket, she carried his body back to Saltillo and gave him a Christian burial.

Sarah ran her hotel until the end of the war. When the army was ready to pull out, she mounted her horse and rode up to the commanding officer, Major Rucker. She asked to join a column of dragoons that had been ordered to California.

"Only married women can march with the army," he replied. "You'll have to marry one of the dragoons."

Sarah rode back and forth along the line of mounted horsemen look-ing for a suitable candidate. In a thunderous voice that shook the parade ground she cried out, "Who wants a wife with fifteen thousand dollars and the biggest leg in Mexico?"

The thought that Sarah might have a husband or two somewhere may have caused the men to hesitate, and at first no one took her up on her offer. After a long silence, a dragoon named David E. Davis stepped forward. "I have no objection to making you my wife if there's a clergy-man to tie the knot."

Sarah turned to the soldier and with a hearty laugh said, "Bring your blankets to my tent tonight and I'll learn you to tie a knot that will satisfy you, I reckon."

Sarah changed husbands as often as most women changed their shoes. She soon fell in love with a man her own size, and before long Davis was just a memory. Although she acquired several husbands along the way, there is no record that she ever divorced any of them.

Sometime in 1849, Sarah arrived in El Paso, Texas. She opened a hotel that catered to the forty-niners and newly arrived soldiers at the fort. As El Paso's first madam, she provided her guests with rooms, meals, and female companionship.

Sarah found her next and last husband among the troops at Fort Bliss—Albert Bowman, a man fifteen years her junior. When he trans-ferred to Socorro, New Mexico, she leased her hotel to the army and went with him. The couple stayed in New Mexico for two years. After Albert was discharged, they moved on to Arizona City, across the Colorado River from Fort Yuma.

The couple became the town's first permanent residents. While Albert worked as an upholsterer, Sarah opened a restaurant and board-inghouse in a dirt-roofed adobe building on the edge of town. By 1864 Sarah and Albert were no longer together. He had run out on her and taken another wife, and his new wife was expecting their first child.

Sarah died from a venomous spider bite on December 22, 1866. She was buried with full military honors at the post cemetery at Fort Yuma, the only woman permitted to lie among her beloved soldiers. In August 1890 the Quartermaster's Department of the US Army exhumed the 159 bodies, including Sarah's remains, from the cemetery and reburied them in the National Cemetery at the presidio in San Francisco.

Despite the fact that Sarah Bowman was everything a frontier woman wasn't expected to be, she will be remembered for her courage under fire and her love and compassion for her fellow soldiers. To quote an old cowboy who met "the Great Western" in an Arizona mining town, "She was a hell of a good woman."

The Red Ghost of Arizona

In 1883 Arizona wasn't quite so wild anymore. A few bands of renegade Apaches still terrorized the countryside, attacking isolated ranches and running off stock. While a few outlaws still roamed the West, the days of the gunfighter were coming to a close.

At a ranch near Eagle Creek, Arizona, two well-armed cowboys rode out into the desert to check on their herd and round up a few strays, leaving their wives behind to attend to the daily chores. About noon, when the sun had reached its zenith, one of the women went down to a nearby spring for water. The other woman stayed behind with the children.

A terrifying scream filled the air, causing the dogs to bark and creating a horrendous commotion. Startled by the clamor, the woman in the house told the children to hide under the bed. Rushing to the open doorway and looking out to see what had caused the commotion, she was amazed to see a huge reddish-brown beast with a hideous creature riding on its back. The monster raced past the house, its cargo swaying back and forth. Shaking with fear, the woman bolted the door, grabbed the children, and hid in the root cellar.

After a long day in the saddle, the men returned home. They expected to find their families waiting for them, but the ranch appeared to be deserted and the cabin dark. The dogs cowered near the barn, afraid to come out and greet them. As if seeking safety from some unseen force, a small herd of horses bunched together at the far end of the corral. The sorrowful bawling of a few stray cattle and the mournful music of howling coyotes gave the blackness of the night an eerie chill.

The men leaped from their horses, drew their guns, and raced for the cabin door. Their apprehension turned to dread as they beat on the door and yelled for someone to open it. Upon hearing the banging and muffled shouts, the woman opened the door and threw her arms around her husband. In a hysterical voice, she described what she'd seen. At first they didn't believe her. They thought she was imagining things until they discovered that the other woman was missing.

The cowboys waited until first light to search for her. In loud voices, they called out her name, but there was no answer. They searched the barns, the outbuildings, and corrals without finding any trace of her. Just as they were about to give up the search and send for the sheriff, they found her lifeless body sprawled across the rocks in a shallow ravine. She'd been trampled to death. Surrounding her corpse were large hoofprints; her clenched fist long strands of red hair.

About a week later, two miners were sleeping in a tent near Clifton, Arizona. Suddenly the stillness of the night was shattered by the sounds of thundering hooves and raucous screams. As the beast raced past the startled miners, their tent collapsed. The miners freed themselves from the fallen canvas in time to see a gigantic creature barrel down the road in the moonlight. The next day, they too found huge hoofprints in the dirt and clumps of red hair clinging to the thorny bushes surrounding their campsite.

What was this ferocious creature that terrorized the countryside? No one knew for sure, but whatever it was, the beast kept the territory in an uproar. With each new sighting, its reputation grew. Some people called it "The Devil's Steed," and one man said he saw it kill and eat a grizzly bear. A drunken cowboy claimed he chased the "Red Ghost" into the desert, and just as he caught up with it, the beast vanished into thin air.

The mystery of the Red Ghost was solved when a local rancher who was rounding up cattle encountered the strange creature. He recognized it as a camel and realized that the burden on its back resembled a human skeleton. Although the rancher had a reputation as an honest man and wasn't given to telling tall tales, no one believed him.

Prospectors searching for gold sighted the animal near the Verde River, and they too saw something tied on its back. They grabbed their guns and fired at it but missed. When the animal bolted and ran, a small object fell from its back and rolled across the ground. What the prospectors retrieved sent shivers down their backs and made their skin crawl. It turned out to be a human skull with flesh and hair still attached.

The following week, the Red Ghost struck again. Several teamsters who had stopped along a deserted road for the night were the next victims. They were awakened at midnight by a series of horrendous screams and a horrific smell that made them throw up their dinners. As they later told the sheriff, "A giant creature about thirty feet tall knocked over two freight wagons, spooked our mules, and tore up our camp. We weren't taking any chances. We hid in the brush until the monster left." The next morning, they found the same strange hoofprints and matted red hair.

Near Phoenix, a young cowboy came across the Red Ghost eating hay in a corral. Like most cowboys, he had to throw a rope on anything that moved. He grabbed his lariat and tossed the loop over the camel's head. The beast turned toward his tormentor, threw back his ears, emitted a roar like a wounded Bengal tiger, and charged straight for the horse. With the cowboy barely holding on, the frightened horse turned and ran. In danger of being pulled from his saddle and trampled to death, the cowboy grabbed his knife, cut the rope loose from his pommel, and rode for his life. The angry camel kept up the chase for about a mile. When the Red Ghost couldn't catch its quarry, it returned to the corral to finish its dinner.

For the next decade, the Red Ghost and its now-headless rider continued to terrorize the citizens of Arizona. It made its last appearance in 1893, when a farmer saw it grazing in his garden. He picked up his rifle and dropped the animal with one shot. Even though it still bore the leather straps that had held the skeleton to its back, the camel had somehow shaken free of its grisly burden. Its reddish brown-color convinced everyone that this was the infamous "Red Ghost." But no one knew where it came from.

In the 1850s the US Army experimented with the idea of using camels as pack animals to resupply their forts and outpost across the Southwest. With the outbreak of the Civil War, the camels were sold off or turned loose to fend for themselves. The Red Ghost of Arizona was one of the last survivors of this failed experiment.

Dilchthe

FOR THE PIONEER WOMAN LIVING IN HER SOD HUT OR THE INDIAN woman in her hogan, life on the Western frontier in 1860 was anything but easy. Brutal weather, disease, deprivation, and death from marauding enemies were their constant companions. The courage and determination of these women is exemplified in the story of Dilchthe, a member of the Warm Springs Apache clan that roamed the deserts and canyons of the American Southwest.

Dilchthe, a middle-aged Apache grandmother, was captured in a raid by Sonoran mercenaries at Esqueda, Mexico, an area south of present-day Douglas, Arizona. The raiders slaughtered all the men in her party and drove the women southwest to the Gulf of California. They were sold into slavery and shipped to a work camp on the Baja Peninsula.

Many of the captives died in the camp, but through sheer determination, Dilchthe survived. Along with other women, she was sold again and put to work as a servant at a nearby hacienda. Despite her age, she worked hard and soon won the trust of her owners. They treated her with kindness and gave her additional responsibilities, but she wanted her freedom. Hiding food and water in places only she knew, she waited until she felt the time was right to make her break. She was determined to escape and return to her family.

In the silence of a moonless night, Dilchthe implemented her plan. Gathering her cache of food into a pack, she slung it over her shoulder, and woke some of the female slaves. The women climbed over the walls to freedom while their captors slept. Through the long night, they trudged across the desert to the Gulf of Mexico, moving ever northward along the coast. Hiding in the daytime and traveling at night, they evaded the mounted vaqueros who were sent out to bring them back. The fugitives conserved their meager supplies, but when their provisions ran out, they ate insects, roots, and desert plants. Dilchthe led them in a northerly direction for almost three hundred miles until they reached the Gulf of California near the Colorado River. They had to cross the river to reach the safety of their homes, but none of the women could swim. Dilchthe insisted they would find a way across, and on the advice of an old Mexican she met along the trail, she guided the women north along the bank of the river.

At the confluence of the Colorado and Gila Rivers, a place that later became the site of the Yuma Territorial Prison, Dilchthe stepped into the cold water and waded toward the distant shore. Just when it looked like she would be swept away in the fast-moving current, she reached a sandbar and climbed to safety. Seeing that she was safe, her fellow travelers plunged into the swirling water to follow her across. The women broke through the thick underbrush that lined the riverbank and made their way into the Arizona Territory.

Even though the women had reached the halfway point of their journey, the hardships continued. Near the Yuma Valley they encountered barren terrain and blistering heat. Some of them wanted to leave the desert floor and climb the mountains to escape the heat, but Dilchthe knew their enemies lived in those mountains and wouldn't hesitate to capture or kill her companions. She convinced them that if they continued to follow the Gila River, it would lead them home.

Three nights later, their camp was attacked by Yuma Indians. The raiders captured one woman and killed everyone else except Dilchthe and another woman, who escaped into the brush. They hid out until their pursuers grew tired of searching for them. When they felt it was safe to venture from their hiding place, the two survivors resumed their journey.

They walked for many days over the hot, dry riverbed. They walked past Gila Bend, Maricopa Wells, and around the villages and camps of their sworn enemies, the Pima and the Papago. Racked with grief from the loss of their traveling companions and weak from hunger, they pushed on for another hundred miles. Finally, too weak to take another step, they collapsed on the sand somewhere near present-day Safford, Arizona.

Knowing her people were nearby, Dilchthe lit a signal fire. The first warrior to spot her fire was her own son-in-law. She ignored the age-old taboo against Apache women looking into the face of their sons-in-law as she grabbed and hugged him. She was reunited with her family and welcomed back into her tribe as a hero.

With Apache courage and determination, Dilchthe escaped her captors and evaded her pursuers. She had walked more than a thousand miles through hostile territory without a map or weapons. With limited provisions, she had helped others to escape, even though most of her companions had met their death at the hands of their enemies. She was just a middle-aged grandmother with the will to live and the determination to reach her people. She was a woman of the West.

Please, General Custer,
I Don't Want to Go

THE SOLITARY FRONTIER SCOUT BEING CHASED ACROSS THE PLAINS BY hundreds of painted warriors is one of the enduring portraits of the Old West. The exploits of these trailblazers are legendary, and many of them were rather colorful characters. They loved to sit around a campfire, spin yarns, and tell tall tales. Their journals, diaries, and the wild stories they told are filled with exaggerations that more often than not have been taken as fact.

Like so many of his contemporaries, Alfred Estlack was a great storyteller. Most of the details known about his life can be verified, but there are some that can't. Whether true or not, Alfred claimed the distinction of advising General Custer not to fight the Battle of the Little Bighorn.

The western frontier offered the promise of open land and a chance at a new life for immigrants who braved the dangers of the unknown. In the fall of 1842, Jesse Estlack, his pregnant wife, Maria, and their infant daughter, Rosa, left their home in Cumberland, New Jersey, for the wilds of Northern Colorado. Alfred was born on the Ute Indian Reservation on April 11, 1843. Maria died in childbirth, Jesse was unable to care for the newborn. Taking the little girl with him, he left his son to be raised by an Indian woman. Alfred didn't see his father and sister again for many years.

Alfred spent his early years learning to be an Indian. When he was eleven years old, his adopted mother told him the story of his birth and how he came to live with the Utes. Alfred had always believed that his father was a famous warrior who had been killed in battle. He was surprised to learn that his real father was a white man who made his home somewhere in the Nebraska Territory.

In 1856 he bade his Indian mother and boyhood friends goodbye and went in search of the man who had abandoned him so many years before. After weeks of traveling around the countryside and questioning everyone he met, Alfred found Jesse and Rosa living in Fort Calhoun, Nebraska. After a brief reunion, he went back to his Indian family, returning to Fort Calhoun many times to visit Jesse and Rosa.

At the young age of thirteen, Alfred was hired to drive a team of oxen for a wagon train hauling freight from Fort Calhoun to Denver. By the end of the first day, the three wagons reached O'Fallon's Bluff, on the Nebraska-Colorado border. Just as the teamsters were making camp for the night, a large war party of Arapaho, Cheyenne, and Sioux rode down on them. Before the teamsters drove off their attackers, one man was killed.

The caravan made a hasty departure for Alkali Station, while mounted warriors dogged their trail. The station was a stage stop and gathering place for freight wagons, and the teamsters party thought they were safe there. That evening more than a thousand warriors attacked them. In the darkness of night, the Indians burned twelve wagons and killed fifteen men. The defenders fought back, and by the next morning they had inflicted heavy losses on the enemy.

The Indians withdrew and the caravan continued on to Denver with what was left of their freight wagons. Four hours out of Julesburg, Colorado, the Indians attacked again, and Alfred was wounded. The fight was short-lived, and the caravan reached their destination without further mishap.

Alfred made his last trip from Fort Calhoun to Denver in 1864. A hundred miles from Denver, the Indians attacked the caravan and ran off most of the stock. Alfred jumped on a horse, crossed the Platte River, and raced down the trail to get help. Fifty miles from Denver, he was spotted by a small war party on the opposite bank. They chased him for several miles, but with the river between them, Alfred outdistanced his pursuers. He escaped to a sod house, where the owner and his family had barricaded themselves behind the thick walls. Throughout the long night,

Alfred Estlack, Indian scout and frontiersman. COUR-
TESY OF JOHN J. (SPARKY) EASTLAKE

they fought off the Indians. When the sun came up, the Indians gave up
the siege and Alfred rode into Denver.

For more than a year, the tribes had been gathering in Colorado to
drive the white man from their land. Large war parties attacked freight
caravans, and the Julesburg Road became littered with burned-out wagons and unmarked graves. Without food, the people of Denver faced
certain death from starvation. Alfred recalled, "The whites ate battered
cakes made from grasshoppers. Hoppers ate up the crops, and we tried
to eat up the hoppers."

John Evans, the territorial governor of Colorado, appealed to Chief
Ouray and the Utes to help save the meager population of Denver from
the marauding tribes. The chief and the tribal council contributed six
hundred warriors to save the whites, and Alfred and two of his friends

hired on as scouts. During some of the fiercest fighting, the Utes defended Julesburg, Alkali Station, and O'Fallon's Bluff.

The first major engagement in the defense of Denver was a one-sided battle that later became known as the Sand Creek Massacre. Alfred was assigned to scout for Colonel John Chivington's 3rd Colorado Cavalry Regiment. The unit was made up of drunks, vagrants, and petty criminals Chivington recruited from the streets of Denver. The colonel led a regiment of the 3rd Colorado Cavalry, a battalion of the 1st Colorado Cavalry, and a battery of assorted artillery pieces on a forced march across the plains of eastern Colorado. He ordered Alfred and the two Ute scouts to locate the hostiles and report back, but they failed to find any renegade warriors. However, they did locate the camp of Chief Black Kettle, a well-known "peace chief." Over the objections of Colonel Chivington, Alfred and the Ute Scouts refused to take part in the attack and hightailed it back to Denver.

Black Kettle's Cheyenne weren't part of the renegade bands that had been terrorizing the countryside. But despite the American flag and a white flag of truce that Black Kettle hung on a pole atop his lodge, Chivington ordered his men to attack. In the predawn hours, the artillery opened fire and one thousand cavalrymen charged into the camp. A few warriors returned fire, and old men, women, and children took shelter wherever they could find it. After hours of senseless killing, Chivington had lost only nine men, but his troops had murdered more than four hundred defenseless Cheyenne. After the slaughter, they scalped and sexually mutilated the bodies, later exhibiting their trophies to cheering crowds in Denver. To justify the massacre, Chivington was quoted as saying, "Nits make lice. Kill them all."

Two weeks later, Chivington was honored with a parade through the streets of Denver. Adoration soon turned to disgust when stories of drunken soldiers butchering defenseless women, children, and old men began to circulate. In an effort to silence these rumors, Chivington ordered the arrest of one of his officers and five enlisted men for cowardice. The men had refused to participate in the battle and spoke openly of the wanton slaughter they had witnessed. The secretary of war ordered the men released, and Congress began a formal investigation of the events at Sand Creek.

Alfred wanted no part of a congressional investigation. In 1865 he left Denver with his friend and fellow scout, Howe Horne. Driving a herd of Mexican mustangs along the South Platte River to Fort Sedgwick, they were surrounded one evening by a small band of Cheyenne while making camp. Since the Indians were on foot and in need of mounts, they attacked the camp. The two men took shelter behind a makeshift barricade, and for the next three days fought off the Indians.

Alfred tried to convince Howe to leave their camp and save himself, but Howe was adamant that "No damned passel of redskins are gonna steal my horses. I'm stayin'." As soon as it was dark, Alfred slipped out of camp, changed clothes with a dead Indian, and escaped on foot. He reached Denver after five days and nights on the trail and led a large rescue party back to their camp. They found the Indians and the horses gone and buried Howe's mutilated body where it lay.

Alfred and his Ute companions spent the next few years in the Nebraska and Colorado Territories scouting for General George Crook. In 1876 they served with Custer's 7th Cavalry until a few hours before the Battle of the Little Bighorn. Scouting ahead of the regiment, they spotted more Indians gathered in one place than they'd ever seen before. They reported back to Custer: "There's ten thousand Injuns down there. We'll all be killed." They didn't wait for Custer's reply. Wheeling their horses around, they skedaddled back to the safety of Fort Abraham Lincoln. That was Alfred's last scouting expedition.

Alfred returned to the Utes, but since tribal law forbade him from taking an Indian wife, he left the reservation. He decided to seek his fortune in the Colorado mining towns of Silver Cliff, Cripple Creek, and Leadville. He tried prospecting and other business ventures.

Life in the mining camps was anything but dull. Robbery, murder, and claim jumping were a way of life in these towns. The miners formed vigilance committees to end the crime wave and drive the undesirables out of town. Under this system of justice, there were no courts, trials, or jails, and only two sentences with no appeals to a higher authority: Get out of town or get hung. Alfred joined the vigilantes and did his part to end the lawlessness.

Major General George Armstrong Custer c. 1865. COURTESY OF
THE LIBRARY OF CONGRESS

By this time, Alfred was getting a little tired of the single life. He
wanted a wife and began courting Miss Calisto Miller, who was alleged
to be one-half Indian. While she was walking down Silver Cliff's main
street one day, Alfred rode up on his horse, swooped her up in his arms,
and proposed to her. They were married in the spring of 1880 and settled
in Littleton, Colorado, where Calisto gave birth to two sons.

Alfred was always looking for new opportunities. In 1886 he liquidated his real estate holdings in Colorado and moved his family to the town of Belleville near Clay County, Texas. Other than the fact that four more children were born to Alfred and Calisto, no information is available for the Estlack family during this time period.

In 1906 Alfred moved to southeastern New Mexico to try his hand at ranching. He herded cattle at some of the ranches in the area, working well into his eighties. He finally retired from ranching in 1928 and spent his remaining years with his children in Vashti, Texas.

Alfred and Calista Estlack, likely in their eighties or nineties. COURTESY OF JOHN J. (SPARKY) EASTLAKE

Well into his nineties, Alfred walked two miles every morning just for the exercise. He seldom talked about his past, never accepted a pension, and never attended church or reunions. He retained his Indian ways and prayed to the Great Spirit every day. In his old age, his loss of memory and hearing created challenges for his family. He would sometimes wander off, and it wasn't unusual for him to show himself in front of his daughter-in-law's houseguests in various states of undress.

Alfred lived to the age of one hundred. In his lifetime, he witnessed the great western migration and experienced the settling of the frontier. He saw the birth of a new century; the invention of the electric light, the airplane, and the automobile; two world wars; and the Great Depression. On November 13, 1943, one of the last frontier scouts passed into history.

Hell Hath No Fury
Like a Woman Scorned

On November 3, 1870, a tall woman of indeterminate age walked across the crowded deck of the transbay ferry *El Capitan* as it pulled away from its Oakland slip bound for San Francisco. She was attired in a raincoat, and a heavy black veil was draped over her head to hide her identity. The woman searched the face of each male passenger until she found the one she was looking for. Drawing a Sharps pistol from her purse, she pointed it at the man who had jilted her. "You have ruined me and my child!" she shouted. A well-aimed bullet struck him in the heart, and he fell dead at her feet.

Who was this mysterious woman who left a trail of husbands and lovers, some dead and some alive, in her wake? She was born Laura Hunt in Holly Springs, Mississippi, on June 22, 1837. Her family was always on the move, never staying in one place for very long. Traveling as far west as Nacogdoches, Texas, they eventually settled in New Orleans. To honor a request from her dying father, at age sixteen, Laura married a man named Stone.

Stone was a New Orleans liquor dealer and commission broker, and, as the saying goes, "he was old enough to be her father." The marriage was marred by domestic quarrels and, due to unforeseen circumstances, it didn't last. Stone was a heavy drinker, and less than a year after taking Laura as his wife, he died from an intestinal infection. Laura attributed his death to his refusal to give up whiskey, even on his deathbed.

Deciding to become a teacher, Laura entered the Convent of the Visitation to study her chosen profession. School and widowhood didn't suit Laura, and after six months, she left the sisters to marry for a second time. Her new husband, Thomas Grayson, was much older than she, and, like her first husband, he too was a drinking man. Unlike Stone, however, Grayson was a violent drunk. His passion for alcohol and firearms became apparent soon after the newlyweds returned from their honeymoon in Vicksburg to make their home with his mother in New Orleans.

Grayson spent his days in the saloons drinking whiskey and courting the dance hall girls. On more than one night when he was feeling happy, he grabbed his pistol and used the poultry in the yard for target practice. He fired his gun at the chickens through the open window, and feathers floated in the night air. After coming home drunk one Saturday night, he drew his pistol and shot every chicken that crossed his path, leaving their blood-spattered carcasses covering the ground. When he was in a particularly foul mood, he would force Laura to lie down on her back on their connubial bed. With bloodshot eyes and a steady hand, he would fire dozens of shots at the headboard, missing Laura's curly blonde locks by a fraction of an inch.

Laura and her mother-in-law lived in constant fear. They'd grown accustomed to sitting by a window each night to watch for Grayson's return from the saloons. He was often too far gone to be dangerous, and the cab driver had to carry him into the house and put him to bed. On one occasion, he was in a blacker mood than usual. Staggering into the house, he pulled a knife from his boot and chased his mother and his wife around the house until he passed out.

Six months with this drunken sharpshooter were enough for Laura. Gathering up her few belongings and any money she could find, and with her mother-in-law in tow, she fled to San Francisco to start a new life. Grayson started divorce proceedings on the grounds of desertion. He spent the Civil War years living in sin with a young German girl, and nothing more is known of him.

San Francisco was a young city bent on trying to find its way, but unfortunately it was caught in the doldrums of an economic downturn. The first great gold rush had collapsed, the banks had failed in 1855, and the silver boom of 1860 hadn't hit yet. Laura and Mary tried to open a boardinghouse, but times were tough and business was bad. Most of the miners had moved on to more promising locations, and Laura decided it was time to move with them. The women deserted the mean streets of the city for Shasta, a town located in the beautiful forested hills of nothern California.

Laura had no intention of staying single very long. She wanted a husband, but not just any husband. She wanted a man who was rich and powerful, one who could give her the finer things in life. She set her sights on Colonel William D. Fair, a prominent San Francisco lawyer. He had the manners of a Southern gentleman, a respectable military title, and was an accepted member of high society.

Laura and the colonel were married in Shasta's Methodist church in February 1859. The wedding was a lavish affair attended by some of the city's most influential citizens, and after a brief honeymoon, the couple settled into their new lives. It wasn't long before Laura realized that her marriage to the colonel was a mistake. The marriage that started on such a high note soon went sour.

At thirty-six years of age, Fair was a successful liar, a charming failure, and a terrible businessman. Even though he claimed he had achieved the rank of colonel after graduation from West Point, the academy had no record of him. Laura's greatest disappointment wasn't in her husband's hopeful lies or fanciful tales but in his inability to provide for her. Despite a failing law practice and an almost nonexistent income, the Fairs managed to keep up appearances, but abject poverty in a small town wasn't the life Laura had envisioned for herself.

In August 1860 Laura gave birth to a daughter she named Lillias Loraine. She thought the baby would repair their marriage, but their relationship remained on a downhill slide. In an attempt to end the grinding poverty that was destroying their lives, Fair moved his family to San Francisco. He reopened his law practice in borrowed office space, but since he was such a poor lawyer, his business floundered. The Fairs were harassed by bill collectors, and their landlord threatened to evict the family from their home.

Until the end of her life, Laura perpetrated the lie that she and the colonel were devoted to each other. In reality, they separated almost as soon as they reached San Francisco. Fair slept on a cot in his office, while

Laura, Lillias, and Mary lived in a rented house. Just before Christmas 1861, Laura went to Fair's office to demand money for food and rent. When he told her he didn't have any, she declared she would never live with him again. After five years of a loveless marriage, the colonel committed suicide. In a note found near his body, he had written that he was ending his life because of his wife's infidelity.

Laura's situation was desperate: Her mother-in-law and daughter were ill, and there was no money to pay for a doctor. She didn't even have enough money for the barest of necessities, and her landlord was suing her for one hundred dollars in back rent. Seeing Laura's distress, an actor friend, McKean Buchanan, convinced her to become an actress and go on the stage. When she protested that she had no acting experience, he insisted that she didn't need any. The public would come out of curiosity to see the widow of a man who had blown his brains out.

The idea was repugnant to Laura, but Buchanan assured her that she'd earn enough money to pay her debts. Coaching her on the finer points of acting, he arranged for her to play the part of Lady Teazle in Sheridan's *The School for Scandal*. As was expected, on opening night the theater was packed with scandal-loving patrons who had come to see this notorious woman they'd all heard about.

Laura turned out to be a gifted actress, and she gave a stellar performance. The theater critics said, "This lady is a debutante. Unused to the stage, Mrs. Fair was cool and self-possessed, and gave an excellent rendition of her part. Compared to the rest of the company, who gave a lackadaisical performance, she carried the play and manifested an astonishing aptitude for the profession."

Despite the glowing reviews, a career on the stage wasn't what Laura wanted. Once she earned enough money to pay off her debts and have sufficient funds to open a boardinghouse, she abandoned the theater. Now that she was finished with poverty and scandal, she wanted the steady income a reputable business would give her. Her dependents included not only Mary and Lillias but also her brother, O. D. Hunt, who had arrived from New Orleans months earlier.

In 1863 Laura opened the Tahoe House in Virginia City, Nevada, a rooming house for men drawn to the silver bonanza of the Comstock

Lode. To save money, Laura put her family to work maintaining the thirty-seven rooms of the inn. Laura's mother-in-law attended to the housekeeping and supervised the chambermaids, while her brother worked the front desk.

Thanks to Laura's charm and business acumen, the Tahoe House prospered. The gentlemen of Virginia City competed for her attentions, and according to a report in a local newspaper, "With so many rigs tied up outside the Tahoe House, it looked like a country funeral."

Across the street from her establishment was a small novelty store owned by one of her tenants, a man named Dale. On July 4 he climbed up on the roof of the boardinghouse and hung a large American flag over her porch. The Civil War was in progress, and since Laura was born in Mississippi, she was sympathetic to the Southern cause. She ordered her brother to cut the halyards and take down the flag.

When her brother refused, Laura grabbed a knife from her desk, climbed out the window, and cut the flag down. Dale tried to stop her, but she stabbed him in the hand and he fell off the roof. He had her arrested, but during the trial, the jury found Dale guilty of malicious persecution and fined him seventy-five dollars. Her lawyer did such a great job of convincing the all-male jury that Laura was innocent and Dale was guilty that the jury didn't even leave their seats to acquit her.

As one of the most attractive women in Virginia City, Laura could have had any man she wanted. With so many dashing young stalwarts and rich gentlemen pursuing her, it seems curious that she would fall in love with a balding, forty-seven-year-old father figure named A. P. Crittenden. Most people saw him as a cold-eyed, tight-lipped individual who took himself too seriously, but Laura envisioned him as her husband and a father to her daughter. Little did she know that he was already married with children.

Crittenden came to Virginia City for the sole purpose of amassing a large fortune as quickly as possible. He was a guest at Laura's boardinghouse, and after she was arrested for stabbing her tenant, he agreed to defend her. Toward the end of 1863, the landlady and her lawyer had become romantically involved. He told her he was single and gave her expensive presents. She fell in love with him and soon became his mistress; but once again, trouble was on the horizon. Laura discovered that her lover was married and demanded that he divorce his wife. Crittenden professed his love for her and promised to leave his wife, a promise he never intended to keep. Six weeks later, he left for California.

Tired of waiting for Crittenden to honor his pledge, Laura decided to take matters into her own hands. Hoping to make her lover jealous, she married Jesse Snyder, one of her boarders. Crittenden learned of the wedding and hurried back to Virginia City. He begged Laura to get rid of her new husband and marry him. Convinced she'd won the battle, Laura divorced Jesse on a trumped-up charge of adultery.

Now that she was free of her unwanted husband, Laura expected Crittenden to leave his wife and marry her, but for Crittenden, divorce was out of the question. He was one of the Kentucky Crittendens, a famous lawyer, one of the leaders of the California Bar Association, and he knew a scandal would ruin him. If anyone ever found out that this woman was his mistress, he was finished.

One day Crittenden received a telegram informing him that his wife and children were arriving by train from Washington, DC. Mrs. Crittenden had been back east to visit relatives and was arriving unexpectedly. She asked him to meet them in two days at the railroad terminus in Oakland. Crittenden was too much of a coward to tell Laura he was meeting his wife and decided to wait until she was asleep before leaving town.

When he was certain that Laura was asleep, Crittenden slipped out of bed, picked up his clothes, and dressed in the dark. Being careful not to wake her, he tiptoed toward the door in his stocking feet. Once outside the boardinghouse, he stopped long enough to put on his boots, climbed on a horse he kept saddled in a nearby corral for emergencies such as this, and hightailed it out of town.

Laura was awakened by the sound of the running horse. She reached for her lover, but he was gone. Jumping out of bed, she pulled a robe around her naked body, lit the oil lamp that hung from a wall bracket, and looked around the empty room. Picking up the telegram Crittenden had dropped on the floor in his haste to escape, she read the words that tore at her heart. His wife was coming home. Once again, her lover had betrayed her.

Bringing to mind the phrase, "Hell hath no fury like a woman scorned," Laura was livid and wanted revenge. Packing a small bag, she boarded the morning stage for California and arrived in time to see her paramour greet his wife and children. From a safe distance, Laura watched him escort his family onto the deck of a ferryboat, never letting them out of her sight. While the family sat talking together on the open deck, Laura confronted the adulterous husband. Grabbing a pistol from her purse, she shot Crittenden through the heart.

Laura was arrested and hauled off to jail to await her trial, but she thought a jury would never convict her. She had heard that during the 1850s and 1860s, women shot men down all the time and escaped scot-free. But times were changing. Laura committed her murder in 1870, and the law demanded a trial.

One of the most publicized trials in the history of San Francisco, Laura's murder case was a cause célébre for equality of women in the battle of the sexes. The courtroom was standing room only. The battle lines were drawn when a group of suffragists led by Susan B. Anthony picketed the courthouse in support of the accused. They claimed that she was temporarily insane due to a female malady and argued that men were using the concept of female hysteria to deny women their rights and keep them under control.

San Francisco's newspapers, the *Chronicle* and *Examiner*, were not about to let a bunch of "silly old women" dictate the outcome of the trial. They called Laura a man-hungry murderer who seduced an upright citizen and destroyed his family. In referring to Anthony and her fellow suffragists, reporters wrote: "The passion of women is dangerous, destructive, and a threat to decent people everywhere."

In presenting their case to the jury, the defense also used the idea of a female sickness to show justification for the murder. They theorized that during the year before the killing, Laura suffered from maniacal attacks due to a delayed menstruation and was unconscious at the time of the shooting. They called three doctors and a nurse to testify that, like so many other women, Laura also suffered from this common malady.

"If Mrs. Fair intended to kill Mr. Crittenden," the defense argued, "she would have done so in a more private setting. She wouldn't have killed him if she'd been sane. She was following an impulse." They attempted to prove that mental illness in women was often linked to their menstrual cycles. "By going into business," they said, "Mrs. Fair took on a man's role, resulting in menstrual irregularity and insanity."

Called to take the witness stand, Laura claimed that as a result of her condition, she suffered from periodic blackouts and did not remember much from the day of the shooting. The women who filled the spectator benches cheered her testimony. Whenever the judge ruled the ladies in contempt, Laura paid their fines. In their closing arguments, the defense portrayed Laura as the victim, claiming it was Crittenden's false promises that drove her insane.

The prosecution countered with equally preposterous theories of their own. They pictured women as dangerous sexual creatures who were subject to control only by moral constraints. "Mrs. Fair is a seductress who will stop at nothing to get what she wants," the prosecutor told the jury. On cross-examination, they destroyed one doctor's credibility and forced another doctor to admit that Laura's symptoms might be the result of sexual excesses.

One of the prosecuting attorneys tried to make Laura admit she was Crittenden's mistress. "How dare she display such unladylike conduct as to shoot her man while he was actually in the presence of his legal wife," the lawyer demanded. The prosecution paraded a large number of reticent males through the courtroom as character witnesses to prove their charges against Laura's chastity. On the stand, Mrs. Crittenden described Laura as a calculating mistress and money-hungry adulteress.

The jury found Laura guilty of murder in the first degree and sentenced her to death by hanging. After the guilty verdict was announced, Susan B. Anthony spoke to a crowd in Laura's defense. She blamed men in general for Laura's incarceration and conviction. "If all men," she said, "protected all women as they would have their wives and daughters protected, you would have no Laura Fair in your jail tonight."

Many people were pleased with the verdict, but they didn't want to see Laura hang. Others felt she was innocent and should be released. The California Supreme Court reviewed her case and ordered a new trial based on the fact that evidence had been improperly admitted during

Laura D. Fair was tried and convicted for shooting her lover, A. P. Crittenden, when he abandoned her and returned to his wife. She was acquitted during her retrial. ARTIST UNKNOWN, JANUARY 2, 1870

Laura's first trial. Laura eventually was acquitted on the grounds of emotional insanity.

In a city known for its excesses, Laura continued to pursue her flamboyant lifestyle. In 1875 the *San Francisco Examiner* reported, "Laura Fair lives in style, gives balls, and speculates in stock. Few ladies are so often named at dinner tables." To women everywhere, Laura D. Fair was a genuine heroine. She had taken on the male establishment and won.

Sam Brown's Folly

FIGHTING SAM BROWN WAS KNOWN ACROSS THE WEST AS A DANGEROUS desperado. According to the folks who knew him, Sam killed enough men to fill up his own Boot Hill. Upon arriving at the Comstock in 1861, he set out to prove that his reputation was not idle gossip.

Sam was a big man, and he slouched when he walked. He never bathed or changed his clothes, and you could smell him coming a mile away. His loathsome appearance was highlighted by a dirty, matted beard filled with food particles and other debris. It grew so long that he parted it and tied it under his chin because it was too much trouble for him to trim.

Sam enjoyed a good fight as long as the odds were in his favor. On his first night in Virginia City, he pushed his way into a crowded saloon and picked a fight with a hapless drunk. Harsh words flew back and forth. Sam whipped out his bowie knife and slashed his defenseless opponent, killing him instantly. One more killing meant nothing to Sam. Wiping the bloody knife on the dead man's clothes, he stretched out on a nearby bench and went to sleep.

Sam never let the law stand in his way. He became outraged when he heard that one of his friends had been taken five miles away to Genoa to stand trial for killing an innocent man. When Assistant District Attorney Bill Stewart announced that he would convict the outlaw and hang him high, Sam vowed to ride over to Genoa, terrorize the court, and free his fellow desperado. Before starting out, he fortified himself with a large dose of liquid courage. In a drunken voice he bragged, "Not only will I clear him of the crime, I'll make the court accept it."

With his spurs jangling, Sam entered the packed courtroom, where his sudden appearance caused an uproar. Afraid that he might shoot up the place just for the fun of it, some of the jurors dove through the open windows while others cowered behind benches. The only man in the courtroom who wasn't impressed with Sam or his reputation was Bill Stewart. Before Sam could draw his pistol, Stewart pulled two derringers from his pocket and pointed them at Sam. "Put up your arms," growled the attorney. Looking down the muzzles of the derringers, Sam did as he was told. Stewart ordered the bailiff to disarm him.

Sam was dragged to the witness stand and sworn in as a hostile witness. "Now, Mr. Brown," Stewart said in a patronizing tone, "you have bragged that you would come down here and swear this defendant free and make the court accept your testimony. I am here to tell you that if you attempt any of your gunplay or give any false testimony, I'll blow your fool brains out."

To ensure that Sam knew he meant business, Stewart kept him covered while he questioned him. Sam admitted that he knew the defendant, that the man had a bad reputation, and that he had no knowledge of the murder. Defense counsel objected to the ruthless tactics of the prosecutor and accused him of intimidating the witness. Stewart replied that he was preventing the witness from intimidating the court.

Ignoring the defense council's objection, Stewart kept his derringers pointed at Sam and asked him if he felt intimidated. Sam would have been branded a coward if he answered in the affirmative. Thinking about it for a moment, the outlaw came up with an answer that made perfect sense to him. "I'm under indictment in Plumas County, California, for assault with a deadly weapon. I dropped into court to hire you to represent me." Stepping down from the witness stand, he offered Stewart five hundred dollars as a retainer. Without ever agreeing to represent him, the lawyer took the money and put it in his pocket.

By this time, it was getting late in the afternoon and Sam needed a drink. He told the judge that if he would adjourn these danged proceedings, Sam would buy the drinks. The judge agreed, and the entire court headed for the nearest bar. True to his word, Sam bought a few rounds for everyone in sight.

On the way out of town, Sam angrily reflected on the events of the day. Stewart had made a fool of him and damaged his reputation, and cost him five hundred dollars to boot. Something had to be done if he was going to regain his bad name. He wanted to kill Stewart, but the lawyer had too many friends. If he was to maintain his place in the community, something had to be done.

Before long, Sam got the opportunity he was looking for. Henry Van Sickles's wayside inn was the perfect place to regain his lost reputation. He dismounted, adjusted his spurs, and walked toward the inn. When Van Sickles heard the jangle of spurs in the courtyard, he rushed out to the porch to greet his guest.

"Shall I put up your horse, Mr. Brown?"

"Hello Van. How are you feeling?"

"Tip-top. Never felt better."

"Guess you're feeling too damned good. I'll take a shot at you just for luck."

Laughing as he drew his pistol, Sam fired half a dozen shots at the innkeeper. Van Sickles ran into the building and out the back door. It was suppertime, and the dining room was filled with hungry guests. When Sam barged into the room with pistol in hand, the diners jumped to their feet and drew their revolvers. Sam backed out the door, leaped on his horse, and raced away.

Van Sickles wasn't about to let Sam shoot up his establishment and get away with it. He grabbed his antique double-barreled fowling piece, added an extra charge of buckshot to each barrel, jumped on his horse, and took off in pursuit. Just as the innkeeper caught up with him, Sam took a shot at him. The shot went wild, and now it was Van Sickles's turn. Discharging both barrels at Sam, he blasted him out of the saddle. The desperado picked himself up, threw a few shots at his pursuer, and ran for his horse. Van Sickles reloaded, climbed onto his horse, and galloped after his quarry. The pursuit continued until the innkeeper was close enough to get off another shot at the fleeing outlaw. The buckshot knocked Sam's hat off his head and burned the side of his face. The outlaw spurred his horse to run faster, but the innkeeper kept after him.

The chase continued for more than an hour until, once again, Van Sickles was in range. He cut loose with both barrels, but his shots went wide. Sam turned in the saddle and returned fire, but his bullets failed to find their mark. He ceased firing and rode for Gold Canyon. If he could reach his hideout at Sun Mountain, he knew he'd be safe.

With the coming of night, Van Sickles lost his quarry. Sam had disappeared into the gathering darkness, and it looked like he might get away. The innkeeper left the road and raced ahead to a place where he might catch the outlaw. Reaching his objective, he dismounted and waited for Sam. Suddenly he heard the creaking of leather and the jangle of spurs.

Van Sickles waited until the outlaw was in range. Stepping out on the road, he pointed his gun at him. "I've got you," he hissed through clenched teeth. "Now I kills you."

At that moment, Sam knew without a doubt that he was going to die. Unutterable fear tore at his insides. With an agonizing scream of despair, Sam begged for his life, but Van Sickles ignored his pleas. Jamming the muzzle of his gun against Sam's chest, he blasted away with both barrels. Sam's lifeless body toppled from his horse and fell to the ground. An inquest was held, and the coroner's jury released its verdict: "Sam Brown has come to his death from a just dispensation of an all wise Providence. It served him right."

Pink Tights and Wild Horses

MANY OF TODAY'S CELEBRITIES ARE AS WELL KNOWN FOR THEIR FLAM-boyant lifestyles and the notoriety that surrounds their personal lives as they are for their professional accomplishments. More than 150 years ago, internationally renowned American actress and poet Adah Isaacs Menken parleyed an unconventional lifestyle into a life of fame, fortune, and despair. Her extraordinary beauty, outrageous style of acting, and daring display of her shapely figure made her a sensation of the Victorian age.

The facts surrounding Adah's birthplace and paternity are shrouded in mystery. Each time she gave an interview, she told a different story. According to one account, she was the daughter of a distinguished old Southern family. By other accounts she was born in Arkansas of a French mother and an American Indian father, or she may have been the youngest daughter of Richard and Catherine McCord of Memphis, Tennessee. On more than one occasion she told reporters she was raised in the Jewish faith.

The most likely story appears to be that she was born in a little village on the shore of Lake Pontchartrain, near New Orleans, on June 15, 1835. It is thought that her father was Auguste Theodore, a highly respected "free negro" of Louisiana, and her mother was a beautiful French Creole. Whatever the truth was, her father died when she was very young, leaving the family in difficult circumstances.

Before his death, Adah's father had been an ardent admirer of *Terpsichore* dancing, a compendium of instrumental dances inspired by the Greek muse. He wanted his daughters to become world-famous dancers, and as soon as Adah and her sister, Josephine, were able to toddle around a room, he engaged the services of a French dancing master. The sisters excelled in ballet, and when Adah was seven years old, they danced before an enthusiastic audience at the French Opera House in New Orleans. Adah and Josephine were an instant success.

For the next few years, they studied and worked hard at their craft. They danced to the adoration and applause of New Orleans high society and in Havana, Cuba, with the world famous Monplaisir Dance Company. Adah was so popular that she was crowned "Queen of the City Plaza" in Havana. Upon completion of a brilliant engagement in Mexico City, the sisters returned to New Orleans, and at the tender age of eighteen, Adah retired from the ballet.

Adah had been dancing before large audiences most of her life, and now she wanted to find other outlets for her creative energy. She enrolled in a private school and before long was fluent in English, Spanish, French, German, and Hebrew. She became an accomplished painter, sculptor, and poet, and she published a volume of poetry titled *Memories* under the pen name of "Indigina."

In 1856 Adah married Alexander Isaacs Menken, a handsome, distinguished gentleman and the son of a prominent Jewish family in Cincinnati, Ohio. Alexander's career as a musician had been floundering for years, and when he lost his money, Adah convinced him to become her manager. It was an affair that was doomed to failure. She made her theatrical debut in Shreveport, Louisiana, in 1857 as Pauline in *The Lady of Lyons* and then accepted the starring role of Bianca in *Fazio: Or, the Italian Wife* at the Varieties Theater in New Orleans. In 1859 she made her New York debut as the Widow Cheerly in *The Soldier's Daughter*.

Adah adored Alexander, and he worshiped her. Like many traditional Jewish men, Alexander wanted a wife who would stay at home and raise their family, but Adah wasn't interested. She wanted the adulation of her audiences, and she loved the attention she received from the "stage-door Johnnys" who waited for her after every performance. Men fell in love with her lovely face and exquisite figure, and rather than disappoint her fans and see them unhappy, she was generous with her love.

On more than one occasion, Adah's in-laws expressed their displeasure with her chosen career and unorthodox lifestyle. Having been raised in the Jewish faith, as time went by, religion was the only thing she and her husband had in common. The couple secured a rabbinical diploma to dissolve their marriage, but Adah continued to use Menken as her stage name.

In New York, Adah met a prizefighter named John C. Heenan. John had been born in the small town of Benicia, California, and was known to the sporting world as "Benicia Boy." As was the custom of the times, Heenan fought with bare fists. He was a brutal fighter who left his opponents broken and bloody.

Adah was fascinated by his brooding good looks and his cruel reputation as a fighter. A brief courtship was followed by a private wedding ceremony in a small cottage near New York City. As outrageous as their behavior in public was, their honeymoon was even more outrageous. John taught her to box, and they spent their nights as sparring partners. Every night after dinner, John used Adah as his punching bag. Adah fought back, but she was no match for this hulking brute. After one month of wedded bliss, John discovered Adah was pregnant by her former husband. He beat her up, dumped her, and divorced her.

In the meantime, although Alexander still loved his wife, she had hurt his pride by remarrying and he wanted to get even. Adah became embroiled in scandal when Alexander revealed to the press that even though their rabbi had dissolved their marriage, they were not legally divorced. In her own naive way, Adah had assumed Alexander would obtain the divorce and she would be free to marry someone else. The scandalmongers had a field day. They wanted her arrested and charged with bigamy. The clamor died down when Alexander did the gentlemanly thing and divorced her.

The baby Adah had wanted for so long died in childbirth. The loss of her baby, the public humiliation of the scandal, and the agony of her divorces were the precursors of a life filled with sorrow and failure. She may have been discouraged, but she never gave up.

Times were tough for Adah now that she was on her own. Unable to find work, she often starved. For a few dollars or a hot meal, she gave readings from Shakespeare or lectures on the theater. Painting her face black, she appeared as Mr. Bones in a minstrel show. When she did impersonations of Edwin Booth performing Hamlet, the public took little notice of her.

Adah wanted fame and fortune and the adulation of her audiences. She told her business manager she wanted to become a great tragedienne and play Lady Macbeth or become a great comedienne and play Lady Teazle in *The School for Scandal*. Her manager, who was something of a diplomat, told her she didn't have the dramatic flair for Lady Macbeth and was too good an actress to demean herself by playing Lady Teazle. He suggested that since her boyish figure was so lovely, and she had such fire in her voice and her eyes, she would be perfect for *Mazeppa* or *The Wild Horse of Tartary*, the drama everyone was talking about.

Mezeppa was based on a poem by Lord Byron and had been performed many times in London and New York. The play climaxed with a scene in which a young Tartar prince is stripped naked and bound to the

Controversial actress Adah Menken

back of a wild stallion. On cue, the horse would dash out of the wing, up a paper-mache cliff, and disappear into the clouds. As the curtain descended, the audience went wild.

To ensure the safety of the actor, tradition dictated that a stuffed dummy resembling Mazeppa would be tied to the horse's back for the ride up the cliff. Adah decided that the play needed dramatic realism. She announced that she would wear flesh-colored tights and ride the horse herself. Riding across the stage on opening night, in the dim glow of the footlights, she appeared to be completely nude. The audience was shocked, scandalized, and horrified. The critics called her performance banal and described her costume as "extremely daring." Her detractors accused her of indecency and nudity.

Critics and audiences be damned. For too long, Adah had borne the animosity of the hateful citizens of this miserable city. Stung by the harsh words of her critics and her enemies, she replied in kind, "New York is too stilted, too smug, too proper to appreciate great art. I'll go to the one place where the audience demands real art. I'll go to San Francisco."

Adah made her San Francisco debut at Maguire's Opera House on August 24, 1863. The press called her "the Frenzy of Frisco," and she was billed as the daring, the sensational, the unprecedented Mazeppa. "She will be stripped naked by her captors and tied to a horse. She will be forced to ride her fiery steed at a furious gallop onto and across the stage and into the distance."

According to the accounts that appeared in the newspapers the next day:

All of the streets leading to Maguire's Opera House were crowded with the most elegant of the city's elite. Ladies in diamonds and furs rode up in handsome carriages; gentlemen in opera capes and silk hats were their attendants. It was a first night such as the city had never before seen. And when, at the climax of the play, Menken vaulted to the back of her full-blooded California mustang and, clad in tights with hair streaming down her back, raced her steed at mad pace across the mountains of Tartary, the enthusiasm of the audience was a mad frenzy never to be forgotten.

The famous and the infamous lined up to see her perform. It was standing room only every night. Her admirers adored her and, in return, Adah was lavish with her love. In addition to being showered with expensive gifts, she received dozens of marriage proposals. American humorist Robert Henry Newell became her third husband.

The two most important topics of conversation in San Francisco at that time were the progress of the Civil War and the success of Adah Isaacs Menken. As her fame spread, she was besieged by imitators. Big Bertha, a circus fat lady who played Juliet opposite the circus thin man's Romeo on a rickety balcony at the Bella Union Saloon, decided she could play Mazeppa better than Adah. Dressed in pink tights and strapped to the back of a large mule, Bertha attempted to ride across the stage. Her 350 pounds were too much for the mule to bear. It tripped over the footlights and dumped her into the orchestra pit. Violins and other stringed instruments flew in every direction, and the musicians scattered to avoid Bertha's bulk when she landed. It took six burly miners more than two hours of pushing and pulling to get her back on her feet.

The citizens of San Francisco were delighted with Adah's bohemian lifestyle. The City by the Bay was a mecca for actresses, artists, and poets, and since Adah was known for her creative talents, she was the darling of high society. The St. Francis Hook and Ladder Company made her an honorary member of its firefighting brigade and presented her with an engraved fire belt. Accompanied by a brass band, the entire brigade serenaded her.

Adah had achieved her goal of fame and fortune. Now she was ready to take on the world. The first stop on her world tour was Virginia City, Nevada. For weeks before her visit, large color posters displaying her half-naked body tied to the back of a black stallion adorned every wall, post, and bar in town. Every man for miles around wanted to see her in the flesh. Before Adah had an opportunity to unpack her bags, three reporters for the Virginia City *Territorial Enterprise* decided to write a negative review of her opening-night performance. They had seen the posters, and as far as they were concerned, she was nothing more than a glorified circus performer. One of the reporters was Mark Twain.

On opening night, every available space was packed with enthusiastic males waiting for Adah's undressed ride up the mountain. As the curtain closed, the audience gave her a standing ovation. The three literary cynics from the *Territorial Enterprise* raced back to their office to write glowing reports of her performance. Mark Twain was so enthralled with Adah's beauty and voice that he wrote a five-page review of her performance. It was reprinted in newspapers across the country.

Adah remained in Virginia City for many weeks. The miners loved her bizarre behavior and treated her like royalty. They presented her with a bar of gold bullion worth two thousand dollars and named a street for her. They gave her fifty shares of mining stock that she later sold for fifty dollars a share. One night in the Sazerac saloon, she stood on the bar and boasted that she could outbox any man in the place. A drunken miner stepped forward and accepted her challenge. Putting on the gloves, she knocked him out in the second round. Another miner lasted for three rounds, and later admitted that Adah's left was a thing with which to conjure.

Adah changed husbands the way most people change shoes. In 1865 she divorced her third husband and, a year later, married a gambler named James Barkley. James hung around long enough to get her pregnant and then disappeared. Adah gave birth to a son, but he died in infancy.

Tired of performing for miners, cowboys, and drunken louts, Adah took *Mazeppa* to Paris. Adah was accepted as an actress, but she wanted the literary world to recognize her as a serious poet. She surrounded herself with an international literary elite that included Alexandre Dumas fils, Algernon Swinburne, and George Sand. The press reported that Adah had affairs with the younger Dumas and Swinburne. Adah created a scandal when she fell in love with the senior Alexandre Dumas, and she might have married him if young Alexandre hadn't stepped in and threatened to horsewhip his father for being a senile Romeo. Heartbroken and in tears, Adah packed up and sailed across the channel to London.

In London, the audiences went wild. They had never experienced anyone like the magnificent Adah. Charles Dickens fell in love with her; princes, dukes, and earls pursued her. Life was rich, full, and exciting,

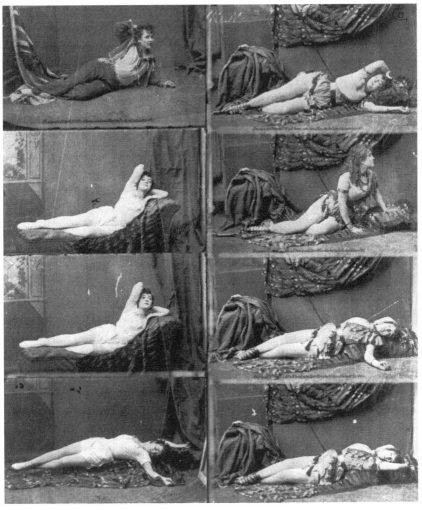

Adah Menken c. 1866. COURTESY OF THE LIBRARY OF CONGRESS

and, as usual, Adah was generous with her love. She spent her fortune on luxuries and gave it away to friends, struggling artists and actors, and various charities.

Adah received a severe injury while performing her famous ride and was forced to retire from the theater. She gave her final performance on May 30, 1868. Since she could no longer perform, the public lost interest in her, and her friends abandoned her. Her money gone and in ill health, she lived in poverty. Her desperate need for money forced her to return to her writing. She published a volume of Victorian poems and raised enough money from its sale to allow her to return to Paris.

Adah knew her days were numbered. She spent her last hours on earth with a sympathetic rabbi discussing faith, hope, and her wasted life. Adah wrote a brief note of farewell to an old friend: "I am lost to art and life. Yet, when all is said and done, have I not at my age tasted more of life than most women who live to be a hundred? It is fair then, that I should go where old people go."

The ravages of peritonitis and tuberculosis had taken their toll. The personal physician of Napoleon III tried to save her, but it was too late. On August 10, 1868, at thirty-three years of age, Adah Isaacs Menken, with the rabbi at her bedside, passed away. She was laid to rest in a pauper's grave in the stranger's burying ground at Pére Lachaise. Her body was later moved to an obscure corner of Montparnasse cemetery. Chiseled in marble, according to Adah's final wishes, were her final words to her creator: "THOU KNOWEST!"

The Texas Salt War

SALT IS A PURE WHITE, CRYSTALLINE SUBSTANCE THAT HAS FLAVORED our food for centuries. But would you kill for it? In the late 1860s, some of the most influential citizens of west Texas and New Mexico, hungry for power and greedy for wealth, precipitated a bloody conflict that became known as "The Texas Salt War."

In the shadow of the Guadalupe Mountains, about 110 miles east of El Paso, salt flats that still cover hundreds of acres provided almost pure salt to frontier settlers and Mexican farmers. The salt was free for the taking, and inhabitants on both sides of the border collected it for their needs. When their meager crops failed, as they often did in this arid land, the Mexican farmers filled their wagons with salt and hauled it to El Paso to be sold for a few coppers. For more than 150 years caravans of slow-moving ox-drawn *carteras* trudged across the desert to the salt flats, and the *salineros* (salt dealers) regarded the salt deposits as a public commodity.

The situation might have continued for many more years, but certain events transpired that set the stage for political machinations, murder, racism, riots, and the only recorded defeat of the Texas Rangers. A cartel of prominent politicians formed a syndicate they called "The Salt Ring." They planned to acquire title to the salt beds and charge the Mexicans a fee for every bushel of salt they took from the deposits. They filed a petition to take possession of the land, but when the court rejected their claim, the members of the ring began to fight among themselves. In a fit of anger, one of the members, Ben Williams, murdered another, Judge Gaylord Clarke. Then in one of El Paso's many saloons, the leader of the Radical Republicans, Colonel Albert J. Fountain, shot and killed Williams.

The violence split the group into opposing factions. Old friends became bitter enemies, and political alliances disintegrated. Fountain fought for control of the syndicate, but it dissolved like a teaspoon of salt in a glass of water. He became the leader of the so-called Anti-Salt Ring and was elected to the Texas Senate. Attempting to secure title to the deposits for the people of El Paso, the new leader of the ring, W. W. Mills, wanted to line his own pockets with the revenues from the sale of the salt. The Fountain-Mills feud contributed to the ruination of the Republican Party in Texas, and effectively ended their political careers. Fountain moved his family to New Mexico and became a major political force in the territory. Mills stayed in El Paso for a few more years and was later appointed US Consul in Chihuahua, Mexico.

These attempts to monopolize the salt trade fed the resentment of the Mexicans. The parish priest of San Elizario, Father Antonio Borrajo, and Louis Cardis, a powerful political leader of the Mexican constituency, fanned the flames of racial hatred. They had been members of the Salt Ring but had been denied their share of the profits. Arousing the ire of the Mexican people on both sides of the border, the hostility between the races broke out into open warfare.

The next stage of the trouble commenced when Missouri lawyer, and political opportunist, Charles Howard joined forces with Cardis in an attempt to crush the Republican machine and establish the Democratic Party in El Paso. Cardis helped secure Howard's election as district attorney; in return for the favor, Howard aided Cardis in his successful campaign for the state legislature. Within two years the men became mortal enemies when Cardis attempted to revive the salt scheme. Howard declared that Cardis was "a liar, a coward, a mischief maker, a meddler, such a thing as could only spring from the decaying carcass of an effete people."

Cardis was reelected to the state legislature and Howard was appointed district judge. The feud turned violent when Howard double-crossed Cardis and filed a claim on the unallocated portions of the salt lake. After the courts honored his claim, Howard posted a notice that the salt was no longer free for the taking and closed the road to the salt flats. Cardis and Borrajo endeavored to coerce Howard to share the spoils, but he threw them out of his office. In the weeks that followed, Howard assaulted Cardis in Austin and San Antonio, but Cardis refused to retaliate. Howard attacked him again at the Fort Quitman Stage stop, and this time Cardis filed charges against Howard and had him indicted.

Howard had two *salineros* arrested for threatening to take salt without paying for it. Judge Garcia ordered one man discharged and the other man turned over to Sheriff Charles Kerber for trial. The imprisonment of a Mexican citizen was the excuse Cardis had been waiting for. He fanned the discontent of the Mexican-Americans in the Rio Grande Valley. A mob stormed the courthouse and arrested the judge and his brother-in-law. Howard and one of his employees sought refuge in the sheriff's home in Ysleta, but an angry crowd soon surrounded the house. The sheriff stepped outside to talk to the mob, but they disarmed him. Dragging Howard and his associate into the yard, they tied them up and took them to San Elizario.

Kerber was convinced that Cardis was the instigator of the trouble. He grabbed Cardis and, though he was unarmed, threatened to get a gun and shoot him if anything happened to Howard. Cardis persuaded the mob to release their prisoners in exchange for Howard's promise to give up his claim to the salt beds and leave the county. Four of Howard's friends signed a twelve-thousand-dollar bond to ensure that he would honor the agreement. Howard retreated to Mesilla, New Mexico, but he swore to come back and even the score.

The situation in El Paso and San Elizario remained tense. Prominent Anglo citizens petitioned Kerber to raise an army to protect their lives and property from marauding gangs. In a letter to the sheriff, the citizens claimed, "The insurgents still maintain their armed organization, and openly state they will massacre every man who worked for Howard's release as soon as they hear the troops are coming. Last night armed men promenaded the town crying, 'Death to the Gringos.'" The sheriff declared his force of 15 men too small to face 360 armed Mexicans, and he decided not to go.

Kerber did his best to restore order, but his best efforts were in vain. Howard blamed Cardis for his humiliation at San Elizario and returned to El Paso to wreak vengeance on him. Grabbing his shotgun, Howard walked into a store where Cardis was hiding and unloaded both barrels into him. Howard was arraigned for murder, placed under bond, and allowed to return to New Mexico.

With Cardis dead, the Mexicans decided to force the issue. On December 1, sixteen wagons and hundreds of armed men headed for the salt beds. On December 12, Howard and twenty-five Texas Rangers rode into San Elizario to confront the *salineros*. That evening, Sheriff Charles Ellis was ambushed and murdered. The next morning, as bullets flew and cannons roared, Father Borrajo urged the mob to kill the gringos.

Howard and the rangers took refuge in an old adobe house. In a scene reminiscent of the siege of the Alamo, six hundred Mexicans surrounded the makeshift fort. The fighting raged for four days until the rangers exhausted their ammunition. Kerber sent for a detachment of soldiers, but without orders from Washington, the troops refused to rescue the rangers.

The defenders awoke on the morning of the fifth day of the siege to discover that the Mexicans had spent the previous night digging entrenchments around the building and tunneling under the foundation. Howard realized that help wasn't coming, and without ammunition they couldn't continue the fight. Howard and the rangers surrendered under a flag of truce. The mob disarmed the rangers and allowed them to leave San Elizario, but despite an agreement to spare their lives, Howard and two of his employees were executed by firing squad. The mob cut off their heads, mutilated their bodies, and threw them down a well.

The violence continued, and rioters looted San Elizario. Within a few days, US Army troops and a posse made up of outlaws, cattle rustlers, bank robbers, and murderers descended on the town. They killed four men, wounded others, and raped some of the Mexican women. The El Paso grand jury handed down more than 280 indictments against the Mexicans for their alleged participation in the riots, while the leaders of the rabble and many of their followers escaped to Mexico. No one was ever arrested or brought to trial.

A congressional investigation attempted to determine the facts and place blame, but the only action they took was to reestablish Fort Bliss, which had been abandoned earlier in the year. With the coming of the railroad to El Paso, San Elizario declined in importance and most of its residents moved on. In his book *The El Paso Salt War*, author C. L. Sonnichsen reflects on the people and events of this vicious chapter of Texas history: "The Salt War like all wars was wasteful and unnecessary, unless to prove to a pessimist that men can die bravely in a bad cause."

The Mysterious Lady in Blue

IN THE EARLY 1600S SPANISH EXPLORERS AND MISSIONARY PRIESTS invaded the American Southwest. The conquistadors came in search of gold; the priests came in search of souls. What they found was an untamed wilderness, an indigenous population with strange beliefs and customs, and a mystery so bizarre that, even in today's enlightened world, is difficult to explain.

The Spaniards were the first Europeans to explore this arid land. Since no white man had ever been there before, they were ill prepared for encounters with Indians who carried crosses, had a rudimentary knowledge of Catholic rituals, maintained altars in their villages, and knew the Catholic liturgy. When questioned about it, the Indians told the priests of a beautiful white woman dressed in blue who came down from the sky, spoke to them in their own language, walked among them, and taught them about Jesus and the Christian God. She said others would follow who would baptize them and instruct them in the faith, after which she disappeared back into the clouds. These weren't the only Indians who spoke of the mysterious lady in blue. From 1621 to 1631, missionaries recorded numerous stories of Indians who claimed to have seen this lady.

Father Eusebio Kino and Father Matheo Manje recorded a story an ancient Indian had related to the priests while they visited a Pima Indian village along the Gila River. According to this old man, a beautiful young white woman dressed in a flowing blue gown appeared in his village and spoke in a language the tribe did not understand. The more she spoke, the louder she became until she was yelling at them. Many of the villagers became frightened. Some of the warriors shot arrows at her until she collapsed on the ground. Believing they had killed her, they ran away. When they returned several hours later, the mysterious lady had disappeared. Three days later, she appeared in the village again and started shouting at them in her strange language. Thinking she was an evil spirit, they hid.

Guided by the chief of the Jumanos, sometime in the 1620s Father Juan de Salas led an expedition of priests and soldiers into southwest Texas. They were met by a large band of Indians who claimed a lady in blue had advised them of the approaching missionaries. More than two thousand natives presented themselves for baptism and religious instruction.

Father Alonso de Benavides, custodian for the missions in New Mexico, California, and Texas, wrote of an encounter with Indians he had never seen before. In July 1629, fifty warriors of the Jumano tribe appeared at the Franciscan convent of the old Isleta Pueblo near present-day Albuquerque, New Mexico. Through an interpreter, they asked to see a priest. They told the good father they had traveled many days and nights to speak with him and that they came from a place far over the mountains, a land the missionaries had never visited.

When Benavides asked what they wanted, their answer confounded him. They requested a priest to return to their village with them to teach them more about Jesus, to baptize every member of the tribe, and to build them a church.

Benavides was suspicious of the motives of these wild savages. Perhaps they wanted to entice the priests out of the safety of the mission so they could murder them. To allay his fears, the Indians told him that they had learned about the priest's Christian God and wanted to worship him.

"How did you learn of God?" Benavides asked.

"A beautiful white lady dressed in blue came to our village and spoke to us in our own language. She told us about the Christian God and directed us to come to the mission."

"Where did she come from?" Benavides wanted to know.

"She just appeared one day," they replied.

"Where did she go?" Benavides asked.

"She just disappeared," they told him.

The Indians stayed at the mission for many days waiting for the priest. On one of the walls of the mission, they saw a painting of a woman wearing a nun's habit. They became excited and pointed out to Benavides that although the lady in the picture was old and fat, she was wearing the same kind of dress their lady wore. The woman in the painting was mother superior of a Poor Clare convent in Spain.

At last, Father Benavides had a clue to the identity of this strange young woman. From the Indians' description of the clothes she wore and

Maria de Agrada teaching the Indians about Jesus Christ.
NATIONAL PARK SERVICE

their reaction to the painting, the priest was convinced the lady in blue was a Poor Clare nun.

But how could that be? Benavides wondered. Poor Clares were cloistered nuns who never left the convent. Was it possible that one of the nuns had somehow made her way to New Spain and was wandering alone across thousands of miles of unexplored territory, walking among the savages, learning their languages, teaching them about Christianity?

Benavides wrote to his superiors in Spain asking if they were sending women to New Spain as missionaries. Their answer perplexed him more than ever. The new lands were too dangerous, they said. They were not sending women to the New World for any reason.

The priest was determined to get to the bottom of this mystery. He returned to Spain in 1631 and met with Maria de Jesus, the abbess of the Poor Clare convent in Agreda. Maria admitted she was the lady in blue and that she had made more than five hundred visits to New Spain.

For the next two weeks, Benavides interrogated her. Telling him how she became a nun, Maria gave him detailed descriptions of the clothing and customs of the tribes she taught. Relating names of tribes and specific individuals, she painted a vivid picture of the Southwestern landscape and told him that she hadn't been outside the walls of the convent since taking her vows.

The eldest daughter of Francisco Coronel and Catalina de Arana, Maria was born in 1602. During her childhood she exhibited an unusual piety and a remarkable memory. At the age of sixteen, she convinced her father to convert the family castle into a convent for Franciscan nuns. Francisco took vows of poverty and joined a monastery, while Catalina became a nun. Maria took her vows on February 2, 1619, and became known as Sister Maria de Jesus de Agreda.

Because Maria was so devout, by the time she was twenty-five years old, she had received special recognition from the pope. By papal dispensation, she was promoted to abbess of her order. She appreciated the honor bestowed on her by the holy father, but she wasn't totally satisfied with her life. Maria didn't want to remain cloistered in the convent while priests and brothers from many religious orders were being sent to the

New World. Maria wanted the same opportunity as her associates to spread God's word, but her superiors denied her that chance.

When asked how she was able to travel thousands of miles and minister to the tribes when she never left the convent, she replied, "God knows." Maria bowed her head as if in prayer, and after a long silence she spoke to the priest in a soft voice. She explained that when she went into her room to meditate and pray, she often fell into a deep trancelike state. In her dreams she was transported to a strange and wild land where she went among the people. She spoke their language, taught them the Gospel, and ministered to their needs.

Benavides wanted to know where she learned to speak the languages of the people she encountered. "I didn't," she replied. "I spoke to them and God let us understand one another."

The priest knew without a doubt that Maria had been to New Spain. He reacted to her descriptions with increasing alarm and advised her to try to stop dreaming. She later told him the dreams had stopped, but she was experiencing terrible nightmares. Satisfied the mystery had been solved, Benavides returned to Mexico.

In his *Revised Memorials of 1634*, Benavides told Maria's story. The document came to the attention of King Philip IV, and he sought her out. For the next twenty-two years, Maria remained the king's spiritual and political advisor. The king said of Maria, "Except for Maria's counsel, the unity of Spain could never have been preserved."

In addition to being the mother superior of her order and advisor to a king, Maria was a prolific writer. Her four-volume work titled *The Mystical City of God* and her book *Divine Virgin Mother, History of God*, in which she described her repeated visions from God, became two of the most widely read and highly acclaimed tomes of the seventeenth century.

Maria de Jesus de Agreda died on May 24, 1665, but her story doesn't end there. Father Damián Massanet wrote of an incident that occurred at his mission in west Texas in 1690. The chief of a Tejas village wanted to trade vegetables and animal skins for a piece of blue cloth. Asked why he wanted the material, he explained that his mother was very old and he wanted to make a shroud to bury her in when she died. The priest told the chief that black was much more suitable for a shroud, but the chief shook his head and insisted on blue.

Puzzled by the Indian's determination, Massanet asked why the tribe favored blue, especially for burial clothes. The chief said, "When my mother was a very young girl, a beautiful white woman dressed in blue descended from the heights and spoke in our language. She taught them about the Christian God, baptized them, and helped them build a church. When she was finished, she disappeared into the clouds. Since that time, whenever one of our people dies, they are buried in blue cloth in the hope that they will once again see the beautiful lady."

In the 1840s a malaria epidemic struck south Texas. The settlers reported that a mysterious lady in blue traveled across the Sabine River Valley giving aid and comfort to the victims of the disease. The last recorded sighting of her apparition occurred during the darkest days of World War II.

The mystery of the lady in blue may never be solved. Skeptics will say the story was a figment of Maria's fertile imagination. Believers in the paranormal will claim Maria had numerous out-of-body experiences or astral projections. Many of the faithful will call it a miracle and say that God sent her to the New World to spread his word among the natives. Where the answer to this enigma lies is up to the reader to decide.

The Last Apache Warrior

As the covered wagons rolled over the trails of the American Southwest and towns sprang up across the desert landscape, the early settlers who invaded this harsh, arid land of Apacheria had more to fear than waterless waste, dust storms, and outlaws. Apache warriors led by Cochise, Victorio, Geronimo, and chiefs of lesser fame pillaged and burned as they attacked the settlers. Treachery by the army and hatred of the Apaches by Anglos and Mexicans alike prolonged the terror of the Indian raids for years and helped spawn the legend of "the Apache Kid."

The Kid was born to chief Toga-de-chuz and his wife in the wilderness near present-day Globe, Arizona, sometime around 1860. Historians are unable to agree on what his Apache name was, or whether he was a White Mountain Apache, a Pinal Apache, or a San Carlos Apache. They do agree that his family was part of Captain Chiquito's band and lived wild and free in Aravaipa Canyon along the Gila River. A land of wooded canyons and running streams, lush vegetation and plentiful game, it was paradise for the Apaches, who had lived and died on this land for centuries.

The Indians resented anyone encroaching on their territory and declared war on any outsider who dared to trespass on their land. Bloody conflicts between civilians and the army on one side and rampaging Apaches on the other raged across the Arizona Territory for years. Small bands of armed warriors burned ranches, towns, and settlements. Tying their captives spread-eagle over open fires or staking them out on anthills to die a slow death, they scalped and mutilated the bodies of their enemies and kidnapped women and children as slaves.

The army was called in to stop these depredations, but they achieved little success. By 1870 the US government realized the military solution was a failure and that more drastic measures had to be taken. They decided the only way to solve the problem was to round up the troublemakers, confiscate their weapons, and confine them to a reservation. If they could teach the Apaches to farm and raise livestock, the Indians might forgo their warlike ways.

Established near Globe, Arizona, to keep the Apaches under control while the whites civilized the countryside, the San Carlos Indian Reservation was located on a windswept strip of land between the Gila and San Carlos Rivers. During summer the mercury soared to 115 degrees Fahrenheit and rain was scarce. Small groves of almost leafless, shrunken cottonwoods lined the banks of the rivers, and scorching desert winds swept across the landscape. In winter the Apaches endured freezing temperatures and the land was often covered with snow. Confinement on the reservation was a slow death for the Indians.

When the army was ordered to round up the scattered tribes and relocate them to the reservation, the Apaches took off for the mountains. The troopers tracked Captain Chiquito's band, convinced them to surrender, and moved them to San Carlos.

The desolation of the reservation was a dead end for the young Apache warrior. He started hanging around Globe doing odd jobs for the cowboys, miners, and soldiers. The townspeople considered him to be friendly and trustworthy. Because of his youth, and since they were unable to pronounce his Indian name, they started calling him "the Apache Kid." Adopting the white man's ways, he soon exchanged the traditional Apache breechcloth and moccasins for the white man's boots and jeans. Learning English, the Kid picked up rudimentary education in the white man's school.

Al Sieber, chief of scouts for the army, took an interest in the Kid and treated him like a son. Wherever Sieber went, the Kid went. Sieber knew the ways of the Apache and recognized that the Apache Kid was a natural leader. Deciding the army could benefit from his talents, Sieber enlisted the Kid as one of his scouts. He excelled at his job and served with distinction. Within two years he was promoted to first sergeant of Company A, Indian Scouts.

In 1882 the Kid fought against his own people at the Battle of Big Dry Wash, the last major battle in Arizona Territory. He joined General

Crook's expedition into the Sierra Madres and went south into Mexico with Crook's forces to fight against Geronimo. With the surrender of Geronimo and his band of renegades, the Kid found himself in a situation that made him one of the most wanted criminals in Arizona history.

The trouble started with a drunken brawl and the death of two men at an Indian dance at San Carlos. Sometime during the festivities, an Apache warrior known as Gon-Zizzie murdered the Kid's father, Togo-de-chuz. The Kid's friends caught and killed Gon-Zizzie, but that didn't satisfy the Kid. He believed his father's enemy, Old Rip, had put Gon-Zizzie up to committing the murder.

Tribal law required the eldest son to exact blood vengeance for his father's death. The Kid asked Sieber for permission to leave the reservation and go after Old Rip, but Sieber refused. Traveling to Fort Apache on business, Sieber and the Indian agent for San Carlos left the young Apache in charge of the guardhouse. As soon as they were out of sight, the Kid took five of his scouts and headed for Old Rip's camp. With one shot through the heart, the Apache Kid killed Old Rip.

The Kid and his scouts traveled to his father's camp to celebrate the victory over his enemy. Joining relatives and other members of the tribe, they danced and got drunk on *tiswan*, a beverage made of fermented fruit or corn. The party lasted for three days.

When Sieber learned that the Kid had disobeyed orders and abandoned his post, he ordered the Kid and his scouts back to the reservation. Hungover and disheveled, they reported to an angry Sieber. He lined them up and commanded the Kid to confiscate their guns and cartridge belts. Once the Kid had disarmed his friends, Sieber told him to place his own rifle and cartridge belt on the ground. He ordered the Kid and the scouts to be locked up in the guardhouse until an army court martial could decide their punishment.

The Indians weren't too happy about being locked up in the white man's jail, and the whites weren't too happy with them being there. Someone in the crowd fired a shot and before long bullets were flying everywhere. A hail of bullets tore Sieber's tent to shreds, and a large .45-70 caliber bullet smashed his left ankle. The captives broke out of the guardhouse and managed to steal some horses, and with twelve other

Apaches they escaped into the desert. Two troops of the 4th Cavalry pursued the fugitives up the banks of the San Carlos River, but the renegades got away.

For the next two weeks, the escapees led the army on a cross-country chase. Loyal Apache scouts located the Kid and his little band of "Bronco Apaches" high in the Rincon Mountains. The soldiers rounded up the stolen mounts, but the Kid and his followers escaped. Survival in the wilderness and escape into Mexico were almost impossible without their precious horses.

Knowing their situation was hopeless, the Kid sent a message to General Miles. If the cavalry would halt its pursuit, he would surrender. Miles ordered his troops back to San Carlos, and on June 22, 1887, eight members of the band gave themselves up. Three days later, the Kid and seven more Apaches surrendered.

A military panel found the scouts guilty of mutiny and desertion under the Articles of War and sentenced them to death by firing squad. General Miles felt the sentences were too harsh and ordered them reduced to ten years at Alcatraz. He later wrote in his memoirs, "The Apache Kid and the others did not fully understand the seriousness of their deed in relation to their enlistment in the Army, that according to Apache custom, the Kid's vengeance on the enemy was not important."

The Kid petitioned President Grover Cleveland for the release of himself and the four scouts, and the president ordered the judge advocate general's office to review the case. The JAG was convinced that prejudice among the officers at the court martial had prevented the men from receiving a fair trial. Secretary of War William Endicott reviewed the findings and authorized the release of the prisoners. They were returned to the reservation.

The good citizens of the territory were outraged by the release of the Apaches. They couldn't believe the courts would allow the Indians to roam free to continue their depredations. A public outcry for protection from these murderers led civilian and military authorities to arrest any Indian accused of a crime and try him in the territorial courts.

Sheriff Glen Reynolds and a large posse entered San Carlos and arrested the Kid and most of the former prisoners. The Kid and three of

Prison photo of Apache Kid taken in 1888 at
Globe, Arizona

the scouts were charged with assault with the intent to commit murder in
the wounding of Al Sieber. Sieber knew these men hadn't fired the shot
that shattered his ankle, but it was his testimony that convicted them. They
were sentenced to seven years in the territorial prison at Yuma, Arizona.

Eight Apaches and one Mexican horse thief were loaded into a
stagecoach for the two-day trip from Globe to the railhead at Casa
Grande. Considered the most dangerous of the prisoners, the Kid and
another Apache, Hos-cal-te, were shackled at both their wrists and
ankles. The remaining Apaches were chained in pairs with one hand

free. The horse thief was left unshackled. Sheriff Reynolds and his deputy, W. A. "Hunkydory" Holmes, rode on top.

On the second day of the trip, the driver, Eugene Middleton, stopped the coach at the steep ascent of Kelvin Grade. Reynolds ordered everyone out except the Kid and his seatmate. The coach headed up the grade and disappeared out of sight. Two of the Apaches jumped the sheriff, grabbed his rifle, and shot him. The other Indians turned on Holmes; after a short struggle, he died of a heart attack. Another prisoner, Pash-lau-te, shot Holmes through the heart to make certain he was dead. The Indians removed the keys from the bodies and unlocked their shackles. They smashed Reynolds's forehead with the rifle butt, but they left Holmes's body unmolested. With the coach some distance away from the onslaught and the prisoners still inside, Middleton continued to guard the Kid and Hos-cal-te. He had no inkling of trouble until he heard the shots and saw the Mexican horse thief racing toward him. The Mexican shouted a warning in broken English and darted into the heavy brush. With Middleton distracted, Pash-lau-te came around the side of the coach and fired Reynolds's rifle at him. The gunshot, coupled with the war cries of the victorious Apaches, startled the horses. They bolted, broke loose from the stagecoach, and scattered into the desert. The bullet hit Middleton in the cheek and exited through his neck. He fell to the sand, stunned and temporarily paralyzed.

Pash-lau-te helped his friends from the coach and unlocked their shackles. Thinking Middleton was dead, they rolled him over on his back to search him for cartridges and valuables. Pash-lau-te wanted to make sure he was dead, but the Kid told him, "Save the cartridges. He is dead anyhow." The Apaches disappeared into the desert in a developing snowstorm.

Waiting until the Indians left the area, the Mexican crept out of his hiding place, snagged one of the coach horses, and galloped to Florence, Arizona, to summon help. Middleton survived through the night, and the next morning, weak from loss of blood, he staggered five miles to Riverside Station to sound the alarm. A posse started on the trail of the fugitives, but a blinding snowstorm forced them to turn back.

By October 1890 most of the escapees had been killed or recaptured. The Kid made good his escape, and for the next several years he terrorized Apaches and whites alike from the Tonto Basin to the Sierra Madres in Mexico. He was blamed for every murder, ambush, and rape that occurred in the Arizona Territory between 1889 and 1894. A five-thousand-dollar reward was offered for his capture, "dead or alive," but it was never collected. The Kid was never apprehended again.

The Kid, with a small band of "Bronco Apaches," raided ranches and freight lines, torturing and killing victims throughout New Mexico, Arizona, and nothern Mexico. No one knew where the Kid would strike next. One rancher who had an encounter with the Kid said it best: "Usually, by the time you saw the Apache Kid, it was entirely too late."

The Apache Kid returned to San Carlos many times to steal young women and other men's wives. When he was tired of them or they were worn out, he sent them back to their families. Running and hiding in the mountains, standing guard at night while the men slept, and performing their normal camp duties required women of great physical endurance. Some of the women weren't up to the challenge, and he had to find replacements frequently.

One of the last reported incidents appears to have occurred at Ed Clark's Galiuro Mountains ranch. Clark noticed moccasin tracks near his corral, and he knew from past experience that Apaches often stole horses from unsuspecting ranchers. When night fell, Clark took his rifle, slipped out of the house, and settled in for an all-night vigil.

Dawn was breaking when he spotted two Indians leading his favorite horse away from the corral. Firing two shots, he killed an Apache woman and wounded an Apache man. The man escaped, leaving a trail of blood behind him. Clark followed the trail for many miles, but it disappeared on the rocky terrain. Clark would later claim, "It was the Kid all right. He crawled away to die somewhere, I know." The body was never recovered, and no one is certain of the horse thief's identity.

Most people believed that Clark killed the Kid, but five years after his purported death, the Mexican government declared that the Apache Kid was the leader of a small band of renegade Apaches in the Sierra Madres. Witnesses reported they saw the Kid in Arizona and in the Yaqui Valley of the Sierra Madres in 1900. Members of a posse claimed they killed the Kid near Kingston, Arizona, in 1905; and there are unconfirmed reports that he died of consumption in 1910. The Kid's nephew, Private Joe Adley, confided to his superiors at Fort Huachuca, Arizona, that his uncle was still alive in Mexico in 1924.

We will never know if the Apache Kid died from a bullet wound or of old age. Perhaps he fled to Mexico and rode with the remnants of Geronimo's warriors, who raided the towns and villages of northern Mexico until 1938. There may yet be Apaches living in the mountains of Mexico, and perhaps they still dream of the old ways as they roam this hostile land.

Julia Bulette, Queen
of the Comstock

Ask any old-timer and he will tell you that it wasn't guns that won the West, it was sex. The West not only had the fastest guns, it also had the fastest women. Like their deeds, their names are legendary. There was Little Gertie, The Gold Dollar, Madame Bulldog, Crazy Horse Lil, Madame Moustache, Silver Heels, Baby Doe, and Big Matilda, to name a few. Some of them amassed great fortunes, but many met a violent end.

One of the most famous women in Nevada's long and colorful past was a prostitute named Julia Bulette. In her short life, this "soiled dove with a heart of gold" became the most popular courtesan of Virginia City, and despite her profession, she achieved a modicum of respectability. The stories that have been told about her over the years have obscured the exact details of her life, but with her untimely death and the execution of her alleged killer, Julia has become one of the enduring legends of the Old West.

The facts concerning Julia's birth and childhood are cloaked in mystery. Some writers say she was born in London and immigrated to Louisiana, where an unhappy marriage drove her into prostitution. Other writers say she was born in France, and recruited in Paris to work in the sporting houses of New Orleans. Recent research indicates that she was actually born near Natchez, Mississippi, in 1832. Most historians do agree that Julia was a Creole and that she worked in the finer establishments on New Orleans's famous Rampart Street. Arriving in northern California sometime in 1853, she plied her trade in the camps and mining towns until she moved on to Virginia City, Nevada, the richest mining community in the West.

In its heyday, Virginia City was the most important settlement between Denver and San Francisco. The saloons, opium dens, and brothels ran twenty-four hours a day, and the mines never shut down. Grubby prospectors became instant millionaires and built magnificent mansions that still stand today as monuments to the opulence of life on the Comstock.

Julia established herself as one of the leading madams of Virginia City, and her house became known as "Julia's Palace." Located on the corner of Union and D Streets, it was the cultural center of the community for the town's men. Unlike many other houses on the line, she permitted no rough-housing or vulgar language. She offered gentle conversation, and taught her customers to enjoy fine wines and skillfully prepared French dishes.

Many of the tales of "fallen angels with hearts of gold" are pure fiction. In Julia's case, the stories are true. Each time an epidemic swept through the city, Julia was there. Ministering to the sick and dying, she gave hope to the hopeless with her presence. She contributed money to a fund for widows and children of the men killed in the mines, and she often sold her furs and jewels to provide food and clothing to poor and needy families. She was a major contributor to the Sanitary Fund, Virginia City's version of the Red Cross. When a large band of Paiutes threatened the town, Julia refused to leave for Carson City with the other women. She stayed behind with the men.

For her generosity and many acts of kindness, Julia was elected an honorary member of Virginia Engine Number One, the only woman in history to be so honored. No parade was complete without Julia riding on the gleaming brass and silver fire engine. Each time the fire alarm sounded, she jumped out of bed to answer the call, often leaving her paying customers to their own devices. Providing coffee and hot meals for the firefighters, on more than one occasion she even assisted with the water pumps.

To the virtuous ladies of the town, Julia was a pariah. They resented her social standing with their husbands, and each time she rode past their fancy homes in her lacquered brougham, they drew their curtains in disgust. These "good" women were scandalized to see her at the opera or

Julia Bulette, Queen of the Comstock. NEVADA HISTORICAL SOCIETY other public places with Tom Peasley, her favorite lover. If she heard the hateful comments they made behind her back, she chose to ignore them.

The ladies of Virginia City wanted to see Julia gone, and they soon got their wish. At 11:30 a.m. on January 20, 1867, a close friend and neighbor, Gloria Holmes, called on her for a prearranged breakfast date. Finding the back door open, she entered the house, walked into the bedroom, and found Julia's battered corpse lying on the bed.

Except for the blood and bruises, Julia seemed to be asleep. Her head rested on a pillow, and her legs and feet protruded from under the covers. The sheet on both sides of her body was smooth, and it was evident that no one had slept with her. Her clothes lay on the floor as if she had stepped out of them before getting into bed.

At the inquest, the doctors testified, "When we arrived at the crime scene at noon, the deceased had been dead for at least six to eight hours. We examined the body and found deep bruises on her forehead and wood splinters in her hair. The marks on her body and on the pillow used to smother her indicate that she fought to save her life. She was severely beaten around the head and shoulders, but the cause of death was strangulation."

Other witnesses came forward and related what they'd seen and heard. A newsboy stated that as he was making his rounds at five o'clock on the morning of the murder, he heard a woman scream as he passed Miss Julia's house. He delivered a newspaper to her door but saw nothing unusual. A Chinese tradesman testified that he had entered the house early that morning, but he wasn't certain of the time. He brought in a load of wood and lit the fireplace. Thinking Julia was asleep, he left without disturbing her.

Julia's funeral was the grandest sendoff the Comstock ever saw. Since she had been a member of Virginia Engine Number One, the service was held at the firehouse on B Street. A brass band, eighteen carriages filled with mourners, saloon girls and soiled doves, and sixty firemen escorted the black-plumed, glass-walled hearse to Flowery Hill Cemetery. The women of the town wouldn't permit Julia to be buried in hallowed ground, so she was interred two hundred yards from the cemetery on a hillside overlooking a saloon.

The band played a funeral dirge as the cortege moved through the streets, but on the way back to town, the joyful strains of "The Girl I Left Behind Me" filled the air. Two thousand men attended the funeral, and her tombstone was the headboard of Julia's bed.

A search of Julia's home revealed that many of her possessions were missing. The murderer had systematically looted the house. The police ruled the motive for the murder as robbery. Over the objections of their wives and girlfriends, the men of Virginia City demanded action, but the law had no idea where to look.

Three months passed before they got their first break. The police had uncovered evidence that linked a Frenchman, John Millain, to the crime. A Mrs. Cazentre of Gold Hill had purchased a dress for forty dollars from a Frenchman fitting Millain's description. Suspecting that the dress might have belonged to Julia, she took it to the sheriff, who in turn questioned some of the local merchants. One of the merchants recognized the dress as one he had sold to Julia Bulette.

At Millain's apartment, police found a trunk filled with Julia's clothing and jewelry. Among the items in the trunk were her velvet opera cape, assorted silk dresses and gowns, a silk breakfast cape trimmed with swansdown, silk handkerchiefs embroidered with Julia's name, and various pieces of lace. Hidden under the clothing was a silver goblet with the initials J.C.B., a set of enameled cufflinks, a silver bar with the name "Julia" engraved on it, a pair of large coral eardrops, a charm bracelet, and a heavy gold ring.

The police had no trouble finding Millain. He was vacationing in the local jail. A few days earlier, he had broken into the house of another lady of the line (as women in Bulette's profession often were called) Martha Camp. When she came home, and caught him rifling through her possessions, he pulled a knife and threatened to kill her. She screamed, and the intruder escaped through the open door. Martha saw him on C Street a few days later and had him arrested on charges of robbery and attempted murder.

Millain denied any knowledge of the murder, but when confronted with the evidence, he confessed. At his trial he pleaded not guilty but admitted that he had taken part in the robbery. "I was part of a three-member gang," he testified. "I remained outside on lookout while my partners entered the house. They came out a short time later carrying the trunk. They left it with me for safekeeping. They left town, and I haven't seen them since."

Millain's lawyer knew there was no way he could win an acquittal, but if he could convince the jury that Millain wasn't present in the house when Julia was murdered, he might save his client from the gallows. He faced the jury and in a bombastic voice that carried to every corner of the courtroom said, "If my client is guilty of anything, it must be insanity. Anyone who showed off the murdered woman's possessions and openly sold an easily recognized dress must be crazy."

Neither the judge nor the jury believed the Frenchman's story. The jury found him guilty of murder in the first degree, and the judge said, "Hang him." His lawyer appealed the case to the Supreme Court of Nevada, but they refused to grant a retrial. Millain was sentenced to hang on April 24, 1867, between the hours of 10:00 a.m. and 4:00 p.m.

To the men of Virginia City, the Frenchman was a monster; to their wives he was an instrument of divine Providence who had rid the community of Julia's evil influence, and they wanted to repay the favor. Visiting him in his cell, they brought him gifts of fried chicken, pies, wine, champagne, and assorted homemade delicacies. They circulated a petition to have his sentence commuted to life in prison but were stopped by an editorial in the *Territorial Enterprise*: "We believe that John Millain will be hung. If he is not, we do not know where a fit subject for hanging is to be found."

On the morning of the execution, the streets of Virginia City were filled with people who came from all over the territory to watch the hanging. A holiday atmosphere permeated the town. On every corner, merchants sold picture postcards of the condemned man. Huge crowds gathered in front of the courthouse; hundreds more lined the route to the gallows.

At 11:30, a carriage with its curtains drawn left the courthouse. Twenty deputies armed with Henry repeating rifles rode on each side of the coach. Hidden from view, Millain and two priests rode inside the coach. As the carriage made its way through the crowd, two more carriages followed, one carrying the physicians who would pronounce him dead; the other, the press. A hearse with a black-draped coffin inside brought up the rear.

The procession halted at the foot of the gallows. The prisoner stepped from the coach and climbed the thirteen steps to his destiny. A reporter for the *Gold Hill News* wrote, "A pleasanter Spring day was seldom seen, and on the sides of the encircling amphitheater of hills were between four and five thousand people, many of them women and children."

A hush fell over the crowd as the sheriff read the death warrant. Turning toward the prisoner, he asked, "Do you have any last words?" Millain stepped forward. In a calm, unwavering voice, he read his farewell statement, first in French and then in English. "In my trial and conviction," he said, "a great injustice has been done to me. Chief of Police Edwards has perjured himself on the witness stand, and abandoned women have been brought in to swear my life away. I have been guilty of some bad deeds during my lifetime, but of this murder, I am innocent."

The Frenchman thanked the sheriff and his deputies for their kind treatment while he was in jail. He forgave the citizens of Virginia City for hanging him, and he thanked the ladies for visiting him in his cell. When he was finished, he knelt down with one of the priests to pray, after which he arose and stood on the trapdoor. The hangman put the noose around the condemned man's neck and placed a black hood over his head. He pulled the lever, and John Millain dropped through the trapdoor into eternity.

Julia is gone now, but not forgotten. In the 1940s the local chapter of E Clampus Vitus erected monuments at Julia's home and her grave. On January 20, 1967, they commemorated the one hundredth anniversary of her funeral with a torchlight parade. Sixty Clampers dressed as nineteenth-century firemen marched through the streets of Virginia City, followed by black-plumed antique hearses and brass bands. At Millionaires Hall, they held a wake complete with whiskey, music, and dancing girls.

Julia was more than a common woman of the line. She was a lady in the truest sense. She was the toast of the richest mining community in Nevada and the pride of the Comstock fire companies. Like so many famous women throughout history, perhaps she also believed that well-behaved ladies never make history.

Fool's Gold

A FEW MILES EAST OF PHOENIX, ARIZONA, NEAR THE TOWN OF APACHE Junction, the forbidding peaks of the Superstition Mountains rise up from the desert floor. This unforgiving landscape is a place of mystery and murder, where treasure hunters have met their deaths at the hands of unknown assailants or vanished without a trace. Despite numerous murders and decapitations over the years, the Lost Dutchman's Gold Mine still lures adventurers to the craggy peak of Superstition Mountain to search for the elusive treasure that drives men mad.

The Pima Indians called this mountain Ka-Katak-Tami, meaning "The Crooked Top Mountain." Its lofty summit towers over the barren waste of the Sonoran Desert that stretches to the far horizon. A few sparse stands of ponderosa pines cling to its jagged cliffs, and from its lower slopes, multiarmed saguaro cacti march across the land in an endless procession. Summer temperatures often exceed 125 degrees Fahrenheit in the shade, and there is no shelter from the searing heat. There is no water, and creek beds and streams dry up. In winter, temperatures drop below freezing and snow covers the ground.

This fragile wilderness is home to mule deer, javelinas, mountain lions, bobcats, coyotes, birds, amphibians, and reptiles. Everything that survives in this harsh environment sticks, stings, bites, or eats meat. Gila monsters, scorpions, and rattlesnakes wait at every turn for the unwary traveler. Perhaps that is why the old-timers called this primitive land "Hell's Backyard."

There are many stories of murder, mayhem, and lost mines in the Superstitions, and it's difficult to separate reality from fantasy. Most historians agree that the Apaches were the first people to claim this barren wasteland, and Francisco Vásquezde Coronado and his conquistadors laid claim to it when they came north from Mexico in 1540 to search for the mythical "Seven Cities of Gold."

The Indians were friendly at first, but due to the harsh treatment they received at the hands of the Spaniards, their friendship turned to anger. They told Coronado that the mountain held much gold, but they refused to show him where it was. Afraid to enter the domain of the "Thunder God" who lived on the mountain, the Indians believed he rumbled ominous warnings from the mountaintop and hurled lightning at anyone who dared trespass upon his sacred ground.

Coronado sent scouting parties into the mountains to search for the gold, but they were never seen alive again. The remaining soldiers fled in terror and refused to return to the mountains when they found the mutilated, headless corpses of their comrades in canyons and ravines. Knowing it was useless to pursue the search for the gold, Coronado ordered his men to strike camp and continue on their way.

In 1748 the king of Spain granted ownership of 3,750 square miles of what later became the state of Arizona to Don Miguel Peralta of Sonora as a reward for service to the crown. The area contained rich mineral deposits, and it isn't certain how Don Miguel discovered the gold.

Over the next one hundred years, the Peralta family made infrequent trips to the mine from their home in Mexico. Their fear of the Apaches kept them from making too many visits. They had found the remains of Apache victims spread-eagled over their campfires and burned to a crisp, staked out over anthills, or scalped and mutilated, and they had no desire to join them. As the years passed, most of the family members died off, and all that was left were a few roughly drawn maps showing the location of the mine.

By 1846 the remaining Peraltas had depleted their silver mines in Mexico and needed to find new sources of revenue to maintain their lavish lifestyle. They decided it was time to brave the dangers of Arizona and work their gold mine. Don Miguel, his four sons, and his great-grandson bade goodbye to their families, and with horses, cattle, burros, and four hundred men, they marched north.

Three months on the trail brought the bone-weary travelers to an area that became the site of present-day Mormon Flats. Making camp on the banks of LaBarge Creek, they set up their arrastras and smelters to crush and process the ore. One of Peralta's ancestors had named the mines Las Minas de las Sombrero (the Sombrero Mines) for a nearby hat-shaped peak. It took Don Miguel and his men a long time to find the mine. Too many other rock formations in the area resembled hats, including one that looked like a giant sombrero that had been tossed up on a ridge. Peralta may have called it "Sombrero," but to the God-fearing miners, it resembled the "Finger of God" pointing toward heaven.

Once they finally located the mine, Don Miguel Peralta organized the peons into small groups. He sent them out to work in the tunnels that had been dug into the mountains by his ancestors or to retrieve the gold from the rich placer deposits in the ancient streambeds. At the end of each day, they carried the ore back to camp to be processed and cached in a storehouse until they returned to Sonora in the spring.

Except for a few skirmishes, when the Peraltas had come from Mexico to work the mine previously, the Apaches had left them alone. But when they came up in 1846, it was different. Something had angered the Indians. There are many versions of what drove the Apaches to attack the well-armed miners. According to one story, some of the men took liberties with the wife or daughter of one of the chiefs. The most accepted version claims that a group of miners working a rich ore deposit had desecrated the Apache's sacred land.

The Apaches warned the miners to leave the "Abode of the Thunder God" or face his wrath. Peralta refused their demands and ordered the miners to continue working. The Indians felt they had no choice but to drive their enemies from their sacred land. Peralta wasn't intimidated by the threats of a few naked savages armed with bows and arrows. His men outnumbered them, and it would be suicide for the Indians to attack.

The Apaches couldn't allow this insult to their honor to go unpunished and the desecration of their holy site to continue, no matter what the cost. The chiefs sent runners to all the neighboring tribes to join them in their fight with the miners. Hundreds of warriors answered the call to battle. They gathered in the hills out of sight and sound of the miners, the staccato beat of the war drums filling the night air. The shamans offered prayers to their gods, and the warriors danced themselves into a frenzy around dozens of blazing fires.

Peralta received word of the impending battle and called his men in from the mine. He ordered them to conceal the entrance and hide the wagons and supplies in canyons and caves. Some of the peons mounted the burros that had been used as pack animals, while others walked. The members of the expedition filled their saddlebags with large quantities of gold, loaded them on the remaining pack animals, mounted their horses, and rode for their lives.

The Apache scouts reported that the miners were escaping, and the war chiefs ordered an immediate attack. The warriors broke into small groups, surrounded the camp, and closed off the escape routes. A signal was given, and a horde of howling Indians charged from all directions. The air was filled with a macabre blend of musket blasts and men's screams as the Apaches rode down on their prey. Unarmed peons scrambled up the rock-strewn walls of the canyon and were the first to die. Apache arrows silenced their screams, and flint knives removed their scalps. When the battle was won, the Indians would return to strip and mutilate the bodies, leaving the remains for the coyotes and buzzards.

The Apaches drove the miners through the canyon to a place where the main body waited to join in the slaughter. The Spaniards spurred their mounts onward, but the weight of the gold-filled saddlebags slowed them down. With the Indians in hot pursuit, they rode as if the Devil himself were chasing them. The dons searched for a place to make a stand but, in their haste to escape, rode into a box canyon.

The miners were encircled and outnumbered. Arrows rained down on them, and in less than ten minutes, the battle was over. Peralta and the men who had accompanied him to Las Minas de las Sombrero were dead. Pack mules scattered into the desert, spilling gold or taking it with them to their death as they plunged over sheer cliffs into canyons and ravines. For many years after the massacre, soldiers and prospectors found the bleached bones of burros with rotted gold-filled leather packs still tied to their backs.

One man survived the massacre and escaped to Mexico with a map of the "Sombrero Mine," but the Peralta heirs were no longer interested.

They feared for their lives at the hands of the Apaches if they returned to the mine. When news of this fabulous gold mine raced across the land, despite the dangers and potential death that awaited them, fortune hunters poured into the Superstitions. Their ranks were decimated by heat, thirst, and death at the hands of Apache war parties.

In 1865 an unlikely treasure hunter, Dr. Abraham Thorne, reported for duty at Fort McDowell, a few miles north of Phoenix. He had lived and worked among the Apaches for many years, and they trusted him. Ministering to the sick and injured, he delivered babies and taught the Indians about hygiene and waste disposal. In 1870 the tribal elders offered to lead Dr. Thorneto a place where he would find gold. They considered him a good man and a friend of the Apache and wanted to reward him. The Indians blindfolded him and led him on horseback about twenty miles into the mountains.

They arrived at their destination, and when the Indians removed the blindfold, he saw an odd-shaped pinnacle of rock in a narrow canyon a mile to the south. Treasure hunters and prospectors who were familiar with the area identified this strange formation as Weavers Needle. There was no evidence of a mine, but heaped against a rock wall was a large pile of almost pure gold the Indians had placed there for him. They helped him fill his saddlebags, replaced the blindfold, and led him out of the mountains. He sold the gold for six thousand dollars and vowed that one day he would return and find the mine.

Thorne adopted a lavish lifestyle, and when the money was gone, he decided it was time to return to the mountain. He convinced some of his friends to purchase mules, equipment, and supplies and join him in his search. Using Thorne's description of the strange rock formation, they stumbled onto the mine. Filling their sacks with gold, they loaded them on mules; but before they could start for home, they were wiped out by an Apache war party. The secret of the lost mine died with them.

The legend of the Lost Dutchman's Gold Mine took another strange twist in 1871 with the appearance of two mysterious adventurers, Jacob Waltz and Jacob Weisner. Waltzwas born to a family of farmers and weavers in Oberschwandorf, Württemberg, Germany, in 1808. He graduated from Heidelberg University with a degree in mining engineering.

Very little information is available on Weisner. It is believed that the two men grew up in the same city, and there is a strong possibility that Weisner was Waltz's nephew. The two families immigrated to America in 1845 and settled in St. Louis, Missouri. Waltz and Weisner were determined to make their fortunes in this new land, and when they heard about a gold strike in North Carolina, they packed their bags and headed south. After a short time, they drifted west to Mississippi, California, and Nevada.

For the next few years, they worked the gold fields of the Sierra Nevada; but even though they found enough gold to meet their needs, it was never enough to get rich. The two Jacobs decided it was time to move on, and in 1862 they set up shop in Wickenburg, Arizona. Waltz filed a dozen small mining claims in and around Prescott, but it's doubtful he ever found anything of value.

There are many stories of how Waltz discovered the mine, but no one is certain which version is true. Waltz was working as a consultant at the Vulture Mine in Wickenburg when he met Ken-tee, an Apache woman who also worked at the mine. The sixty-year-old man took her as his mistress, and she moved in with him.

The mine owners noticed that they were losing small quantities of ore from the mine. They suspected Waltz and Ken-tee of high-grading (stealing choice pieces of ore) and held an inquiry. Although the owners found no trace of the gold when searched Waltz's living quarters, he and Ken-tee were fired and thrown off the property.

With no place else to go, they camped out on the desert in the shadow of Superstition Mountain. Ken-tee revealed the hidden location of the mine to Waltz and related the legend of the mountain. As a young girl she had heard the stories that were handed down by her ancestors. They told how the Thunder God protected his domain and how he gave the Apaches the gold to use in time of desperate need. Ken-tee led Waltz over a secret trail to the mine, and they returned to Phoenix with seventy thousand dollars in gold.

The Apaches suspected that Ken-tee had betrayed their secret and sent out their scouts to find her. In a running gun battle that lasted for more than two days, Waltz was wounded in the shoulder. He managed to escape, but Ken-tee was captured and tortured. The Indians cut out her tongue to keep her from ever speaking again; she bled to death an hour later.

Waltz returned to Phoenix, and for the next two decades, he and Weisner lived like royalty. They paid for their food, drinks, and lodging with pure gold nuggets. Some said the two men stumbled upon the mine by accident, while others claimed this was the stolen loot from the Vulture Mine. Many people believed they had murdered two Mexican miners and stolen their gold or robbed stagecoaches in eastern Arizona. No one knew where the gold had come from or how Waltz had come to be called "the Dutchman." It was a nickname he carried to his grave.

The most popular version of the story has Waltz and Weisner searching for gold in the Sonoran Desert. In the small Mexican town of Arizpe, they rescued the great-grandson of Don Miguel Peralta from certain death in a knife fight. He related to them the story of a gold mine in Arizona and how his family had almost wiped out in a massacre. He showed them a map and offered to share the gold if they would join him and help protect the expedition from the Apaches.

Reaching the mountain after three months of arduous travel, they began their search. Even with the map, it took them days to locate the mine and retrieve the gold. They managed to evade the Apaches and return to Mexico with sixty thousand dollars in gold. Peralta's fear of the Apaches was so great that he vowed never to return to the mine. He offered to sell them the map and the mine for their share of the gold. He had fallen on hard times and needed money to operate his ranch. Waltz and Weisner agreed to the offer, and Peralta signed over his rights to the mine.

The Dutchman and his partner purchased mules and enough supplies to last six weeks and returned to the mine. They set up camp and began to extract and refine the high-grade ore, caching the gold in pits and holes near the claim so they could retrieve it in a hurry if they were attacked.

After weeks of backbreaking labor, their food ran low. Waltz rode out of the mountains to a nearby settlement to replenish their supplies, and Weisner stayed behind to guard the camp. Upon his return, Waltz found the camp in ruins, the ground covered with pools of dried blood, and no sign of his partner. Waltz hoped to find him hiding at the mine, but the

Indians had destroyed that too. He gathered up some of the gold, filled his pack, and left the mountain.

Perhaps Waltz was sick with remorse for having left his friend to the mercy of the Apaches. Waltz returned to their camp and searched for Weisner. He found his friend spread-eagled over a campfire and burned to death. Knowing what the Apaches would do to him if they caught him, Waltz once again fled from the mountain. He came back to the camp three days later and buried Weisner near the mine.

One story that has never been verified suggest that Weisner was badly wounded in the Indian attack but managed to crawl to the Gila River. Some Pima Indians found him and brought him to Dr. John Walker, who tried unsuccessfully to nurse him back to health. Before Weisner died, he gave Walker a deer hide map and the location of the mine. According to this version of the story, Walker spent many years searching for the mine, but he never found it.

The Apaches may have killed Weisner, or he may have died from his wounds at Walker's ranch. But most historians and Western writers believe that Waltz shot his lifelong friend to protect the location of the mine. Whatever the truth may be, the Dutchman disappeared for long periods of time and always came back to Phoenix with thousands of dollars in gold. Each time someone tried to follow him to the mine, he managed to throw them off his trail.

Waltz became tired of being followed into the mountains, and he hated the rumors and innuendos. Leaving the Superstitions behind, he settled in Lehi, a small Mormon settlement on the banks of the Salt River. His home was a one-room adobe shack, and his only companions were a few scraggly chickens. He became a recluse, shunning most human contact. His only real friend was Julia Elena Thomas, a mulatto woman who owned a small bakery and soda fountain in Phoenix. Thinking he was a poor farmer, she bought a few eggs from him to help him out. They spent considerable time together, and even though he was over eighty, they may have been romantically involved.

On one of his visits to her bakery, he found Julia in tears and her son, Reinhold, sulking at her feet. Her husband had run off with another woman, leaving her a large mortgage, a stack of unpaid bills, a ten-year-old boy, and no money. The bank was ready to foreclose on her store, and she had nowhere to go.

Jacob returned the next day with a tin box full of gold worth about fifteen hundred dollars. It was enough money to pay her bills and keep her business afloat. He told her it came from his mine in the Superstitions, but because it held too many sad memories for him, he hadn't been there for years.

In 1891 torrential rains fell over the Southwest. The Verde and Salt Rivers overflowed their banks and flooded Waltz's home. After chasing the chickens to the roof of his shack in an effort to save them, he climbed a tree to escape the rising water. Tying himself to its branches, Waltz spent the next two days and nights in the icy water. As soon as the water receded, he lowered himself to the ground and sloshed through the mud to his cabin.

Two of Waltz's neighbors stopped by to check on him. They found him sitting on his cot, his legs covered with an old horse blanket, a lighted candle nearby. They helped him to his feet and took him outside. They set Waltz and a large box astride a horse and led him to Julia's home.

Julia tried to nurse her friend back to health, but his condition continued to deteriorate. He attempted to tell her how to find the mine, but he had suffered a paralyzing stroke and his speech was slurred. He died of pneumonia on October 25, 1891, and the secret of his lost mine died with him. Beneath his deathbed, he left a trunk full of gold and a list of clues to the location of the mine.

Since 1881, hordes of treasure seekers have invaded the sacred mountain of the Apaches; few have returned to tell the tale. No one knows how many victims the mountain has claimed. The headless corpses of those who sought the Dutchman's gold mine litter the canyons and ravines of this desolate hell. The Apaches say that the Thunder God is wreaking vengeance on those who dare to violate his sacred domain. Others claim it is the ghost of Jacob Waltz or the spirits of those poor souls who died in their quest for the treasure that guard the secret of the Lost Dutchman's mine.

Somewhere in the Sonoran Desert, near the town of Apache Junction, the jagged peaks of the Superstition Mountains beckon to all who dare to tempt fate. The Dutchman's lost mine is still out there, waiting for someone to solve the mystery and claim the prize.

The Man with Nine Lives

In the fertile Rio Grande Valley, the sunbaked town of Socorro, New Mexico, sits astride Interstate 25. The town is quiet now, but in the last half of the nineteenth century, it was a trading, drinking, and gambling center for more than four thousand miners, cowboys, soldiers, and itinerant travelers. Dozens of saloons lined its dusty streets, and the law was only as strong as the men who enforced it.

Southwestern New Mexico was an untamed country where Geronimo ruled the land and the likes of Billy the Kid rode the outlaw trail. It was a time and place where cowboys did what they wanted, when they wanted, where they wanted, and few dared to stand up to them. Into this boiling cauldron of lawlessness, a self-appointed deputy, Elfego Baca, stepped forward to earn his place in the history and legends of the American West.

Elfego Baca was born in 1865 in Socorro, New Mexico, and even his arrival was sudden and dramatic. As the story goes, his mother, Juanita, while pregnant with Elfego, was playing a Mexican softball game known as *las iglasias*. When she jumped up to catch a fly ball, Elfego popped out and entered the game.

All his life, Elfego was a great storyteller. He claimed that when he was about fifteen years old, he met the infamous Billy the Kid. Looking for excitement, they went to Albuquerque, but Billy thought the town was too quiet. Elfego drew his pistol and fired it several times into the air. He created a disturbance, making so much noise that a deputy sheriff ran the two of them out of town.

In the 1880s many ranchers, including John Slaughter, drove their cattle from Texas into New Mexico. Each time the Texas cowboys from the nearby ranches came into town, they terrorized any Mexican they encountered. In the town of Frisco (now called Reserve), on the far western edge of the county, the Texans reportedly held one Mexican down and castrated him. When one of his friends protested, so they tied him to a post and used him for target practice.

Elfego was incensed that Deputy Sheriff Pedro Sarracino refused to arrest the perpetrators. "You should be ashamed of yourself," Elfego said, "having the law on your side, to permit the cowboys to do what they do without consequence."

"My job is available to anyone who wants it," replied the deputy. "If you think you can do a better job as deputy, the job's yours." Refusing to discuss it further, he turned and walked into the nearest saloon. If Sarracino wouldn't do the job, Elfego would do it for him. He pinned a phony mail-order badge on his shirt, grabbed his Colt .45, and rode the 150 miles from Socorro to Frisco.

Ignoring any danger to himself, Elfego charged down the main street of town. Charlie McCarty, a rambunctious cowhand from the Slaughter Ranch, was yahooing up and down the street, shooting at anything that moved. The townspeople took shelter from the flying lead wherever they could find it.

Elfego was determined to put a stop to McCarty's fun and return some semblance of order to the town. "Why do you stand around and do nothing?" he demanded of the residents. "Why do you let him get away with this?"

"But, señor, if we dare arrest him or harm him," they replied, cowering in fear, "the cowboys from the Slaughter Ranch and the other ranches will come and get us."

"This is one Mexican the Texans aren't going to push around," Elfego replied. He asked around and found a few men who were brave enough to join him. They pulled the drunken McCarty from his horse and took his gun away. Elfego stuck McCarty's revolver in his own belt and dragged him off to an adobe shack on Frisco's main plaza to await trial.

Elfego knew it wouldn't be long before Slaughter's cowboys would show up to rescue their friend, and he was ready for them. With Parham, the ranch foreman, in the lead, a dozen Texans rode up to the shack and demanded McCarty's immediate release. Elfego refused their demand and threatened to shoot them if they weren't gone by the count of three.

Legend has it that the cowboys were joking that "Mexicans can't count" when Elfego yelled through the closed door, "One! Two! Three!" and opened fire on them. The Texans scattered like cockroaches at an exterminator's picnic. One cowboy was shot in the knee, and Parham's horse fell on top of him, crushing the foreman to death.

The cowboys regrouped at a safe distance from the shack and sent riders to the surrounding ranches for reinforcements. By next morning, a mob of angry cowboys had gathered in Milligan's Saloon. Fortifying their courage with rotgut whiskey, they rode to the plaza and surrounded the shack. Before any shots were fired, the Texans sent a delegation to talk to Elfego and asked a local justice of the peace to arrange a speedy trial for McCarty.

McCarty was found guilty, fined five dollars, and released into the custody of the vengeful cowboys. Even after he was freed, he was still complaining that Elfego had kept his gun, and the Texans wanted revenge for the death of the foreman. The mob returned to Milligan's Saloon to nurse their collective grudge against "that dirty Mexican." After a few more drinks, they poured out of the saloon, mounted their horses, and went looking for him.

Elfego didn't wait for the Texans to catch him. He drew his guns and ran down an alley to the dubious protection of a small jacal (a flimsy structure of thin wooden posts plastered with mud). Arriving at his makeshift fort, the cowboys surrounded the hut. A drunken roper named William Herne jumped from his horse, grabbed his rifle, and kicked at the door with his booted foot. He ordered Elfego to "come out of there and be damned quick about it."

Elfego's answer wasn't long in coming. Two bullets through the closed door hit Herne in the gut. His friends picked him up and dragged him away. At 9:00 a.m. on October 30, 1884, eighty angry cowboys opened up on the jacal.

Elfego noticed that the floor of the structure had been dug down about a foot and a half below ground level. As a hail of bullets tore through the walls of his fragile shelter, he lay down in the safety of the recessed floor and waited. Moving low toward the jacal, one of the cowboys exposed his position. Elfego brought him down with one shot. Two Texans met the same fate when they tried to rush the hut.

The cowboys assaulted the jacal throughout the rest of the day and into the night. To confuse his attackers, Elfego placed his Stetson in plain sight. The cowboys wasted a lot of lead on that empty hat. Elfego rose up and returned their fire, and a few more Texans were wounded.

One brave cowboy, using part of a cast-iron stove for protection, approached the jacal. With one shot, Elfego creased the Texan's skull, causing him to drop his armor and crawl back to his friends. Another attacker got close enough to toss a burning kerosene-soaked rag onto the dirt and *latilla* (branch) roof. One entire wall collapsed on the determined defender.

The cowboys were certain the fire had "cooked Elfego's goose," but they decided to wait until morning to dig him out. Standing outside the jacal in the early dawn, they couldn't believe what they saw. Tendrils of smoke rose from the chimney of a wood cook stove, and there stood Elfego next to a plaster statue of Nuestra Señora Dona Ana (Our Lady of Dona Ana). He was nonchalantly flipping his breakfast tortillas and drinking his morning coffee.

Mortified that Elfego wasn't dead, the Texans cut loose with every gun they had. Eyewitnesses said they fired more than four thousand rounds into the jacal. With all that lead coming at him, Elfego must have done a lot of praying to the Señora. The only things that remained unscathed were Elfego and the statue. The door of the jacal had almost four hundred bullet holes in it, and most of the walls had been shot away.

Just when it looked like the end of the road for the young Mexican, Deputy Sheriff Frank Rose showed up. With rancher Jim Cook and one of Elfego's friends, Rose walked up to the door of the hut. He told Elfego that if he would give himself up, Rose would escort him to Socorro to stand trial.

Elfego agreed to the deputy's terms, but only if he could keep his guns and ride in the back of a buckboard, with all accompanying cowhands in plain sight at least thirty feet behind him for the entire trip to Socorro. Cook ordered his men to put down their weapons and let the deputy sheriff and his prisoner pass. He assured them that Elfego would stand trial, and most likely be found guilty of murder and hung.

Thirty-three hours after the first shot was fired in a battle that became known as "The Baca Cowboy War," Elfego reached the relative safety of a Socorro jail. He was tried twice and acquitted of all charges.

In 1885 Elfego realized his lifelong dream when he was elected sheriff of Socorro County. Each time the court handed down an indictment, he used his reputation to intimidate the lawbreaker. Instead of sending his deputies out to arrest the accused man, he sent a letter:

> *I have a warrant for your arrest. Please come in by March 15 and give yourself up. If you don't, I'll know you intend to resist arrest, and I will feel justified in shooting you on sight when I come after you.*
> *Very Truly Yours,*
> *Elfego Baca, Sheriff*

Few dared to challenge Elfego, and most of the outlaws turned themselves in voluntarily. In his book *The Shooters*, Leon Metz wrote, "Most reports say he was the best peace officer Socorro ever had."

In 1888 Elfego was appointed US marshal, and during the next two years, he read for the law. He was admitted to the bar and practiced law in El Paso. When New Mexico gained statehood, he ran for Congress and, even though he lost the election, remained a powerhouse in local politics.

During the Mexican Revolution, Elfego was hired to defend one of Mexico's most famous generals, José Salazar. The general was arrested for violating the law prohibiting revolutionaries from crossing into the United States. The government didn't want them to return to their own country at some future date to fight again. The US Army refused to allow Elfego into Fort Bliss to defend his client, but he appealed to Washington, DC, and his request was granted.

Using his usual courtroom tactics, Elfego tried to intimidate the army, without success. His client was indicted for perjury, denied bond, and transferred to the Bernalillo County Jail in Albuquerque. Knowing that Salazar would be found guilty, the lawyer and six of his friends broke the general out of jail. A few days later, they were arrested and charged with jailbreak.

Believing that one of their coconspirators, Celestino Otero, might betray them, Elfego decided to take care of the problem himself. On January 31, 1915, he caught up with Otero in El Paso and shot him dead. Elfego was arrested and tried for murder. On the witness stand, he claimed that Otero had fired first. In rebuttal, the prosecution claimed that Elfego had purchased the gun at a local pawn shop and placed it in the decedent's hand.

Otero's widow testified that Elfego and her husband had been involved in the jail break, and that Elfego had killed him to shut him up. Her testimony was thrown out when it was revealed that she had been a prostitute before and after her marriage.

In an effort to ensure that Elfego would go free, his brother, Francisco, hinted to the witnesses and the jury that he would seek revenge against anyone who harmed his brother. The all-white jury returned a "not guilty" verdict.

Elfego held a succession of public offices, including county clerk, mayor, and school superintendent of Socorro, and district attorney for Socorro and Sierra Counties. He opened a detective agency and for a short time worked as a bouncer for a casino in Juarez, Mexico. He published a small newspaper he called *Lo Tureca* that he sold by subscription, charging two dollars a year to good citizens, five dollars a year to bootleggers, and five dollars a month to Prohibition agents.

Elfego passed away on August 27, 1945. He was born at a time when horses were the primary means of transportation and died as eight-cylinder automobiles roared past his Albuquerque home.

Elfego Baca never backed down from a fight. In all of his eighty years, he faced death more than most men of his time. With nothing more than a six-gun and an iron will, he accomplished the impossible.

Where Did the Camels Go?

IN THE MID-NINETEENTH CENTURY, THE US ARMY HAD A SERIOUS problem in its western sector. The distance from one fort to the next was about ninety miles, and roads across the desert were almost nonexistent. The army needed pack animals that could travel across the waterless waste of the Southwest to resupply these outposts. Mules were too ornery; horses couldn't bear the intense heat and died in droves. The westward expansion required new methods of hauling freight.

The idea of using camels originated with George Crossman, a second lieutenant in the Quartermaster Corps. He believed that for strength in carrying burdens, patient endurance of labor, and ability to survive deprivation of food, water, and rest, the camel was far superior to other animals. No one took him seriously until his friend Major Henry C. Wayne convinced Senator Jefferson Davis of Mississippi that the army should give camels a try.

The idea intrigued Davis. In his capacity as chairman of the Senate Committee on Military Affairs, he tried to convince his colleagues in Congress to support the importation of camels for the army on an experimental basis. It wasn't until Davis was appointed secretary of war in 1852 that he was able to make an official recommendation that Congress create a US Camel Corps to help build and supply a wagon route from Texas to California.

Davis made a fiery speech to get Congress to approve the necessary funding for the project, but his words fell on deaf ears. For the next three years, long-winded congressmen debated this crazy idea, and the press loved it. Who ever heard of using camels as pack animals in place of mules? The debates raged on until Congress gave in and appropriated thirty thousand dollars to purchase the camels.

Davis appointed Major Wayne to procure the camels, and on June 3, 1855, the USS *Supply*, under the command of Lieutenant David Porter, set sail for the North African city of Tunis. With more enthusiasm than knowledge, Porter and Wayne bought the first beast offered to them, only to discover it was old and sick. It didn't take them long to realize that healthy camels were in short supply. The Crimean War was raging, and all the healthy camels had been shipped to the front to carry troops and supplies. They upped anchor and set sail for Malta, Turkey, and Greece. Camels were in short supply there too, so it was on to Egypt, where they found a plentiful supply.

By now Porter and Wayne were savvy camel traders. They had learned that one-hump dromedaries were best for riding, but two-hump Asian Bactrian camels were better suited for carrying heavy loads. They recognized crooked camel dealers who not only inflated their prices but also artificially inflated a sick camel's hump to give it the appearance of a plump, healthy animal.

Dealing with corrupt government officials was another matter. Regulations forbade anyone from taking camels out of the country. After weeks of negotiations and exorbitant bribes, thirty-three camels were loaded aboard the USS *Supply* for the two-month journey home. The deck was modified to accommodate the large number of beasts, and the camels were lashed down in a kneeling position to prevent injury from the constant storms that battered the ship. The drovers who were hired to care for the animals succumbed to seasickness and were useless. The USS *Supply* arrived at the port of Indianola, Texas, with thirty-four camels; one of the females having given birth during the voyage.

The camels were given six weeks of rest at a temporary camp before being transferred to their permanent base at Camp Verde, sixty miles west of San Antonio. In the winter of 1857, forty-four camels that had been purchased in China were added to the herd.

Over the next year, the camels were put to the test against mules and horses; each time, they proved to be superior. Between 1856 and 1860, expeditions traveled as far south as the Big Bend Country in Texas and as far west as California. The most famous expedition was commanded by Lieutenant Colonel Edward Beale. In June 1857, Secretary of War Jef-

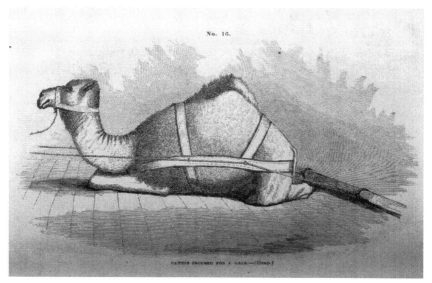

Illustration of how camels were secured on the ship during transport to the United States, from the 1875 report to the secretay of war

ferson Davis ordered the Camel Corps to survey the unexplored territory between El Paso, Texas, and the Colorado River. The caravan consisted of twenty-five camels, forty-four soldiers, horses and mules, and two camel drovers named Greek George and Haji Ali. The soldiers had a hard time pronouncing Haji's name, so they called him Hi Jolly.

At first the camels were a big disappointment for Beale. The soldiers' inexperience with these strange-looking creatures made them difficult to handle, and they often arrived in camp hours later than the horses and mules. After a few days on the trail, however the column settled down. The camels soon outstripped the other animals in traveling over terrain where horses and mules balked.

Heat, thirst, sandstorms, and Indian attacks sapped the energy of man and beast. Over a period of weeks, the caravan became lost. Water supplies dwindled to nothing. Horses and mules died, and only the camels were fit to go on. The camels found a river twenty miles from camp and led the expedition to it. Men, mules, and horses slaked their thirst. They rested and recuperated for two days before pushing on to the Colorado River. Beale wrote in his journal: "My admiration for the camels increases daily. They pack water for others for days under a hot sun and never get a drop. They pack heavy burdens of corn and oats for months and never get a grain. They eat worthless shrubs and not only subsist, but keep fat."

Brigadier General Edward Beale

Perhaps Beale was too optimistic. The soldiers despised the mangy brutes. Camels had a stench that didn't wash off easily. Horses and mules were frightened of them and often bolted, and the camels were bad-tempered and held grudges against anyone who ill-treated them. The soldiers grumbled about their ability to spit the contents of their stomachs with the accuracy of a Kentucky marksman.

The experiment ended with the outbreak of the Civil War. The camels were auctioned off to circuses, mining companies, zoos, and individuals, and many of the animals were released into the desert to fend for themselves. Beale purchased some of them for thirty dollars apiece and allowed them to live out their lives in comfort on his Texas ranch. Hi Jolly kept a few and started a freight line between the Colorado River ports and the mining camps to the east. When his business failed, he released his last camel into the desert near Gila Bend. Hi Jolly died in 1902 and was buried in Quartzsite, Arizona.

Western entrepreneurs with an eye for a quick buck used the beasts to supply remote mining camps. On a trip to Missoula, Montana, the stench of the camel caravan was enough to stampede a mule train. The mules took off running through the center of town, and their cargo of whiskey barrels flew in every direction. The contents from the smashed casks flowed like water and turned the dirt streets into a sea of alcoholic mud. The camels were banished from the northern mining camps forever.

California businessman Otto Esche imported camels from China to establish a freight line from San Francisco to Salt Lake City. Esche's venture failed, and he abandoned the camels in the Nevada desert. They created so many problems for travelers that the state legislature banned them from public roads.

More than half a century has passed since these beasts were turned loose in the arid deserts of the Southwest. Even though they are long gone, there are those who claim they still see camels silhouetted against a starlit sky as they plod across the desert sands. It is in the realm of fantasy that the ghosts of "Uncle Sam's camels" continue to roam the parched land of the yucca, mesquite, and Joshua trees. I've never seen one, but every time I drive across a long stretch of empty desert, I keep looking.

Henry Starr, King of the Bank Robbers

On the morning of March 27, 1915, Henry Starr and six well-armed horsemen rode into the sleepy prairie town of Stroud, Oklahoma. Not since 1892, when the Dalton Gang had been brought down in a shootout with local citizens in Coffeeville, Kansas, had anyone tried to rob two banks at the same time.

Out of all of the desperados who rode the outlaw trail, none was more successful than Henry Starr, the "Cherokee Badman." In his thirty-two-year career, he robbed more banks than the James-Younger Gang, the Daltons, and the Doolins put together. During all of his criminal activities, he killed only one man, a US deputy marshal who was trying to arrest him. And he was the first outlaw to use an automobile to rob a bank.

Henry was born near Fort Gibson (Indian Territory) on December 2, 1873, to a half-breed Cherokee named George Starr and Mary Scot Starr, a woman of Irish and Cherokee blood. Mary was highly educated and came from a respectable and virtuous family, but George's side of the family was littered with famous outlaws. Henry's grandfather, Tom Starr, was a notorious outlaw in his own right. His uncle, Sam Starr, was married to "Outlaw Queen" Belle Starr, whom Henry found to be "crude and reprehensible." He was quick to inform people that she was his aunt by marriage and not by blood.

In the late nineteenth century, the Indian Territory where Henry spent his youth was a wild, lawless place. Thieves, murderers, and outlaws found refuge in this rugged land and could hide out from the law for months at a time.

In 1866 Henry's father died, leaving Mary with three children and a farm. There were plenty of men who were looking for a woman with property, and it didn't take long for her to find a new husband. From the very beginning, Henry hated his stepfather and considered him inferior because he had no Indian blood in his veins. He referred to him as "a sallow, malarial, green-eyed reprobate who saw a fine chance for exploitation of rich lands, with free range and no taxes." Not long after his stepfather moved in, Henry moved out.

At age sixteen, Henry had his first scrape with the law while working at a ranch near Nowata in Indian Territory. He was driving a wagon to town when two deputies caught him with whiskey. Arresting him on a charge of introducing spirits into the Territory, they hauled him off to court. In his defense, he claimed he didn't know the whiskey was in the wagon and was released a short time later.

Henry's next brush with the law came when he was arrested for stealing a horse. In his autobiography he claimed, "The horse wandered onto the ranch where I was working. I kept and cared for the animal for almost a month. When the horse's owner, Charles Eaton, came to reclaim the animal, he offered me his profuse thanks, but soon swore out a warrant for my arrest." In December 1891, eighteen-year-old Henry Starr was arrested and sent to Judge Parker's jail in Fort Smith, Arkansas.

Henry insisted that he was innocent, but no one was listening. The longer he sat in his cell, the angrier he became. In describing his time in jail, he wrote: "Most of the good went out of me and I became a soured, sullen man, brooding over this great wrong that was done to me."

When Henry's case was called, Judge Isaac Parker, known as the "Hanging Judge," dismissed the charges. In his opinion, Eaton's case was weak and failed to prove that Henry had stolen the horse. Henry was released and sent on his way.

Henry returned to Nowata, bitter and frustrated. If he was going to be treated like a criminal, he might as well become one. "There was the road for me," he wrote. "It stretched out before me and I knew what I had been longing for. I took to it right gladly, feeling the spirit of exultation and freedom surge within me as my resolve was made."

Determined to make good on his resolution, Henry hooked up with Ed Newcome and Jesse Jackson, two young cowboys wanted by the law for various crimes. The gang made a career of robbing stores and railroad depots and escaping with small amounts of money for their trouble.

In July 1892 they held up the Nowata train depot and relieved the agent of seventeen hundred dollars. On the way out of town, Henry's horse collided with an unseen barbed-wire fence. He was arrested and sent back to Fort Smith. Once again, Henry faced the wrath of Judge Parker. He pleaded "not guilty" and was released on two thousand dollars' bail.

Once back in the Territory, Henry had no intention of returning to Fort Smith to stand trial. Judge Parker issued a warrant for his arrest and sent US Deputy Marshal Floyd Wilson and Railroad Detective H. E. Dickey to track him down.

The lawmen followed Henry's trail to the "XU Ranch" near Nowata. He had worked there as a cowboy, and they thought he might be hiding there. The owner of the ranch, Arthur Dodge, told them that he hadn't seen Henry for weeks and had no idea where he was. They spent the rest of the night searching the surrounding area.

The next day the lawmen were still at the ranch. Dodge rode in and told them he'd just seen Henry down by Wolf Creek. Without waiting for his partner, Wilson jumped on the rancher's horse and took off to confront the fugitive. Dickey had to stay behind to saddle his horse.

Wilson caught up with the fugitive and ordered him to "hold up." Since Henry didn't recognize him, he pulled his Winchester from its scabbard and swung down from his saddle. Keeping his weapon pointed at the ground, he waited to see what the rider wanted.

Wilson halted about thirty feet away and called out for Henry to surrender. Henry ignored the order and walked toward his horse. The deputy dismounted from his horse, raised his rifle, and fired a warning shot over the outlaw's head. In retaliation, Henry opened fire, hitting the lawman twice. Badly wounded, Wilson dropped his rifle and fell to the ground. He managed to draw his pistol, but before he could fire it, Henry hit him with two more shots, dropping him to the ground. In the first act of murder Henry ever committed in his long criminal career, he walked up to the fallen lawman and pumped several more bullets into his body. Dickey arrived too late to assist his partner.

Henry made good his escape and teamed up with Frank Chaney, a farmer from the Territory. Riding hard and fast, they robbed the train depot and two stores in Choteau. A few days later, they hit a depot and store in Inola. Their take from these robberies was less than five hundred dollars.

Looking for more lucrative targets, the outlaws decided the real money was in the banks. In March 1893 they rode into Caney, Kansas, a small town a few miles north of the state line. With their guns drawn, the two men entered the Caney National Bank.

Chaney walked into the vault carrying an old two-bushel flour sack. "I've kept this sack on my farm for seven years just for this purpose," he said with a smile. He stuffed the bag with stacks of money and exited the vault. The outlaws locked the bank's customers and employees in a back room and ran for their horses.

In less than twenty-four hours, the bandits covered a distance of ninety miles and outran any posse that might be chasing them. When they stopped to count their loot, they discovered they had taken the bank for five thousand dollars. They decided that if it was that easy to relieve the banks of their money, then that is where they would direct their attention.

Henry's next target was the People's Bank of Bentonville, Arkansas. As Henry, Kid Wilson, and three other men rode into town and entered the bank, someone recognized them and spread the alarm. Gunfire erupted and the outlaws grabbed what money they could and ran for their horses. With a posse chasing after them, they raced out of town. Losing their pursuers in the rugged hills of the Territory, they stopped long enough to divide their spoils. Splitting eleven thousand dollars five ways wasn't much money, considering the danger the outlaws had placed their lives in to get it.

With the law getting too close for comfort, the gang split up. Intent on reaching California, Henry, May Morrison (a young lady later identified as his wife), and Kid Wilson boarded a train at Emporia, Kansas. They stopped in Colorado Springs to "replenish the lady's wardrobe" and do a little sightseeing. They took rooms at the Spaulding House, and while Henry's wife was asleep, the outlaws enjoyed a late dinner. Recognizing the outlaws, the restaurant owner sent for the police. Taking no chances, four burly policemen jumped them from behind and hauled them off to the city jail.

Henry's worst nightmare was about to come true. He was returned to Judge Parker's court to stand trial. Charged with thirteen counts of robbery and one count of murder, Henry was found guilty and sentenced to be hung by the neck until dead. His lawyers appealed his conviction to the US Supreme Court, and Parker's decision was overturned. Henry was granted a new trial.

Henry spent his time in the confines of a squalid cell in the Fort Smith jail, waiting for his second trial. On the afternoon of July 26, 1895, Crawford Goldsby, alias Cherokee Bill, attempted a jailbreak. Bill managed to get his hands on a gun and in the ensuing riot shot and killed a guard. Barricading himself in his cell, he shot back each time the guards shot at him.

Henry and Bill had ridden the outlaw trail together and he didn't want to see his friend killed. Calling out to the guards, he said, "If you promise not to kill Bill, I'll go into his cell and get his pistol." Since no other solution presented itself, the guards agreed. The order was given to hold their fire.

Henry entered Bill's cell and sat down on an empty cot. He told Bill it was useless to continue to resist. He might get a few more guards, but he was never going to escape. Bill gave up his revolver and Henry tuned it over to the guards. Even though the law was a little more sympathetic toward the outlaw for his cooperation, it didn't help him in court.

At his second trial, Henry was found guilty and sentenced to hang. His lawyers appealed, and once again the Supreme Court overturned Parker's ruling, setting his murder conviction aside and granting him a new trial.

Things were a lot different at Henry's third trial. Judge Parker was dead, and a new magistrate sat on the bench. Henry pleaded guilty to manslaughter and was sentenced to three years hard labor in a federal penitentiary. He also received seven years and seven days for seven counts of robbery, and five additional years for one count of train robbery.

In the fall of 1901, Henry's mother visited Washington, DC, and was granted an interview with President Theodore Roosevelt. Sitting with the president, she related her son's story in the hope of winning his release from prison. Roosevelt was impressed with the woman's sincerity, and he admired Henry for his courage in the Cherokee Bill incident. He sent the bandit a telegram asking him if he could behave himself if he were released. Henry assured the president that he was through with the criminal life and that if released, he would go straight. After serving only three years of a fifteen-year sentence, Henry walked out of prison a free man on January 16, 1903.

Henry returned to Tulsa and went to work in his mother's restaurant. He married his second wife, Miss Ollie Griggin, and before long she gave birth to a son. They named him Theodore Roosevelt Starr in honor of the man who had freed Henry from prison.

Henry had every intention of keeping his promise to the president, but unfortunately his past came back to haunt him. He was still wanted by the State of Arkansas for the Bentonville robbery, but there was no way to extradite him as long as he stayed in Indian Territory. Once Oklahoma gained statehood, Henry was fair game for a prison cell in Arkansas.

Believing he wouldn't get a fair trial and having no desire to return to jail, he hid out in the brush of the Osage Hills. He later wrote, "I preferred a quiet and unostentatious internment in a respectable cemetery rather than life on the Arkansas convict farm."

Henry needed money, and as far as he was concerned, the easiest way to get it was to rob banks. He teamed up with his old partner, Kid Wilson, and together they held up the State Bank in Tyro, Kansas. A posse chased after them, but they got away.

With the law on their trail, Oklahoma and Kansas were getting too hot for the outlaws. They decided to move on to California, but on reaching Amity, Colorado, they thought the local bank looked too good to pass up. They helped themselves to eleven hundred dollars and split up a short time later. No one knows what became of Kid Wilson, but Henry drifted on down to Arizona.

Henry tried to keep a low profile, but the law caught up with him. On May 11, 1909, he was apprehended and returned to Colorado to stand trial. He was convicted and sentenced to no less than seven and no more than twenty-five years of hard labor at the Colorado State Prison in Canon City. On the way to prison, he was informed that Ollie had divorced him.

Just as before, Henry was a model prisoner. With his charm and charisma, he soon won over the warden, the chaplain, the guards, and everyone else at the prison. He was such a model prisoner that, within one year, he was made a trustee. Five years after his conviction, he was paroled with the stipulations that he report to a parole officer once a month and never leave the state.

Henry wanted to keep his word, but there were still banks to be robbed. Less than a year after being released, he broke his parole and slipped over the state line into Oklahoma. From September 8, 1914, to January 13, 1915, the Starr Gang hit fourteen banks and made off with more than twenty six thousand dollars. It was the worst spate of robberies in the history of Oklahoma. In response to the crisis, the state legislature passed the "Bank Robber Bill," appropriating a fifteen-thousand-dollar reward for the capture of any bank robber and a one-thousand-dollar reward for the capture of known outlaws.

While every lawman in the state of Oklahoma was looking for him, Henry was busy planning his most daring robbery yet. He would rob two banks at the same time. He recruited a gang of six men and rode into Stroud, Oklahoma. One man stayed with the horses while Henry and two of the bandits entered the Stroud State Bank. At the same time, the other three outlaws walked into the First National Bank of Stroud.

Henry pulled a rifle with a sawed-off barrel from under his coat; his companions drew their revolvers and threatened the bank's customers and employees alike. Henry scooped sixteen hundred dollars out of the cash drawer, but the tellers refused to open the safe, where the real money was kept. Furious over their failure to get into the safe, the outlaws grabbed three hostages and marched them into the street at gunpoint. A few minutes later, the second group of outlaws emerged from the First National Bank with forty-two hundred dollars and more than a dozen hostages.

Using the captives as human shields, the outlaws made their way toward their horses. The townspeople opened fire on them. Afraid of being hit by stray bullets, the hostages dived for cover, leaving the bandits out in the open. Even though they couldn't see the men who were shooting at them, the outlaws began to blaze away with their own guns as they ran for their horses.

The outlaws mounted their horses and, with Henry bringing up the rear, attempted to escape. As they raced through town, a seventeen-year-old boy named Paul Curry squeezed off a shot at the retreating bandits. Hit in the left leg just below the hip, Henry fell from his horse. Curry jacked another round into the chamber of his rifle and called out to the fallen outlaw, "Throw away your gun or I'll kill you." Henry tossed his revolver away and gave up.

Before the gang escaped, a second outlaw was wounded. He continued riding until he passed out and toppled off his horse. The bandits abandoned him to the posse and kept going. The wounded outlaw, Louis Estes, was placed under arrest and brought back to town. The Starr Gang had accomplished what the Daltons had failed to do.

Henry and his fellow robber were lodged in the Chandler, Oklahoma, jail. While a doctor tended to their wounds, Henry admitted who he was. At the trial, Estes testified against Henry and was sentenced to five years in prison. Henry didn't even bother to fight the charges. He pleaded guilty, and the judge sentenced him to twenty-five years of hard labor in the state penitentiary at McAlester, Oklahoma. He was granted parole and released from prison on March 15, 1919.

Henry was now forty-five years old and had spent seventeen years of his life in prison. Determined to go straight and start a new life, he decided to become a movie producer. Borrowing money from his friends, he wrote, directed, and starred in *A Debtor to the Law*, a silent film about the double bank robbery in Stroud, Oklahoma. The movie was a roaring success, as were his next two films. All three movies were financial blockbusters, but he never made a penny off them. His partners swindled him out of his share.

Broke and despondent, Henry went back to the only life he knew. On the morning of February 18, 1921, Henry and three associates in a high-powered touring car drove into Harrison, Arkansas. Entering the People's State Bank, Henry cleaned out the cash drawer while his assistants kept everyone covered.

Henry ordered the cashier to open the vault, and once it was open, he stepped forward to help himself to its contents. The director and former president of the bank snatched up a rifle that was concealed near the vault and fired point-blank at the bandit. The single shot tore through Henry's right side and shattered his spine. Not wanting to be the next target, the other outlaws ran out of the bank, jumped into their car, and took off at high speed. That was the last anyone ever saw of them.

Henry hovered between life and death for the next four days. On February 22, 1921, the king of the bank robbers fell into a coma and died. Before lapsing into unconsciousness, he bragged, "I've robbed more banks than any man in America."

For more than three decades, Henry Starr rode the outlaw trail, and his passing marked the end of an era. He was the last of the old-time desperados and the greatest bank robber the Old West ever produced.

The Gentle Giant of Texas

From its earliest days, Texas was known for its colorful characters. They cast a giant shadow on a hostile land that was as big and tough as their reputations. With courage and determination, men like Sam Houston and Davy Crockett made their marks on history, but their exploits pale in comparison to the adventures of William A. A. "Bigfoot" Wallace, the most famous Indian fighter, Texas Ranger, and frontier scout in the history of the Lone Star State.

Depending on which story you choose to believe, there are two versions of how William got his nickname, "Bigfoot." Never one to repeat the same story twice, he once told his biographer that when he was in Austin in 1839, someone ransacked his neighbor's home. Because he had big feet and wore moccasins, they confused his tracks with those of an Indian named Bigfoot, and he got blamed for the crime.

According to the second version, William's jailers gave him the name while he was a prisoner of the Mexican Army. They couldn't find shoes big enough to fit him, so they had to make special footwear. I don't know which story is true, but more about that later.

William was born into a family of large men in Lexington, Virginia, on April 3, 1817. One of his uncles was seven feet tall; his brother Andrew was six feet, six inches tall. As William grew to manhood, he stood six feet, two inches and weighed 240 pounds. He claimed he was descended from Scottish Highlanders William Wallace (Braveheart) and Robert Bruce, who fought to drive the English from their land.

William spent his youth working in his father's orchards. When word came that the Mexican Army had massacred his older brother Sam and his cousin William, along with Colonel Fannin and more than four

William "Bigfoot" Wallace. HERITAGE AUCTION GUILD, 1872

hundred defenders at Goliad, William swore to go to Texas and kill Mexicans. His father tried to dissuade him from going, but William wasn't having any of it. "The Mexican Army are scoundrels of the worst sort and I'm goin' to Texas to fight 'em," he said.

William arrived in Galveston, Texas, in October 1837, but he didn't stay long. He moved inland to the settlements along the Colorado River and, with winter approaching, settled in the town of La Grange. One winter was enough for him. To hear him tell it, "The winter was so cold that the whiskey in the only saloon in town froze, leading the townspeople to speculate that it was heavily watered down."

As soon as the weather turned warm, William headed back to the Gulf Coast. He made his way among the settlements but preferred the solitude of the open plains. An undisciplined nonconformist, William considered Texas a hunter's paradise. Comparing his new home to the rest of the United States and Canada, he once said, "I would not swap Texas for the whole shooting match."

William returned to La Grange and tried his hand at farming, but he was too much of a frontiersman to make a success of it. It was much more fun to go hunting than it was to push a plow. The one time he hitched his saddle horse to a plow and made a furrow, it was a dismal failure, and neither he nor the horse ever got the hang of it. He did plant a few rows of corn, but the rains never came. All he got for his trouble were thirteen shriveled ears of corn, enough for one meal.

One dark night, a band of Comanche stole William's mules and horses from the corral, but they missed the old mare that was staked out in a clearing on the other side of the cabin. Discovering that the Indians had taken his stock, he grabbed his rifle, jumped on the mare, and gave chase. Topping a hill about a mile from the ranch, he smelled the unmistakable aroma of barbecued horsemeat. It galled him to think that the Indians were eating his horses. He wasn't about to let them get away with that.

Riding toward the Indian camp, William found himself in the middle of a hickory grove. He didn't know how he was going to deal with these "painted devils," but he knew he couldn't ride into their midst and recover his horses without some kind of protection.

Seeing the nuts scattered on the ground gave him an idea. He tied the cuffs of his shirt and the bottom of his buckskin pants with rawhide and stuffed them with nuts. He looked like an oversized Santa Claus, and he waddled when he walked. He was a sight to see as he mounted his horse and rode toward the Indians.

William halted about a thousand yards from the camp, rolled off his horse, and crawled through the tall grass until he was close enough to see the enemy. He was so determined to recover his stolen stock that the sight of forty-two Indians sitting around a campfire wasn't enough to stop him. He raised his rifle and fired into the gathering, killing one of the Comanche.

While William reloaded his rifle, the Indians grabbed their bows and arrows and came after him. As he later related it, "With my rifle in position, I raised up in all my majesty and all my stature and all my hickory nuts, and after one look at me, the Indians halted like they were paralyzed."

After a few moments of confusion, the Indians loosed their arrows at him. Each time an arrow hit a hickory nut, it split the nut and the arrow fell to the ground. In a short time, the ground was covered with arrows, but William was unharmed. He walked toward his quarry, and they backed off. Convinced that he must be an evil spirit, they dropped their weapons and ran for the hills.

William untied the rawhide from his clothes, and thousands of pieces of hickory nut fell to the ground. In retelling the story he said, "You can kick me to death with grasshopper legs if a single, solitary hickory nut in the whole passel hadn't been split open." A few days later he returned to the Indian camp with a wagon and gathered up the nuts. He took them home and fed them to the pigs he kept out back of his cabin.

William was getting tired of farming his few acres and decided it was time to move on. The town of Austin had just been selected as the new capital of the Republic of Texas, and there was plenty of work at high wages for anyone who wanted to help build the new city. Using his skill with a broadax, he got a job hewing logs into lumber for the new buildings being constructed on Congress Street. He earned two hundred dollars a month plus room and board, and it didn't take him long to realize he could make a lot more money by going into hostile territory, cutting the logs, and rafting them up the Colorado River into town.

William was a great storyteller, and it was during his stay in Austin that he said he earned his nickname "Bigfoot." According to his story, a small band of Indians led by a rather large Indian also known as "Bigfoot" often raided the settlements near Austin, killing the settlers and stealing their horses. They called him "Chief Bigfoot" because he stood six feet, eight inches tall and weighed more than three hundred pounds.

One day, a neighbor returned from town to discover that his home had been ransacked. Finding large moccasin tracks around his home, he accused William of the crime. Since the moccasins that made these tracks were much larger than the ones he wore, William knew they belonged to Chief Bigfoot. He was absolved of the crime when he placed his feet in the tracks and showed the rancher the difference in size. From that day on, whenever anyone mentioned Bigfoot, people would ask, "Do you mean 'Bigfoot' Wallace or the Indian"?

Even though William arrived too late to take part in the war for Texas independence, it wasn't long before he got the opportunity to fulfill his original purpose for moving to Texas. Deciding that Austin was too civilized to suit him, he pulled up stakes and moseyed on down to San Antonio.

San Antonio and the surrounding countryside were dangerous places in 1840. To the south, the Mexican Army was threatening to invade Texas. In the north and west, marauding Indians were killing anyone who dared to enter their territory. In the east, the Cherokee were making life difficult for the settlements, and a blood feud between two groups of settlers known as the Modulators and the Regulators was about to break out into open warfare. As far as the Texans were concerned, there was only one agency that could make everyone behave. They needed the Texas Rangers.

To meet these challenges, Sam Houston commissioned John Coffee "Jack" Hays, to raise a company of Rangers. Hays was the perfect man for the job. He'd already proved his mettle at the battle of Plum Creek and was considered one of the finest Ranger captains who ever lived.

Captain Hays was pretty particular about who joined his company. He enlisted the best Indian fighters in the West, and he was never defeated in battle. He required each man in his company "to have courage, good character, be a good rider, a good shot, and own a horse worth one hundred dollars." William's reputation as an Indian fighter preceded him, and Hays signed him on the spot.

William spent the next two years chasing cattle rustlers, outlaws, and horse thieves; fighting hostile Indians and range wars; and settling cattle disputes and feuds. Horse thieves were hung from the nearest tree; Indians were shot on sight. Remembering how his kin had died at Goliad, he gave the Mexican outlaws special attention.

While the Rangers were protecting the frontier, the Mexican Army was marching into San Antonio. The Mexican government refused to recognize the Republic of Texas, and in March 1842 four hundred battle-hardened soldiers under the command of General Ráfael Vásquez entered the city. Fearing the Texans might overwhelm his position, he withdrew his troops from the city. With William in the lead, the Rangers trailed the enemy until they crossed the Rio Grande.

The second Mexican invasion came on September 11, 1842. General Adrian Woll and a force of fourteen hundred slipped into Texas and captured San Antonio. The troops interrupted a session of the district court and took everyone in attendance into custody. The judge, jury, clerks, lawyers, witnesses, and a few prominent citizens were placed in chains and marched off to a Mexican prison. To avoid capture, the Rangers quickly left town and scattered into the hills.

At Salado Creek, a few miles from San Antonio, General Mathew Caldwell and a handful of Texans waited to engage Woll's troops. As soon as the Rangers regrouped, they raced to within shouting distance of the Mexican lines. Keeping just out of range of the enemy's guns, the Rangers taunted the invaders to come out and get them. Woll was outraged at the disrespect these frontier buffoons had for his army. The time had come to teach them some manners.

With Woll at the head of the column, four companies of cavalry, twelve hundred infantrymen, and a few artillery pieces chased the Rangers to Salado Creek, where the Texans were waiting for them. In his autobiography William claimed, "General Woll had 1,500 soldiers against 196 white men and a Negro named Tom."

What should have been an easy victory for the Mexicans soon turned to defeat. They fired their cannons at the Texans waiting for them in a pecan grove, but all they succeeded in doing was break a few branches and knock some leaves off the trees. Woll ordered his troops to charge, but the Texans were ready for them. A wall of fire halted the Mexican advance. They regrouped and charged, but once again they were driven back. With the Texans hot on their tail, they retreated back to San Antonio.

Years later, William recalled that during the battle, he spotted a Mexican soldier wearing his favorite pants. He had stolen them when the Mexicans took San Antonio. Unable to get a clear shot at the thief, he picked out another soldier who was as big as he was, shot him off his horse, and took his pants. Since they were of excellent material and an almost perfect fit, he put them on and continued fighting.

The defeat at Salado Creek and the sight of five hundred Texans massed on the banks of the San Antonio River were enough to convince Woll that it was time to move on. The Texans caught up with Woll's troops at Hondo Creek, near the site of present-day Castroville.

Expecting their comrades to follow them, the Rangers rode into the Mexican camp and tried to capture the enemy's cannons. The charge might have been successful if the rest of the Texans had followed them, but instead they hung back; the Rangers were forced to retreat. Try as he might, William couldn't get his mule to turn and go the other way until a Mexican bullet singed its nose. The frightened animal finally turned tail and ran for its life.

Later that afternoon, the Texans regrouped on the east side of the creek. They set out pickets and settled in for the night. They'd planned to resume the attack in the morning, but sometime during the night, the Mexicans escaped. The Texans held a council of war and decided that further pursuit was useless. Breaking camp, they started for home while the Rangers returned to their headquarters in San Antonio. With the Mexicans back in their own country, William resigned from the Rangers.

William was content to hunt, fish, and pursue his own interests until Sam Houston sent out a call for able-bodied men to join an expedition to avenge Woll's invasion of Texas. He reenlisted in the Rangers under his old friend Captain Jack Hays and joined General Alexander Somervell's campaign to teach the Mexicans a lesson. With very little resistance from the inhabitants, the Texans captured the towns of Laredo and Guerrero.

Houston had ordered Somervell to continue the invasion only if circumstances assured a reasonable chance of success. Since almost one-third of his men had returned to their homes after taking the towns, Somervell decided that his army wasn't strong enough to cross the river to take on the Mexican Army.

Somervell ordered his men to disband and return to their homes, but many of the Texans felt betrayed by the order and refused to follow it. They had joined the expedition to seize and plunder the towns on the Mexican side of the river, and they weren't going home until they got what they came for. One hundred eighty-nine men, including Captain Hays and most of his Rangers, followed Somervell to Gonzales, while the remaining three hundred Texans elected to cross the river and attack the Mexican settlements.

Constituting what became known as the Mier expedition, on December 22, 1842, the column moved down the Rio Grande to a suitable campsite in preparation for their incursion into Mexico. Leaving a force of forty-five men to guard the camp, the Texans crossed the river. Encountering no opposition, they occupied the town of Mier and demanded that the people of the town deliver supplies and provisions to their camp.

To ensure that the supplies would reach their camp, they took the alcalde (mayor) hostage and retreated back across the river. All day long on Christmas Eve they waited for the supplies that never came. From a captured Mexican peasant, they learned that the Mexican Army had moved into Mier and prevented delivery of the goods.

The Texans needed those supplies, and they were determined to get them. On Christmas Day, 261 Texans crossed the Rio Grande and attacked the town. It didn't matter that they were outnumbered ten to one; they continued to fight until their ammunition ran out.

Under a flag of truce, the commander of the Mexican forces, General Pedro de Ampudia, sent a captured prisoner to the besieged Texans to inform them that he had seventeen hundred soldiers ready to wipe them out and three hundred more on their way from Monterrey. If they surrendered, he would treat them as prisoners of war. If not, no quarter would be given. Remembering the fate of his relatives at Goliad and the defenders of the Alamo, William expected the same treachery from de Ampudia. He was the last man to surrender.

The battle lasted for more than twenty-four hours. Each time the enemy charged, the Texans drove them back. When the smoke cleared, the Mexicans counted six hundred dead and two hundred wounded. The Texans counted sixteen dead and thirty wounded.

Santa Anna sentenced the prisoners to death by firing squad, but de Ampudia reversed the order and spared their lives. He ordered his cavalry to march them first to Matamoros and then to Monterrey until they could be transferred to Perote Prison in Mexico City. The wounded were left behind in Mier.

The march to prison was sheer hell. Sick and starving, the bedraggled prisoners were forced to walk hundreds of miles over rocks and burning sand until they were almost barefoot. They did get some relief when they were loaded into wagons at Saltillo to continue their journey.

At Hacienda Salado, a hundred miles south of Saltillo, the Texans overpowered their guards, stole their horse and mules, and scattered into the hills in a desperate attempt to escape. For three days and three nights, they traveled north until they reached Saltillo. To avoid their pursuers, they circled around the town and headed into the mountains.

The fugitives might have made good their escape, but they made the mistake of trying to cross the mountains in the dry season. The country was barren and lifeless, and after six days of terrible deprivation, they were reduced to eating their horses and mules, snakes and grasshoppers, and anything else they could find. They became disoriented; some of them just wandered away, while others dropped in their tracks from lack of water. In describing his trek into the mountains, William told his listeners, "I dried some of the mule meat in the hot sun and carried it on my back. In a few days I was so thirsty that my tongue had swollen to the roof of my mouth and I couldn't eat anything."

The Texans left an easy trail to follow, and the Mexicans soon rounded them up and returned them to Hacienda Salado. Santa Anna ordered the prisoners lined up and shot, but the officer in charge refused to carry out the order. Political pressure from other countries outside Mexico forced Santa Anna to halt the executions.

Santa Anna was livid that his efforts to kill his enemies had been thwarted. He issued a decree that every tenth prisoner who participated in the break was to be executed. In an episode that became known as the "drawing of the black beans," the Mexicans allowed the prisoners to draw lots to see who would live and who would die.

Filling an earthen jar with 159 white beans and 17 black beans, the Mexicans passed it to the prisoners. Commissioned officers were ordered to draw first. Then the enlisted men were lined up in alphabetical order and given the jar. William was one of the last to draw.

William stepped forward and reached for the jar. His hand was so large that he had to force it into the opening. Deciding that the black beans were larger than the white ones, he latched onto the smallest one he could reach. He withdrew his hand and pulled out a gray bean. After several minutes, the Mexican officer in charge determined the bean was white, and William's life was spared.

The men who drew the beans of death were unshackled, led to a courtyard reserved for executions, and shot at dusk while the survivors were marched more than eight hundred miles to Perote Prison. Before they reached the prison, William was in agony. Since he was such a big man, his shackles were too small for him. They cut into his flesh, swelling his arms and legs and turning them black.

After walking for many weary miles, he wore out his moccasins and his feet swelled to twice their size. According to the rumors that still persist today, the Mexican guards were sent to fetch him a pair of sandals. Because they all had small feet, they were unable to find a pair that fit, so a boot maker was called in. He later commented that the big man had big feet, and the name stuck.

William remained a prisoner until September 16, 1844, almost two years to the day since he'd joined Somervell's campaign. Returning to

Texas, he built a cabin on the banks of the Medina River near Castroville. When the United States went to war with Mexico in 1846, he was one of the first to volunteer. He was commissioned a first lieutenant in the Rangers and led his troops into battle in Monterrey.

Once peace was declared, William returned to his cabin on the Medina River. For a short time he was the only inhabitant on this untamed frontier, but when too many settlers started moving in, he packed his belongings and headed south. On a wild stretch of land on Chicon Creek near the Hondo River, William built his last homestead.

William remained with the Rangers for a few more years. With each Indian battle, his fame spread. In 1850 he drove a mail coach from San Antonio to El Paso—a job no one else wanted because everyone else who tried it had either been killed or scared off by the Indians. He took six armed guards along on each trip and half a dozen mules to replace the ones the Indians killed. Large bands of Apache and Comanche lay in wait along the trail and attacked his coach as it went by. He always got through, but his coach was so shot up that he had to lay over a day or two in the settlements along his route to repair it.

Sometime in the early 1870s William retired from the Rangers and settled down on his ranch on Chicon Creek. With his horses, chickens, and two old mongrels named Sowder and Rock, he was content to sit on an old rawhide chair under a tree near his cabin and tell stories to anyone who happened by. In describing his last few years of his life, William said, "I now reside on San Miguel Creek in Frio County and I live on prickly pear and red pepper." To honor this brave Texan who had fought so hard and so long for Texas, the people of Connally's Store a few miles from his home changed the name of their town to Bigfoot.

The most famous Texan in the history of the state died of pneumonia on January 7, 1899. The next day, he was buried in Longview Cemetery in Devine, Texas. On orders from the state legislature, his body was disinterred one month later and moved to his final resting place at the state cemetery in Austin. Under a clear blue sky of the land he loved, he was buried with full military honors.

In paying final tribute to the man who meant so much to the people of Texas, State Representative Edward Rex Tarver said, "His name and fame are indelibly impressed on every page of the history of Texas. His whole life was a sacrifice to duty."

William is gone now, but the epitaph on his tombstone stands tall for all to see. It reads:

BIG FOOT WALLACE
Here lies he who spent his
manhood defending the homes of Texas
Brave honest and faithful

Fetterman's Folly

THE INFAMOUS BOZEMAN TRAIL WAS ONE OF THE MOST DANGEROUS roads west in the 1860s. John Bozeman and his partner, John Jacobs, discovered the trail in 1863 while searching for a more direct route from Fort Laramie to the gold fields of Montana. A shorter, better-watered wagon road than alternative routes, the trail branched off from the Oregon Trail in a northwesterly direction, passed through northern Wyoming, forded the Powder and Tongue Rivers, crossed the Big Horn Mountains, and ended at the gold fields in Virginia City, Montana.

The US government ignored the fact that the trail crossed the traditional hunting grounds of the Lakota and the Cheyenne and opened it up to westward travel. Chief Red Cloud, war chief of the Oglala Sioux, vowed to defend his people's territory. He was determined to shut the trail down, and the US Army was determined to keep it open.

In 1866 Colonel Henry B. Carrington and seven hundred soldiers of the 18th Infantry were ordered to the Northern Wyoming Territory. It was Carrington's bad luck to arrive at Fort Laramie with all those troops and supplies in the late spring of 1866. A peace conference between the Sioux and representatives of the US government was in progress. Red Cloud was livid when he discovered that Carrington had orders to establish a string of forts across the Powder River country. He was outraged that the army was bringing in large numbers of troops before the Lakota had agreed to a military road through their country. Red Cloud and his chiefs stormed out of the council, and he promised to kill any whites who sought to use the trail or occupy Indian lands.

Carrington may have been the wrong man for the job. He was an engineer, not a cavalryman. Most of his time in the army had been spent building fortifications, and he had no experience fighting Indians. Most of Carrington's officers had fought in the Civil War, and they believed the Indians were a bunch of ignorant savages who could be defeated by a disciplined regiment of US soldiers. They considered Carrington a coward because of his unwillingness to engage the Indians in battle.

In defiance of Red Cloud's warning, in early July 1866, Colonel Carrington and the first detachment of troops marched into the Powder River country to implement their orders. Once Fort Reno was restored, the column moved on to Piney Creek. Carrington ordered his men to begin construction on Fort Philip Kearny. He sent a small detachment to build Fort C. F. Smith on the Big Horn River, about ninety miles from Fort Kearny.

Just as she had always done, Margaret Carrington accompanied her husband to his new duty post. A long wagon train loaded with mowing machines, shingle- and brick-making machines, door sashes, glass, nails, locks, rocking chairs, sewing chairs, churns, and washing machines followed the troops on their march. Some of the wagons contained boxes of canned fruit, live turkeys and chickens, and a brace of swine. One wagon was filled with musical instruments for the post band. Colonel Carrington believed it would be a peaceful winter, and that with such a large number of soldiers garrisoning the fort, Red Cloud wouldn't dare attack.

While Fort Kearny was under construction, George Grummond and his wife, Frances, were in Tennessee waiting for their marching orders from the army. He had been a brevet lieutenant colonel of volunteers during the Civil War and was recently married. Receiving a commission as a lieutenant in the US Army, he was assigned to the 18th Infantry stationed at Fort Philip Kearny.

George and his pregnant wife arrived at Fort Laramie in time to join the second detachment bound for Fort Kearny. At Kearny they were assigned to temporary quarters, two "A" tents set up and joined together. The first tent contained their trunks, two dilapidated camp chairs, and a battered mess chest. Two worn-out hospital bunks and a small heating stove filled most of the available space in the second tent. A narrow passageway led to the cook stove that was hidden behind a large tarpaulin.

The first night in their new home, the temperature dropped, and as the snow fell, it drifted into the tent. Frances was awakened from a sound sleep when her body heat caused the snow to melt and trickle down her face. The pillows, bedding, and furniture were covered with snow. She shook the snow out of her stockings and shoes and, shaking from the cold, succeeded in building a fire in the cook stove.

Frances had limited experience as a cook, but she managed to whip up bacon that was edible and coffee that was almost fit to drink. She tried to bake biscuits, but the results of her mixture of flour, salt, and water not only resembled a pile of stones but were as hard as the rocks that lined the parade ground of the fort. "No hatchet chanced to be conveniently near to aid in separating them in halves," she said. "Impulsively I seized the butcher knife, but in the endeavor to do the hatchet work with it, the blade slipped and almost severed my thumb, mingling both blood and tears."

The fort was completed in early December, and the Grummonds moved into their new quarters. In her journal, Frances described their new home:

The house was made of pine logs, recently felled and not quite dry and small pine poles covered with clay for the roof. Beneath were three, yes, actually three rooms. In my haste to move I tacked blankets around the bed space. Pieces of sheeting answered for window shades and old newspapers covered the kitchen windows. The company tailor sewed gunnysacks from which corn had been hurriedly emptied and I soon had a carpet. My residence seemed palatial.

With the arrival of Captain William J. Fetterman at Fort Kearny, all the major players were now in place for the bloody events that would soon unfold. Fetterman was a war hero, and like Grummond, he too had served as a brevet lieutenant colonel in the Union Army. Arrogant and impetuous, he despised Carrington's passive strategy against the Indians and his lack of ability to command. Carrington ignored Fetterman's boast that with eighty men, he could ride through the Sioux Nation. Fetterman openly accused Carrington of cowardice and timidity.

The first signs of trouble came on December 6, when a large war party attacked an unescorted wood train four miles from the fort. One column commanded by Carrington and a second column commanded by Fetterman set out from the fort to rescue the wood-gathering party and engage the enemy. The soldiers encountered more than a hundred warriors, and after a pitched battle in which two of his men were killed and five wounded, Carrington retreated to the safety of the fort.

About a mile and a half from the fort, a small war party attacked another wood train. Carrington ordered two companies consisting of twenty-seven cavalrymen and fifty infantrymen to assemble on the parade ground. Fetterman was placed in command and Lieutenant Grummond volunteered to lead the cavalry unit.

From past experience, Carrington was aware of Fetterman's penchant for taking unnecessary risks. He gave the captain a direct order: "Take your detachment and support the wood train. Relieve it and report to me. Do not engage or pursue Indians at its expense. Under no circumstances, pursue the Indians over Lodge Trail Ridge." As soon as the column marched through the open gate, Carrington ran up to the sentry walk and ordered Fetterman to halt. In a loud voice, he repeated his order: "Under no circumstances, Captain, must you cross Lodge Trail Ridge."

The column moved out at a fast pace, and as they approached the wood train the Indians broke off their attack and fled over Lodge Trail Ridge. Red Cloud had set a trap for the unwary soldiers, and now he was ready to spring it. These Indians attacking the wood train were decoys.

Fetterman disobeyed orders and led his forces in pursuit of the hostiles. Reaching the crest of the ridge, they were surrounded by more than two thousand Indians. Red Cloud gave the signal, and the braves charged the straggling column. With their escape routes cut off, the soldiers fought back with guns, knives, and bayonets, but their ammunition was soon exhausted and they resorted to using their gunstocks as clubs. Fetterman's command was wiped out in twenty minutes.

Back at the fort, Frances waited for her husband to return. She later related that her heart was filled with strange forebodings. Some of the women of the post tried to cheer her up and assure her that everything would turn out okay. Describing the events of that terrible day, she wrote: "Suddenly out of silence so intense as to be torture to all who watched for any sound however slight, from the field of exposure a few shots were heard, followed up by increasing rapidity, and showing a desperate fight was going on at the very place where the command was forbidden to go, then followed by a few quick volleys, then scattering shots, and then, dead silence."

Carrington knew something was wrong when he heard the gunfire. He ordered a second detachment to go to Fetterman's aid. The column stopped short of the battlefield when they saw thousands of Indians moving across the valley. They waited until the Indians disappeared before moving up to the ridge. The ground was strewn with mutilated bodies. They returned to the fort after dark with forty-eight of the dead.

Lieutenant Grummond's body was not among the remains they had recovered. Carrington listened to the reports and knew without a doubt that the young lieutenant had been killed in the attack. He asked his wife, Margaret, to inform Frances that her husband would not be coming home. In later years, Frances remembered the scene vividly. "Mrs. Carrington tenderly took me in her arms and led me to her home where in silence we awaited the unfolding of this deadly sorrow. Henceforth, my home was with Mrs. Carrington."

That night, Carrington doubled the guard in case the Indians decided to attack. At dawn he assembled his officers and informed them that as soon as it was light, he would lead a strong force to recover the remaining bodies. He told them that if they didn't recover their dead, the Indians would think they were weak and couldn't defend the fort.

Before mounting his horse to lead the troops to the ridge, the colonel entered his quarters to inform Margaret and Francis of what he intended to do. Frances later wrote: "Mrs. Carrington was sitting near a window and I was lying down. When the door opened we sprang trembling to our feet." Colonel Carrington spoke to his wife and then turned to Frances. "Mrs. Grummond, I shall go in person and will bring back to you the remains of your husband." "They are beyond suffering," she replied with tears in her eyes. "You must not imperil other precious lives and make other women as miserable as myself."

Carrington rode to the ridge with eighty men and a dozen empty wagons. He left secret instructions with the officer of the day: "If in my absence, Indians in overwhelming numbers attack, put the women and children in the powder magazine with supplies of water, bread, crackers, and other supplies that seem best, and, in the event of a last desperate struggle, destroy all together, rather than have any captured alive."

Margaret and Frances waited and watched throughout the long day. Toward evening, the wagons bearing their gruesome cargo crawled through the gate. Frances tried to run to the wagons, but Margaret held her back. She didn't want Frances to see the mutilated body of her husband. His head was almost severed from his body and he had been scalped, his fingers cut off and his corpse filled with arrows and bullets.

Frances later wrote in her diary:

> *And then the horrors of the following days, the making of coffins and digging in the hard, frozen earth for a burial place when the cold was so intense that the men worked in fifteen-minute relief and a guard was constantly on the alert lest Indians should interrupt. . . . One-half of the headquarters building, which was my temporary home, was unfinished, and this part was utilized by carpenters for making pine cases for the dead. I knew that my husband's coffin was being made, and the sound of hammers and the grating of saws was torture.*

The pine cases were numbered and lowered into a fifty-foot-long by seven-foot-wide pit. Christmas morning 1866 was a day of sadness and mourning.

News of the massacre spread fast. It was the main topic of conversation in every city and town in America. Newspapers vilified Carrington, and the public condemned him. Even though Fetterman had disobeyed orders and led eighty good men to their death, Carrington was relieved of command.

Brigadier General Wessels took over as commanding officer of Fort Kearney. Carrington and his detachment of troops, along with their wives and children, were ordered to Fort Casper. It didn't matter to the army that it was January and they would have to make the journey in the middle of a howling Wyoming winter.

Since Frances no longer had a husband in the army, she was ordered to leave the fort with the wagon train. Without a husband and being seven months pregnant, it was a difficult time for her. She agreed to join the wagon train, but only after Carrington allowed her to take George's body back to Tennessee. Carrington ordered the pine box disinterred and placed in one of the wagons. The few women remaining in the fort purchased her furniture and dishes to give her enough money for the journey home.

Because they would have to endure the subzero temperatures and incessant blizzards of Wyoming in winter, Carrington ordered extensive preparations for the journey. The canvas covers on the wagons were doubled, with a tiny window at each end. The sides and the ends of the wagon beds were walled up, and a hinged door was placed at the back of each vehicle for entry. A small sheet-iron stove with a smoke vent through the wagon cover sat near the door. A cord of wood and a pile of pine knots filled one corner of the wagons. The women and children bundled up in beaver hoods, buffalo boots, and any other fur they could find. At 1:30 p.m. on January 23, 1867, in the blowing snow of a winter day, the column passed through the gates of Fort Kearny for the last time.

Snowstorms and blizzards raged across the Wyoming Territory for weeks. A sheet of ice covered the hills and valleys, and the trails were blocked with drifting snow. The first afternoon and into the night, the column pushed its way through a blinding snowstorm and massive snowdrifts. An advance party was sent out to shovel the deepest drifts, but it did little to alleviate the situation. By ten o'clock that night, they were only six miles from Fort Kearny. Stopping for the night, Carrington circled the wagons on an unsheltered bluff, while the fierce wind piled snow against the wagons and blew sentries off their feet.

By one o'clock in the morning, the snow had tapered off and the wind had died down to a stiff breeze. A full moon cast its light over the frozen landscape, and the aurora borealis danced in the heavens. The air was bitter cold. In Margaret Carrington's wagon, the thermometer read thirteen below zero. Carrington ordered the bugler to sound reveille and wake everyone up, and by 3:00 a.m. they were on the move.

At dawn the column encountered a herd of buffalo wallowing in the snow. All day long they trudged through the snow, surrounded by hundreds of buffalo. The drivers were ordered not to crack their whips for fear the buffalo might become frightened and stampede the wagon train.

The exhausted travelers halted for the night at Crazy Woman's Fork. They circled the wagons in a grove of trees beside a stream and placed pickets on a surrounding bluff. The men dug through the snow to find wood for the campfires to conserve the pine knots and firewood stored in the wagons. They used axes to break their bread, and as the coffee was taken from the fire, it formed into a frozen slush before it could be swallowed. The turkey Margaret had cooked before they left the fort had frozen into a block of ice. Using a hatchet to chop pieces from it, she placed them on the stove to soften them up before she could feed her family.

Reveille sounded at one o'clock in the morning, and the weary travelers tumbled out of their beds. Half-frozen men staggered down to the stream to break through the ice for water to refill their casks. The tiny stoves in the wagons did nothing to dispel the cold, and the women wrapped themselves in buffalo robes and beaver hoods, garnering what heat they could. The temperature on Margaret's thermometer dropped to forty below, and the mercury in the bulb congealed.

The teams were hitched up, and the column crossed the icebound river toward a sixty-foot bluff. Only one wagon at a time could go up the steep inclines. A detail was ordered to climb to the top and then, using rope, haul each wagon up the cliff. As dawn broke over the eastern horizon, the last wagon rolled over the crest of the bluff. It took all day for the column to travel twenty miles to the warmth and safety of Fort Reno. Late in the afternoon, the first wagon crawled through the gate, ending a three-day, sixty-five-mile journey through the frozen hell of a Wyoming winter. After three days of rest at Fort Reno, the column took the trail to Fort Casper.

Frances and the pine box containing her husband's remains arrived in Tennessee in March 1867. A few weeks later she gave birth to a son. Not long after returning home, Frances read in the newspapers that Margaret Carrington had died. She sent a letter of condolences to Colonel Carrington, and he responded. Henry B. Carrington and Frances Grummond were married in 1871.

The army abandoned the forts along the Bozeman Trail in August 1868. As soon as the soldiers were out of sight, the Indians burned them to the ground. True to his word, Red Cloud closed the trail and drove the white man from his country forever.

The Grandest Storyteller
of Them All

LIKE THE MAJESTIC ROCKY MOUNTAINS THAT TOWER OVER THE WEST-
ern landscape, the mountain men of the American frontier cast a long
shadow over the land they roamed. Fearing neither man nor beast, these
rugged individualists explored the uncharted wilderness of a new land.
Living by their wits, they befriended savage Indians while harvesting
the beaver pelts for a fashion craze that was sweeping Europe: men's
beaver felt hats.

In addition to their skills as hunters, trappers, and Indian fighters,
many of these men were master storytellers. They told improbable tales
of their heroic adventures and the fantastic sights they encountered. Like
his more famous contemporary, Jim Bridger, James Pierson Beckwourth
was one of the grandest storytellers of them all.

James Pierson Beckwourth, the son of Sir Jennings Beckwith, a
descendent of minor Irish nobility, and Miss Kill, an African-American
slave, first saw the light of day on April 6, 1798. In the early years of the
nineteenth century, Sir Jennings gathered up his thirteen children and
their mother and moved to the frontier outpost of St. Louis, Missouri.

Sir Jennings raised the boy as his own son, but in the eyes of the law,
James was still a slave. Not wanting his son to suffer the burden of slavery,
Sir Jennings appeared in court on three different occasions to execute a
"Deed of Emancipation."

As a young boy, James spent his time hunting, fishing, and learning
about the wilderness and the Indians who lived there. He was appren-
ticed to a blacksmith, but for a young man who craved adventure, it was

an unhappy time. He stayed long enough to learn his trade, but after a few heated arguments with his boss, he took off for New Orleans. As a free black man in the Deep South, James had a difficult time finding any kind of employment. Changing his name from Beckwith to Beckwourth, he returned to St. Louis in time to join General William Ashley's Rocky Mountain Fur Company.

In 1832 the Rocky Mountain Fur Company advertised for adventurous men to explore the far west and trap for furs. Men like Jim Bridger, Jedediah Smith, Thomas Fitzpatrick, and Étienne Provost signed on. James joined up as the company's blacksmith.

As the company moved westward, James became a skilled frontiersman. Living in the wilderness, he became an expert hunter, trapper, and fur trader. He may have also taken part in the exploration of Wyoming's South Pass and of the Bear, Weber, and Green Rivers. It is known that in 1825 he was hunting and trapping in the Cache and Salt Lake Valleys of Utah.

Getting the furs to market presented a real dilemma for the mountain men and the fur companies. Prior to 1825, they either had to haul their pelts back to St. Louis, to Astoria at the mouth of the Columbia River, to Santa Fe, New Mexico, or to Fort Lisa on the Big Horn River. It was always a long hard journey over dangerous terrain. Faced with the threat of attack from unfriendly Indians, they were never certain if the trading posts would even be there when they reached their destination.

To solve the problem, General Ashley arranged to meet the trappers at Henry's Fork in the Green River Valley of Wyoming. He bought their furs for whatever he considered fair and for exorbitant prices sold them the supplies they needed to survive in the wilderness. It was also an opportunity for old friends to get together and blow off steam in an anything-goes celebration; thus the fur rendezvous was born. In his autobiography, James described the rendezvous:

It may well be supposed that the arrival of such a vast amount of luxuries from the East did not pass off without a general celebration. Mirth, song, dancing, shooting, trading, running, jumping, singing, racing, target shooting, yarns, frolic, with all sorts of extravagances

James Beckwourth, mountain man, fur trader, and explorer.
PORTRAIT OF JAMES P. BECKWOURTH, LIBRARY OF WESTERN FUR TRADE,
HISTORICAL SOURCE DOCUMENTS, 1856

that white men or Indians could invent were freely indulged in. The unpacking of medicine water contributed not a little to the heightening of our festivities.

Many of the mountain men were famous for their tall tales. It was at the first rendezvous that James established his reputation as a master storyteller. Like his friend Jim Bridger, he related stories of his heroic deeds and unbelievable sights, often embellishing the details with each telling.

Because James was so good at telling tall tales, no one was ever certain of what was real and what was fantasy. In 1856, with the help of T. D. Bonner, a wannabe journalist and temperance reformer with a drinking problem, James published *The Life and Adventures of James P. Beckwourth*. In his autobiography, he claimed that while on a trapping expedition with Jim Bridger in 1828, he was captured by a party of Crow warriors. When an old Crow woman insisted that he was her long-lost son, he was adopted into the tribe and lived with the Indians for almost eight years.

For the Crow Nation, war was a way of life. The only way to become someone of importance in their eyes was to demonstrate courage in battle and great prowess in stealing horses from their enemies. On more than a few occasions, James rode into battle with them. He was such a fierce warrior that the Crow made him a war chief. To hear James tell it, on the death of Chief Arapooish (Rotten Belly), he was named chief of the entire Crow Nation. During his sojourn with the tribe, he was married at least ten times; when he returned to his own people, he left his wives behind.

By the summer of 1836, the fur trade was in deep decline. After years of heavy trapping, the beaver were almost gone. Silk had become the material of choice for men's hats, and so the demand for beaver pelts was almost nonexistent. Since the Rocky Mountain Fur Company no longer needed his services, James became restless and returned to St. Louis. "The Gateway to the West" had changed in his absence. His father had passed away the year before, and St. Louis was too civilized for his taste. The frontier town he remembered from his youth no longer existed.

In an effort to renew his contract with the Rocky Mountain Fur Company, James made a brief visit to the Crow Nation in 1837. Unfortunately, it coincided with an outbreak of smallpox that almost wiped out the Plains Indians. James's enemies and some Western writers have accused him of deliberately infecting the Indians to kill them off. Killing an enemy by bashing in his skull or defeating him in hand-to-hand combat were honorable ways to die, but using a plague to murder thousands of men, women, and children just wasn't his style.

James was always looking for new adventures and new ways to enhance his reputation. In Florida, the Second Seminole War was raging with no end in sight. The US Army wanted men who could live and fight like Indians, and the mountain men were exactly what they needed. James joined the Missouri Volunteers but met with disaster on the way to Florida.

Arriving in Florida, the men boarded a number of small ships bound for Tampa Bay. Driving their horses into the holds, they set sail on what should have been a short voyage. As they crossed the bay, a series of savage storms struck the fleet, causing James's vessel to flounder on a reef. Men and horse remained stranded for twelve days until the army sent a steamer to rescue them.

James stayed in Florida for ten months. He scouted the enemy and carried dispatches for the army. The endless war ground on and James became increasingly bored. Describing his time in Florida, he wrote:

Now we had another long interval of inactivity, and I began to grow tired of Florida. It seemed to be a poor country dear even at the price of the powder to blow the Indians out of it, and certainly a poor field to work for renown. I wanted excitement of some kind—I was indifferent of what nature, even if it was no better than borrowing horses of the Black Feet. The Seminoles had no horses worth stealing or I would have exercised my talents for the benefit of the United States.

Once back in St. Louis, it took James five days to find suitable employment. His old friend Louis Vasquez had built a fort on the Platte River in Colorado, and he hired James to act as his intermediary with the Cheyenne, the Arapaho, and the Sioux. For weeks they followed the Santa Fe Trail until they reached the fort. As agent in charge, James used his extensive knowledge of the Plains Indians to establish a successful trading relationship with them.

Thanks to James's expertise as a trader and two ten-gallon kegs of whiskey, Vasquez enjoyed a profitable trading season. Due to circumstances beyond their control, however, the second season was disappointing. In 1840 Vasquez sold his operation and, once again, James was unemployed.

Never one to be out of work for very long, James took employment with the Bent brothers. He continued to trade with the Indians, but he was restless. His life had become too confining, and he decided it was time to move on. After crossing the rugged mountain passes to Taos, New Mexico, he opened his own trading post. He traded with the Cheyenne and the other tribes in the area, and before long he married Luisa Sandoval, a Mexican woman from a good family.

Life in Taos was a little too tame for the rugged frontiersman. In 1842 James and Luisa opened a trading post on a deserted spot on the Arkansas River in southern Colorado. In a few short months, twenty families moved into the area, creating a thriving community they called Pueblo.

The Bent brothers weren't too happy with James. He had opened a trading post in what they considered Bent country, and they saw him as a threat to their trading empire. They wrote an irate letter to the superintendent of Indian affairs complaining about "those renegade Americans and Mexican Traders." They pleaded for the government to build a military fort in the area and drive these "upstarts" out of the territory, but their entreaties fell on deaf ears.

In 1844 James took off for California. He arrived in Pueblo de Angeles with the intention of expanding his business. Unfortunately, he found himself in the middle of the Anglo revolt against the Mexican government. When war broke out between Mexico and the United States, James and his friends decided it would be a good time to return to Colorado.

To ensure they didn't go home empty-handed, James and his friends raided most of the haciendas and ranches from San Gabriel to San Bernardino, rounding up hundreds of horses. James later wrote: "Along with five friends, we collected eighteen hundred stray horses we found roaming the California ranches and started with our utmost speed from

Pueblo de Angeles. This was a fair capture and our morals justified it, for this was war."

Returning to Pueblo, James discovered that Luisa had remarried. To induce her to marry him, her new husband had shown her a forged document expressing James's desire to be free of her. Remorseful, she offered to go back to him, but he wasn't interested; he was enjoying the single life too much to tie himself down to one woman. He settled his affairs and left for California.

If his autobiography is to be believed, James always seemed to show up just in time to witness or take part in some great historic event. The following events illustrate this point. He arrived back in California in late fall 1848, just as gold fever gripped the state. He was also first on the scene of one of California's most infamous and brutal murders.

Eking out a living in the gold fields was too slow for James. He wanted excitement and found it carrying dispatches from Monterrey to Nipomo and back. Early one morning as he traveled on his route, he stopped at Mission San Miguel to visit his old friend William Reed. To his surprise, the place looked deserted. He dismounted and cautiously entered the house. Mr. and Mrs. Reed, their newborn baby, the midwife and her teenage daughter, and the Indian servants and their children had been hacked to death. In telling of the incident, he wrote:

> *In going along a passage, I stumbled over the body of a woman; I entered the room and found another, a murdered Indian woman who had been a domestic. I was about to enter another room, but I was arrested by some sudden thought which urged me to search no further. It was an opportune admonition, for that very room contained the murderers of the family, who had heard my footsteps and were sitting at that moment with their pistols pointed at the door ready to shoot the first person that entered.*

James leaped on his horse and rode for help, returning a short time later with a large posse. In the house they found eleven bodies thrown together in one pile. The murderers had tried to set the house on fire in an attempt to destroy the evidence of their crime, but the fire went out before it could do any damage. The posse caught up with the murderers near Santa Barbara. The murderers were tried on the spot and, in a burst of gunfire, given a taste of vigilante justice.

James's greatest accomplishment was the discovery of a pass through the Sierra Nevada, northwest of present-day Reno. Named Beckwourth Pass in his honor, the trail was much less hazardous than the infamous Donner Pass. It became the main road for prospectors heading into the gold fields of nothern California and the immigrants who followed a few years later.

In 1866 the US government hired James to act as an interpreter in peace negotiations with the Crow Nation. James was so respected by the Indians that during a visit to a Crow encampment, they asked him to be their chief. He thanked them but declined their offer. They decided that if they couldn't have him in person as their chief, they would find a way to always have his spirit with them. At his farewell dinner, the medicine man served him poisoned food. They buried him on Crow land in Montana near the present site of Bighorn Canyon National Recreation Area.

Even though his accomplishments rivaled the adventures of such men as Kit Carson, Jedediah Smith, and Jim Bridger, James Beckwourth never achieved the national recognition many of his contemporaries received. Was it because he was black and didn't fit into the white man's stereotyped ideas of mountain men, or was it because he told such improbable tales that no one believed him? Wherever the truth may lie, there is no question that James Pierson Beckwourth changed the face of the American West forever.

The Man Who Almost Drowned San Diego

How often have we heard someone say, "Everybody talks about the weather, but nobody does anything about it?" In centuries past, Native Americans performed sacred dances to call on their gods to change the weather. In more recent times, when the farmers of the American West were faced with drought, they hired a pluviculturist. Known in the lexicon of the day as "cloud coaxers," "water magicians," "moisture accelerators," and "wizards of hope," most people just called them "rainmakers."

The most famous rainmaker of his day was a sewing machine salesman named Charles Hatfield. His uncanny ability to seemingly make rain out of nothing in drought-stricken areas of the world was legendary. From Canada to California, from Alaska to Italy, he was hailed as a genius or damned as a charlatan. Though few have ever heard of him, history will remember him as the man who almost drowned San Diego.

Charles started life in Fort Scott, Kansas, in 1875. Sometime in the 1880s his father bought a farm in Oceanside, California. He quit school after completing the ninth grade and took a job as a salesman for the New Home Sewing Machine Company. When he wasn't selling sewing machines, he was busy reading an 1871 edition of *The Science of Pluviculture*, a how-to book on how to make it rain.

Charles began to experiment with the different techniques he found in the book, and by 1902 he was ready to make it rain. He created a secret mixture of twenty-three chemicals that included hydrogen and powdered zinc in large galvanized evaporating tanks which he claimed attracted rain, and he dubbed himself a "moisture accelerator." Following the instructions in the book, he released his compound into the air near the windmill on the farm owned by Charles and his brother. To his surprise, it started to rain.

In 1904 Charles took up residence in Glendale, California. He continued to sell his sewing machines and refine his secret rainmaking formula, hoping for a chance to show the world what he could do. He needed someone who could get him the publicity he needed to further his work, and real estate promoter Fred Binney was just the man for the job.

To attract attention to the rainmaker, Binney ran a series of ads in most of the California newspapers. The adds read: "For $50, Charles Hatfield will come to your community and lend nature a little assistance to cure your drought woes." Dozens of skeptical farmers paid the fee, and in return Charles promised to deliver eighteen inches of rainfall to the people of Los Angeles between December 1904 and April 1905.

Charles brought his brother, Paul, to assist him, and together the two men hauled their supplies to the summit of Mount Lowe. They constructed a twenty-foot-tall wooden tower, and as soon as the preparations were complete, Charles climbed to the top and released his secret formula into the atmosphere above La Crescenta. It started to rain almost immediately, and before long it was coming down like a pent-up waterfall.

It rained for the next several weeks, and by mid-March Charles was just a fraction of an inch short of his promised goal. The Weather Bureau claimed that it was going to rain anyway, but that didn't stop Charles from taking the credit. The farmers were so happy with the results that they paid him double his required fee. He pocketed one thousand dollars in cash and a lot of publicity. Calling himself "The Professor," he hit the lecture circuit, earning money by explaining his rainmaking techniques.

The rainmaker's next job took him to the gold fields of Alaska. Most of the mining in Alaska and the Yukon was done by placer mining, which required an unlimited supply of fast-running water to separate the gold from sand, gravel, and small rocks that were washed down through a sluice.

The summer of 1905 was one of the driest summers ever recorded in the Klondike. The miners had tried everything from constructing a seventy-two-mile-long wood flume and iron pie ditch known as the

Yukon Ditch to using water-efficient rocker boxes to alleviate the situation. Since none of their remedies seemed to work, it was time to resort to more drastic measures. They called in the rainmaker.

In August 1905 Charles entered into a simple contract with the Alaskans to bring his equipment to the Klondike in 1906. According to the terms of the contract, a panel of seven men would determine how much rainfall Charles would have to provide. If he succeeded in meeting their goal, he would be paid ten thousand dollars. If he failed, he would receive only enough money for his transportation and living expenses.

Charles accepted the offer, and in June 1906 the rainmaker and his brother passed through the town of Whitehorse on their way to Dawson. With tongue in cheek, a reporter for the *Weekly Star* wrote: "Residents might get him to give us a shower here—just a little one for fifteen cents or two for a quarter." When the sternwheeler *Selkirk* docked at Dawson, a large crowd dressed in raincoats and boots came out to greet him. Everyone in the crowd seemed to be carrying umbrellas. They'd all heard about Charles's ability to make it rain, and they were taking no chances on getting wet.

Charles set up his headquarters on the outskirts of Dawson and, with the help of his brother, built a twenty-four-foot tower on the summit of King Solomon's Dome. Mixing up a batch of his magic formula, he carried it up the tower. Standing on the platform, he released large plumes of smoke skyward.

Every day for weeks, Charles climbed the tower to release his mixture into the sky. Except for an occasional shower or two, nothing happened. Even though Charles couldn't make it rain, he did get blamed for a hailstorm that wiped out most of the flower and vegetable gardens in Grand Fork.

Perhaps it wasn't Charles's fault that his formula didn't work. According to Chief Isaac of the Han tribe, four of his medicine men were dancing and praying to stop him from making rain. The chief offered that if Charles would pay him five thousand dollars, he would order his medicine men to teach the rainmaker how to make it rain.

Charles failed to deliver what he promised, and by late July the Alaskans had lost their patience. They gathered in groups and began to mutter against him. Before they could take action to rid their community of this nut who claimed he had the secret of making rain, Charles shut down his project, collected his expense money, and got out of town.

The Alaskan fiasco should have ended the rainmaker's career, but so many people believed in his ability to make it rain that job offers continued to pour in from all over the world. When he succeeded, he was hailed as a hero; when he failed, which wasn't often, he simply packed up his gear and moved on to the next job.

Drought has always been a constant threat for the water-starved American West. In 1915 San Diego was experiencing one of the worst droughts in its history. They built the Morena Dam in 1897 to guarantee an ample water supply for the city, but due to inadequate rainfall, they never had enough water to fill it up. "If we don't get some rain soon," said the city planners, "San Diego might just dry up and blow away."

To the citizens of Southern California, Charles was a hero. He had successfully fulfilled hundreds of rainmaking contracts and saved many of them from financial ruin. They believed that if anyone could make it rain, he could. Fred Binney and his friends at the San Diego Wide Awake Improvement Club sent a letter to the city council. They wrote: "The Morena Dam Reservoir is barely one-third full and the city's growth hinges on an ample water supply. We think the council should consider hiring Charles M. Hatfield to make some rain."

The council thought it was a good idea, but since Charles's rainmaking techniques couldn't be proven scientifically, it was out of the question. Unless something happened to change their minds, they were not about to spend the taxpayers' dollars on a wild scheme that was chancy at best.

Binney and the Improvement Club persisted until the council relented. They sent a delegation to the rainmaker's home in Eagle Rock to ask him to make it rain and fill up the reservoir behind the dam. Charles agreed to use his expertise to end the drought, but only under certain conditions. Any amount of rain under forty inches was free, but the city would have to compensate him at the rate of one thousand dollars an inch for anything between forty and fifty inches. Anything over fifty inches would be free.

Since his proposal was met with skepticism and disinterest on the part of the city, Charles modified his offer, agreeing to fill the reservoir to capacity for a flat fee of ten thousand dollars. If he was unable to fulfill his promise within one year's time, they wouldn't owe him a dime. With nothing on the line but their political futures, the council hired him to make rain.

As soon as the council gave its okay, Charles and his brother went to work. They constructed two twenty-foot towers near the Lake Morena Reservoir, sixty miles from San Diego. They added an eight-foot extension to each tower for the evaporating tanks and other paraphernalia, and by January 1, 1916, they were ready to begin.

Using a mixture that was 300 percent stronger than usual, Charles released his chemical vapors skyward. For the first four days, nothing happened; but on January 5 it started to rain, and rain, and rain. The downpour forced the temporary closure of the Panama-California Exposition and cancellation of races at the Agua Caliente Racetrack in Tijuana, Mexico.

Day after day, it rained and rained and rained. Once-dry riverbeds overflowed their banks, washing out bridges and flooding farms and homes. Dozens of homes were swept away into the San Diego River. Policemen manned rowboats to rescue stranded homeowners and motorists. Raging floodwaters cut off the city's water supply; cats, dogs, horses, cattle, and hundreds of snakes floated through the streets.

Sections of the coastal highway and major roads into San Diego disappeared under the onslaught of raging floodwaters. Telephone and telegraph lines vanished as if they had never existed. Helpless passengers clung to the roofs of submerged trains as miles of track washed away. Now that San Diego was cut off from the rest of California, the only way to get food into the city was by the occasional relief steamer.

In a matter of days, the Sweetwater and Lower Otay Lake Dams filled to capacity and overflowed. There was more than enough rain to fill the Morena Reservoir twice over and then some.

The Californians must have wondered if this incessant rain would ever stop. On January 20 they finally got some relief. The clouds parted and the sun shone for the first time in two weeks. However, the respite lasted a mere four days, and the worst was yet to come.

In a storm that lasted six long days, the sky opened up and deluged the already drowned city. The runoff from the Morena Reservoir and the excessive rainfall flowed into the already overfilled Lower Otay Reservoir. The pressure of all that water was too much for the weakened walls of the dam. On the night of January 27, it burst like a punctured balloon, and a wall of water fifty feet high roared through the jagged opening.

Thirteen billion gallons of turbid water rushed down the valley on its seven-mile journey to San Diego Bay, killing at least twenty people. Trees, houses, and anything else that stood in the floodwater's path were swept along in the angry torrent. All but two of the area's 112 bridges were torn from their foundations. Most of the roads and railroad tracks that had been spared in the earlier devastation were now victims of nature's latest fury.

The Hatfields were so busy fulfilling the terms of their contract that they were unaware of the destruction. Imagine their surprise when they were confronted by a group of farmers who wanted them to stop the rain. Charles thought they were joking and ignored them, continuing to vent his mixture into the air.

In the eight weeks since the rains had started, forty-four inches had fallen at Morena. As soon as it stopped, Charles checked the level of the Morena reservoir. Not only was it filled to capacity, but more than four feet of water flowed over the top of the dam. Charles had met the terms of the contract, and he wanted to be paid.

Before leaving for San Diego to collect their money, the brothers dismantled their towers and buried the chemicals where no one would find them. It wasn't until they started for the city that they saw the extent of the damage. To avoid being lynched by angry farmers along the way, they became the "Benson Brothers."

When Charles asked for his money, the city refused to pay him on the grounds that he had never signed a contract with them. When he threatened to sue, the council agreed to pay him the ten thousand dollars if he would accept liability for the estimated sixty deaths and the 3.5 million dollars in damages as a result of the floods.

Being a man of common sense, Charles turned down their offer and tried to settle for four thousand dollars. When the council refused, he took them to court. Two different courts ruled that "The rain was an act of God and not Charles Hatfield." He continued to sue the city until 1938, when the courts threw his case out as a dead issue.

Rainmaking certainly wasn't a dead issue for the people who needed Charles's unique services. While waiting to settle his suit with the city, because of his perceived success in San Diego, his career as a rainmaker blossomed. The ranchers and farmers of Southern California continued to hire him to bring much-needed rain to their parched land.

In 1922, at the request of the Italian government, Charles went to Naples to end a drought that had plagued them for years. In 1929 the Bear Valley Mutual Water Company in California used his services to fill Bear Lake, and in 1930 the Central American Banana Growers asked him to make it rain to drown out the jungle fires that threatened their plantations in Belize.

Other than the fact that Charles was married, very little is known about his personal life. His nephew, David, once told an audience that the Hatfields' most successful feat took place in the California desert in 1922. In Sand Canyon, the brothers hauled in a large quantity of chemicals, built a tower, and waited two days for the rain. "It rained for about a day," said David, "but in one hour the weather bureau recorded 250 inches of rain. The canyon was destroyed, thirty miles of railroad tracks were wiped out, and a prospector living twenty miles away had to run for his life."

The Great Depression, the construction of Hoover Dam, and hundreds of irrigation canals across California convinced Charles that it was time to retire. His wife divorced him and he returned to Eagle Rock to resume his career as a sewing machine salesman. According to David, "The Hatfields were offered large sums of money for their secret formula, but they refused to sell. They decided it was too devastating a force to unleash to any one individual or group of bureaucrats who might misuse it. They looked around and saw very few people of integrity, men who stood by their words at all cost. The secret will die with us."

Always on the lookout for a good story, Broadway and Hollywood finally took notice. In 1956 Charles was invited to attend the Hollywood premier of *The Rainmaker*, starring Burt Lancaster and based on the hit Broadway musical *110 in the Shade*.

When Charles died in Pear Blossom, California, on January 12, 1958, he took his secret formula to the grave. He claimed that during his lifetime, he performed more than five hundred successful rainmaking events and never had a failure.

We will never know for sure if Charles Hatfield could really make it rain, but one thing is certain. He will always be remembered as "the man who almost drowned San Diego."

BIBLIOGRAPHY

THE COMIC OPERA OUTLAW OF CALIFORNIA

Enss, Chris. *Outlaw Tales of California: True Stories of the Golden State's Most Infamous Crooks, Culprits, and Cutthroats.* Guilford, CT: TwoDot, 2008.

Jackson, Joseph Henry. *Bad Company: The Story of California's Legendary and Actual Stage Robbers, Bandits, Highwaymen, and Outlaws from the Fifties to the Eighties.* Lincoln: University of Nebraska Press, 1997.

Seacrest, William B. *California Desperados: Stories of Early California Outlaws in Their Own Words.* Clover, CA: Word Dancer Press, 2000.

———. *California Badmen: Mean Men with Guns.* Sanger, CA: Word Dancer Press, 2006.

STAGECOACH MARY

McConnell, Miantae Metcalf. *Deliverance Mary Fields, First African American Woman Star Route Carrier in the United States.* Columbus Falls, MT: Huzza Publishing, 2016.

Wagner, Tricia Martineau. *African American Women of the Old West.* Guilford, CT: TwoDot, 2007.

THE OUTLAW PRIEST

Bosanko, Ivan. *Brown's Hole.* Baltimore: PublishAmerica, 2004.

Kouris, Diana Allen. *The Romantic and Notorious History of Brown's Park.* Greybull, WY: Wolverine Gallery, 1988.

Mcclure, Grace. *The Bassett Women.* Athens: Swallow Press/Ohio University Press, 1985.

THE GREAT TRAIN ROBBERY OF 1895

Bell, Bob Boze. "The Blast at Steins Pass: Black Jack Ketchum's Gang vs. Three Express Guards." *True West Magazine,* July 15, 2014.

Marriott, Barbara. *Outlaw Tales of New Mexico: True Stories of the Land of Enchantment's Most Infamous Crooks, Culprits, and Cutthroats.* Guilford, CT: TwoDot, 2007.

McClintock, James Harvey. "Train Robbers of Arizona." *Legends of America.* www .legendsofamerica.com/az-trainrobbers/. Accessed May 20, 2019.

Trimble, Marshall. *In Old Arizona: True Tales of the Wild Frontier.* Phoenix, AZ: Golden West Publishers, 1985.

Vigilante Justice

Larson, Elizabeth. "Virginia Slade, Wife of Jack Slade." *Overland Trail*. www.overland
    .com/dale html. Accessed May 20, 2019.
Reasoner, James. *Draw: The Greatest Gunfights of the American West.* New York: Berkley
    Publishing Group, 2003.
Schindler, Harold. "Here Lies Joseph Slade." *Salt Lake Tribune*, June 6, 1994.

The Gentleman Bandit

Baumgart, Don. "Legendary Stagecoach Robber Black Bart Led a Merry Chase."
    Nevada County Gold. www.nevadacountygold.com/article/legendary-stagecoach
    -robber-black-bart-led-a-merry-chase. Accessed May 20, 2019.
Finkelstien, Norman H. *The Capture of Black Bart, Gentleman Bandit.* Chicago: Chicago
    Review Press Incorporated, 2018.
Hoeper, George. *Black Bart: Boulevardier Bandit: The Saga of California's Most Mysterious
    Stagecoach Robber and the Men Who Sought to Capture Him.* Fresno, CA: Word
    Dancer Press, 1995.
Pierce, J. Kingston. *The Plundering Po8.* San Francisco: Your History Sasquatch Books,
    1995.

Whatever Lola Wants, Lola Gets

Burr, Chauncy C. *The Lectures of Lola Montez: With a Full and Complete Autobiography
    of Her Life.* Philadelphia: T. B. Peterson Brothers, 1858.
Miller, Ronald D. *Shady Ladies of the West.* Tucson, AZ: Western Lore Press, 1985.
Seymour, Bruce. *Lola Montez: A Life.* Durham, NC: The Marathon Group, 1996.
Varley, James F. *Lola Montez: The California Adventures of Europe's Notorious Courtesan.*
    Spokane, WA: Arthur Clark Company, 1996.
"Very Important Passengers: Lola Montez." *The Maritime Heritage Project*. www
    .maritimeheritage.org/vips/montez.html. Accessed May 20, 2019.

Diamonds in the Dust

Bagley, Will. "Sack of Gems Made Fools out of Many." *Salt Lake Tribune*, August 6,
    2000.
Elliott, Ron. *American El Dorado: The Great Diamond Hoax of 1872.* London: Acclaim
    Press, 2013.
Harpending, Asbury. *The Great Diamond Hoax and Other Stirring Events in the Life of
    Asbury Harpending.* New York: Freedonia Books, 2002.
Lyman, George D. *The Great Diamond Hoax of 1872.* Chicago: Charles Scribner &
    Sons, 1937.
Yadon, Laurence, and Robert Smith. *Old West Swindlers.* Gretna, LA: Pelican Publish-
    ing, 2011.

THE MAN WHO ALMOST STOLE ARIZONA

Cookridge, E. H. *The Baron of Arizona*. New York: John Day Publishers, 1967.

Court Papers, James Addison Reavis. Federal Court, Santa Fe, NM (1882–1886).

Powell, Donald M. *The Peralta Grant: James Addison and the Barony of Arizona*. Norman: University of Oklahoma Press, 1960.

THE LIEUTENANT WAS A LADY

Massey, Mary Elizabeth, and Jean V. Berlin. *Women in the Civil War*. Lincoln: University of Nebraska Press, 1994.

Silvey, Anita. *I'll Pass for Your Comrade: Women Soldiers in the Civil War*. New York: Clarion Books, 2008.

Tsui, Bonnie. *She Went to the Field: Woman Soldiers of the Civil War*. Guilford, CT: TwoDot, 2006.

Velazquez, Loreta. *The Woman in Battle*. Richmond, VA: Dustin, Gilman & Company, 1876.

THE LEGEND OF OOFTY GOOFTY

Asbury, Herbert. *The Barbary Coast: An Informal History of the San Francisco Underworld*. New York: Garden City Publishing, 1933.

Anderson, Ivy, ed. *Alice: Memoirs of a Barbary Coast Prostitute*. Berkley, CA: Heyday Publishers, 2016.

Jensen, David. *Inside the Barbary Coast*. Bloomington, IN: Xlibris, 2001.

Riley, Brendan. *Lower Georgia Street: California's Forgotten Barbary Coast*. Mount Pleasant, SC: Arcadia Publishing, 2017.

NORTON I, FIRST EMPEROR OF THE UNITED STATES

Asbury, Herbert. *The Barbary Coast: An Informal History of the San Francisco Underworld*. New York: Garden City Publishing, 1933.

Barker, Malcom E. *Bummer and Lazarus: San Francisco's Famous Dogs*. San Francisco: London Born Publications, 2001.

Carr, Patricia E. "Emperor Norton I." *American History Illustrated*, 1975.

Hansen, Gladys C. *San Francisco Almanac: Everything You Want to Know about Everyone's Favorite City*. San Francisco: Chronicle Books, 1995.

SHE WAS A HELL OF A GOOD WOMAN

McNeeley, Regina Bennett. "Sarah Bowman." *Handbook of Texas Online*. https://tsha online.org/handbook/online/articles/fbo30. Accessed May 21, 2019.

Elliott, J. F. "The Great Western: Sarah Bowman, Mother and Mistress to the U.S. Army." *The Journal of Arizona History*, vol. 30, no. 1. Spring 1989, 1–26.

Grant, Ulysses S. *The Complete Personal Memoirs of Ulysses S. Grant*. CreateSpace, 2009.

Greenberg, Amy S. *A Wicked War: Polk, Clay, Lincoln, and the 1846 U.S. Invasion of Mexico*. New York: Knopf, 2012.

Phillips, Lisa, and Reyna Martinez. "Sarah Bowman and Tillie Howard: Madams of the 1880s." *Borderlands*, vol. 18. 1999. http://epcc.libguides.com/cphp?g=54061. Accessed May 21, 2019.

Roberts, Robert B. "Historic California Posts, Camps, Stations, and Airfields: Fort Yuma." California Military Department. www.militarymuseum.org/FtYuma.html. Accessed May 21, 2019.

THE RED GHOST OF ARIZONA

Estlack, Russell. *Please General Custer, I Don't Want To Go*. Conshohocken, PA: Infinity Publishers, 2005.

Froman, Robert. "The Red Ghost." *American Heritage*, vol. 12, issue 3. April 1961. https://american heritage.com/red ghost. Accessed June 13, 2019.

Trimble, Marshall. *Arizoniana: Stories from Old Arizona!* Phoenix, AZ: Golden West Publishers, 1988.

DILCHTHE

"An Apache Woman's Tale." *The Foothills*. thefoothillsaz.tripod.com/id38.htm. Accessed June 13, 2019.

Dary, David. *True Tales of the Old Time Plains*. New York: Crown Publishers, 1979.

PLEASE GENERAL CUSTER, I DON'T WANT TO GO

Estlack, J. C. "Al Estlack Picks Last Indian Bullet from Leg as He Recalls the Old Days." *Littleton Colorado Booster*, March 1937.

Healey, Donald W. *The Road to Glorietta: A Confederate Army Marches through New Mexico*. Berwin Heights, MD: Heritage Books, Inc., 2009.

"John M. Chivington (1821–1894)." *New Perspectives on the West*. www.pbs.org/weta/thewest/people/a_c/chivington.htm. Accessed May 21, 2019.

Paddock, Buckley B. *A Twentieth Century History and Biographical Record of North and West Texas*. University City, MO: Lewis Publishing Company, 1906.

Alfred Estlack obituary. *Clarendon Enterprise*. Clarendon, TX. November 21, 1943.

HELL HATH NO FURY LIKE A WOMAN SCORNED

Brown, Dee. *The Gentle Tamers: Women of the Old West*. New York: Putnam, 1958.

Lamott, Kenneth Church. *Who Killed Mr. Crittenden?* New York: David McKay Company Inc., 1963.

Neville, Amelia Ransome. *The Fantastic City: Memoirs of the Social and Romantic Life of Old San Francisco*. Cambridge, MA: Houghton Mifflin Co, 1932.

Streeter, Holly. *The Sordid Trial of Laura D. Fair: Victorian Family Values*. Digital Georgetown | Georgetown Law Library. https://repository.library.georgetown.edu/handle/10822/1051402. Accessed May 21, 2019.

SAM BROWN'S FOLLY

Lyman, George D. *The Saga of the Comstock Lode: Boom Days in Virginia City.* New York: Charles Scribner and Sons, 1934.

Pioneer Nevada. Harold's Club of Reno. 1951.

PINK TIGHTS AND WILD HORSES

Brody, Seymour. *Jewish Heroes and Heroines of America from Colonial Times to 1900.* Hollywood, FL: Lifetime Books, 1996.

Brown, Dee Alexander. *The Gentle Tamers: Women of the Old Wild West.* New York: Putnam, 1958.

Dickson, Samuel. "Adah Isaacs Menken, 1835–1868." *The Virtual Museum of the City of San Francisco.* www.sfmuseum.org/bio/adah.html. Accessed May 21, 2019.

Stoddard, Charles Warren. "La Belle Menken." *National Magazine*, February 1905.

THE TEXAS SALT WAR

Cool, Paul. *Salt Warriors: Insurgency on the Rio Grande.* College Station: Texas A&M University Press, 2008. http://muse.jhu.edu/chapter/312111. Accessed May 21, 2019.

Sonnichsen, C. L. "Salt War of San Elizario." *Handbook of Texas Online.* https://tsha online.org/handbook/online/articles/jcs01. Accessed May 21, 2019.

———. *The El Paso Salt War of 1877.* El Paso, TX: C. Hertzog and the Texas Western Press, 1961.

THE MYSTERIOUS LADY IN BLUE

Anderson, Dorothy Daniels. *Arizona Legends and Lore: Tales of Southwestern Pioneers.* Phoenix, AZ: Golden West Publishers, 1991.

Chipman, Donald. "Agreda, Maria de Jesus de." *Handbook of Texas Online.* https://tsha online.org/handbook/online/articles/fag01. Accessed May 21, 2019.

Eckhardt, C. F. "The Mystery of the Lady in Blue." www.texfiles.com/eckhardt/lady inblue.htm. Accessed June 8, 2019.

Sharp, Jay W. "The Blue Nun—María Jesus de Ágreda: Mystical Missionary to the Indians." *DesertUSA.* www.desertusa.com/desert-people/lady-in-blue.html. Accessed June 8, 2019.

THE LAST APACHE WARRIOR

Dearment, R. K. "The Sheriff Who Took On the Apache Kid." Historynet, October 3, 2012. www.historynet.com/the-sheriff-who-took-on-the-apache-kid.htm. Accessed June 9, 2019.

Hurst, James W. "The Apache Kid." *Desert USA.* www.desertusa.com/desert-people/apache-kid.html. Accessed May 21, 2019.

Hutton, Paul Andrew. *The Apache Wars: The Hunt for Geronimo, the Apache Kid, and the Captive Boy Who Started the Longest War in American History.* New York: Penguin Random House, 2016.

McKanna, Clare V. *Court-Martial of the Apache Kid: Renegade of Renegades.* Lubbock: Texas Tech University Press, 2009.

Wilson, Jim. "The Legend of the Apache Kid." *Shooting Times*, April 5, 2005.

JULIA BULETTE, QUEEN OF THE COMSTOCK

Best, Hillyer. *Julia Bulette and Other Red Light Ladies.* Racine, WI: Western Printing, 1959.

Daniels, Zeke, and Ben Christy. *The Life and Death of Julia C. Bulette, "Queen of the Red Lights," Virginia City, Nevada.* Virginia City, NV: Lamp Post, 1958.

Enss, Chris. "Wild Women of the West: Julia Bulette." *Cowgirl Magazine*, July 17, 2018. http://cowgirlmagazine.com/wild-women-julia-bulette/. Accessed June 13, 2019.

Miller, Ronald Dean. *Shady Ladies of the West.* Tucson, AZ: Westernlore Press, 1985.

FOOL'S GOLD

Glover, Thomas E. *The Lost Dutchman Mine of Jacob Waltz, Part 1: The Golden Dream.* Phoenix, AZ: Cowboy Miner Productions, 2000.

Paul, Lee. "The Dutchman's Lost Gold Mine." *Angelfire.* www.angelfire.com/trek/forthetruth/dutchman.html. Accessed May 21, 2019.

Storm, Barry. *Thunder God's Gold.* Tortilla Flats, AZ: Southwest Publishing, 2012.

Taylor, Troy. "The Lost Dutchman Mine." *American Hauntings.* www.prairieghost.com/dutchman.hmtl. Accessed May 21, 2019.

THE MAN WITH NINE LIVES

Bryan, Howard. *Incredible Elfego Baca: Good Man, Bad Man of the Old West.* Santa Fe, NM: Clear Light Publishing, 1994.

Hardin, Jessie Wolf. "The Guns of Elfego Baca." *The Free Library.* www.thefreelibrary.com/The+Elfago+Baca.-a0102274458. Accessed May 21, 2019.

McCafferty, Regis. "Elfego Baca and the Cowboys." *Dark Canyon.* http://darkcanyon.net/elfego_baca_and_the_cowboys_part_1.html. Accessed May 21, 2019.

Sager, Stan. *Viva Elfego! The Case for Elfego Baca, Hispanic Hero.* Santa Fe, NM: Sunstone Press, 2008.

WHERE DID THE CAMELS GO?

Bonsai, Stephen. *Edward Fitzgerald Beale: A Pioneer in the Path of Empire 1822–1903.* Ithaca, NY: Cornell University Press, 2009.

Jacobs, Ellen. "Army Camel Corps." www.drumbarracks.org./original website/Camel Corps.html. Accessed June 10, 2019.

Weise, Kathy. "Edward Fitzgerald Beale—Blazing the West." *Legends of America*. www
.legendsofamerica.com/we-edwardbeale/. Accessed June 10, 2019.
Woodbury, Chuck. "U.S. Camel Corps Remembered in Quartzite, Arizona." *Out West*,
2003. www.outwestnewspaper.com/camels.html. Accessed September 21, 2009.

HENRY STARR, KING OF THE BANK ROBBERS

Bovson, Mara. "The Last Outlaw: End of Henry Starr's Era in Bank Robberies." *New
York Daily News*, August 29, 2010. www.nydailynews.com/news/crime/outlaw
-henry-starr-era-bank-heists-article-1.200857. Accessed June 11, 2019.
Reasoner, James. *Draw: The Greatest Gunfights of the American West*. New York: Berkley
Publishing Group, 2003.
Trimble, Marshall. "Outlaw Henry Starr." *True West*, March 13, 2017. https://truewest
magazine.com/outlaw-henry-starr/. Accessed June 11, 2019.
Weiser, Kathy. "Henry Starr, The Cherokee Bad Boy." *Legends of America*, September
2017. www.legendsofamerica.com/we-henrystarr/. Accessed May 23, 2019.

THE GENTLE GIANT OF TEXAS

Boardman, Mark. "On the Trail of Bigfoot—Wallace, that is, the Legendary Texas
Ranger." *True West*, July 14, 2015. https://truewestmagazine.com/on-the-trail-of
-bigfoot/. Accessed June 11, 2019.
Duval, John C. *The Adventures of Bigfoot Wallace, Texas Ranger and Hunter*. J. W. Burke
& Co., 1870.
Moore, Steve. "Texas Ranger William A. A. 'Bigfoot' Wallace (1817–1899)." *Texas
Ranger Dispatch Magazine*, Summer 2005.
Weiser, Kathy. "'Bigfoot' Wallace: A Texas Folk Hero." *Legends of America*. www.legends
ofamerica.com/we-bigfootwallace/. Accessed June 11, 2019.

THE GRANDEST STORY TELLER OF THEM ALL

Augherton, Thomas. "James Beckwourth: A Mountain Man Found Freedom in the
Fur Trade." *True West*, January 13, 2015. https://truewestmagazine.com/
james-beckwourth/. Accessed June 11, 2019.
Bonner, T. D. *The Life and Adventures of James P. Beckwourth: Mountaineer, Scout, and
Pioneer, and Chief of the Crow Nation of Indians*. New York: Harper & Brothers
Publishers, 1856.
Mulroy, Kathleen. "From Slave to Early Explorer: James Pierson Beckwourth." *Montana
Senior News*, February 1, 2019. https://montanaseniornews.com/james-pierson
-beckwourth/. Accessed June 11, 2019.
Nichols, Jeffery D. "James P. Beckwourth and the Mythology of the West." *History
Blazer*, March 1955.

The Man Who Almost Drowned San Diego

Fuller, Theodore W. *San Diego Originals*. San Diego: California Profiles Publications, 1987.

Lundberg, Murray. "Charles Hatfield, the Klondike Rainmaker." Explore North. www.explorenorth.com/library/yafeatures/rainmaker.html. Accessed May 23, 2019.

Shea, Bob. "Rainmaker's Renown Was Worldwide, but Most Famous Deluge Was Here." *Eastern Empire Guardian* (La Morena, CA), September 3, 2003.

Vargo, Cecile Page. "The Great Pluviculturist." *Explore Historical California*. www.explorehistoricalif.com/ehc_legacy/hatfield2.htm. Accessed May 23, 2019.

Wallechinsky, David, and Irving Wallace. *The People's Almanac*. New York: Bantam Dell, 1981.

INDEX

About the Author

Russell Estlack is a native of Wildwood, New Jersey. He enlisted in the US Air Force and served during the early years of the Cold War. During his military service, he was assigned to remote locations to track Soviet submarines and underwater nuclear explosions. He also spent more than a year on the East German border as a technical advisor to the West German Air Force.

Estlack graduated from New Mexico State University with a BS in Tourism Management. Later, as a field engineer for the Bendix Field Engineering Company, he was actively involved in the Apollo moon landings and the space shuttle program. He has lived in the American Southwest for many years and is intimately familiar with the people and places he writes about. Estlack and his wife live among the magnificent red mountains of St. George, Utah.